TO THE LAST MAN

A MEMOIR

LLOYD K. WALUND

sweetgrassbooks
an imprint of Farcountry Press

ISBN 978-1-59125-327-7

Design by Steph Lehmann

sweetgrassbooks
an imprint of Farcountry Press

Produced by Sweetgrass Books
PO Box 5630, Helena, MT 59604; (800) 821-3874; www.sweetgrassbooks.com

Produced and printed in the United States of America

27 26 25 24 23 1 2 3 4 5

DEDICATION

This book is dedicated to the men and women of the United States Army 34th Infantry Division, past and present, who have served our country in times of our greatest need, and in peacetime. May this account remind all who read it of the unselfish willingness of our finest men and women to pay the supreme sacrifice for the security and peace that we enjoy in the United States of America.

TO THE LAST MAN

A MEMOIR

LLOYD K. WALUND

sweetgrassbooks
an imprint of Farcountry Press

CONTENTS

were also there
Sped never did forget the "Rodney."
We pulled out to sea again
and Col. Swenson called us together
to give us the dope. We were
to invade the city and port of Algus
North Africa. Each man was told
in the finest detail just what
his job was. The Bn. Was to get
off the cruiser Sheffield and Board
two destroyers some where in the
Mediteranion. L Co. and part of J Co.
were to board the Destroyer "Broke"
K Co. a small part of J Co. and a platoon
from "M Co. were to board the
Destroyer "Malcolm." That night
about 7 o'clock we boarded the boats

FOREWORD

Lloyd K. Walund was many things to our family. Dad, Husband, Grandpa, and role model to name a few. He was also a proud and decorated World War II Army Veteran. Growing up with this man we all adored and admired, we were aware of his service, but we never fully understood the enormity of his experience. He didn't speak much about his nearly 600 days of frontline combat with the 34th Red Bull Division, but fortunately, he wrote about them.

As children, we remember the countless evenings Dad spent in his cozy den, his distinguished medals hanging on the wall nearby, writing each detail of this story in long hand with his exceptional penmanship. Eventually, the manuscript was typed into a spiral bound copy that Dad presented to each of us, along with a personal note. We held this gift sacred, a cherished family treasure to each of his children and grandchildren. Dad's sense of humor, patriotism, humility, and strong character were clearly the result of some of his wartime experiences, as were the many values he imparted to us throughout our lives.

As the years have passed, we have come to understand the importance of sharing Dad's story with a wider audience. *To the Last Man* is his remarkable personal account of valor and courage, of a young man willing to sacrifice everything for the greater good. The fact that our father safely returned home from this war is astonishing. We are blessed and privileged that we were able to call him Dad, Husband, and Grandpa. Mostly, we call him our hero. May we never forget the sacrifices made by the men and women of "The Greatest Generation" during the immense conflict which was World War II. It is with tremendous love, respect, and gratitude that we share this deeply personal gift that our dad has graced us with.

The text included here is reprinted verbatim from our father's final manuscript, preserving his spellings and usage. We have added chapter names throughout the book to aid the reader in finding his or her place in the story.

**Jim, Gail, Vicki, Connie, Patti, Ken and Lori,
the children of Lloyd Kenneth Walund**

And

**Amanda, Holly, Rory, Jason, Dan, Pat, Sean, Casey, Conor, Michael,
Colin, Kiley, Kjersti, Brett, and Noah, the grandchildren**

BYWORD

This byword was written and dated in 1992 as part of an effort that produced an earlier version of this book. That effort produced a number of bound, printed documents that were distributed to Lloyd's children, grandchildren, and other family members at that time, and was foundational in the completion of the current version of To the Last Man. *The byword has provided lasting and profound value into the production of* To the Last Man. *The present publication includes dust jacket testimonials written exclusively by the children of Lloyd K. Walund.*

Lloyd Walund is one of the few—if not the only—surviving member of the famed 34th Red Bull Division. He lives quietly with his wife of 41 years, Dorothy Burnett Walund, near Anaconda, Montana. He has seven children and ten grandchildren.

Lloyd was born near Forbes, North Dakota, on February 22, 1920. He volunteered for the Armed Services and was inducted into the United States Army on April 18, 1941. He was shipped overseas as a member of the 34th Red Bull Division on April 30, 1942. He returned to the United States on March 21, 1945, and was honorably discharged from the Army on May 18, 1945.

In the fifty years that have passed since this story began to unfold, the world has seen a great many changes, not all of which we enjoy. Unfortunately, some of these changes have affected our values. In that regard, it is important that we be made aware of at least a few of the thousands of heroic and courageous actions that have in some small way allowed each of us to grow and prosper in this fair land. Those who received so little, yet who gave so much, are indeed worthy of our everlasting gratitude.

It would indeed be a tragedy if the stories of some of these brave and courageous men were left untold. This is one of millions of stories that could and should be told, as it tells of a time and place and happenings that we dare not forget.

The minimal effort that has gone into assembling this narrative is simply a tribute to those many brave men who did not come home, but especially to one man who did and still lives to share our lives. 🐂

"TO THE LAST MAN"

Clint Burnett
June 1992

AUTHOR'S PREFACE

In making an account of these wartime actions, major events and engagements are sometimes written as if they occurred on a day-to-day basis. Less eventful events may have transpired in the interim between the high points. However, to put it into a more story-like form, a linkage of day-to-day basis is used.

The turnover of a combat division in wartime is, of course, such that many men who played an integral part are not mentioned by name. Many more are mentioned by nickname only, as that seemed to be the thing at that time. Often it seemed like there was a constant rotation of personnel. Only a minute number went on for an extended period of time—not only enlisted men, but commissioned officers as well.

For example, the table of organization called for a commissioned officer, first or second lieutenant, to lead a platoon. However, due to casualties or other reasons, a big share of the time the platoon sergeant or right guide wound up leading the platoon. In both the commissioned and N.C.O. ranks, situations found these men performing assignments, two, three, or four grades above their rank, and their rank seldom caught up with them.

In making a report on combat situations and conditions with any accuracy, one can only report on what takes place in his own immediate area or sector. Often times one is unable to account for what takes place within his own platoon, let alone the overall picture. Geographic and terrain features of places where major events took place seem to stand out vividly in memory.

One thing the rigors of war does to an infantry man is that so many little simple things are so greatly appreciated. Things such as a hot meal, a place to sleep out of the miserable weather, no one shooting at you and the comradery of your fellow soldiers. Everyone seemed to like everyone else. The only common dislike was for the enemy against whom this war was waged.

The Front to an infantry man and the first aid men that are attached to it is unlike the Front known by other units. Other units were able to perform their tasks in a capable manner without the animal-like existence of the infantry man. When an infantry man achieved his objective, nothing was over. He then, in most likelihood, would curl up in a muddy hole with rain or snow pouring over him and open up a can of distasteful C rations for his meal.

Always on the alert for a counter attack, he considered himself lucky if artillery and mortar shells were not raining down on him. If he was not pinned down in this manner for an extended period, he would then attack again. Pushing forward, if he saw a man to his right or left, he was happy. This meant that chance were that he was an ally. However, anybody in front of him was the enemy, and he'd shoot the son-of-a-bitch before he got it himself.

After an extended period of combat, I think most infantry men became somewhat emotionally calloused. By that, I mean passing by slain and wounded and pushing forward for the sake of self-preservation with little thought of the fallen men. However, if any of these men were ones with whom you were closely associated, you were shattered by remorse. In some cases, losing a close buddy could have such an adverse effect that it was very difficult to carry on.

In some places in this account, rough, harsh language is used. I am not particularly proud of some things that transpired in non-combat situations. Not that they were anything real bad, but more or less acts of mischief. It seemed that whenever the situation would permit, you had to let off steam to vent your frustrations. It was sort of like a safety valve.

Some of the more gruesome facts in this account are actually minimized to some extent to make them more believable. However, to stray from the facts would not be telling it like it was. I always believed in calling a spade a spade. Anything else is nothing but fiction. I swear this is a true account as I seen it through my eyes.

I am thankful to God that I came through all this combat as well as I did, along with my buddies. I am proud of the fact that I was an infantry man in the 34th Red Bull Division and was able to play a part in its incredible record of combat time in World War II. I would only be projecting false modesty if I didn't bring out the fact that I was able, through the grace of God, to stick through about 90 percent of the combat time compiled by the Red Bull Division.

In relating these facts, the reader will undoubtedly find errors in spelling, punctuation and lack of eloquence in writing. I am not a journalist or an author. So with a ninth grade education I put this manuscript together. No ghost writer was involved.

Lloyd K. Walund

Forward

This, I wish to dedicate, to the people of America, and the world. Not to bring back the horrors of war to people who have grief and anguish from it's effects nor to paint a black picture for people who would prefer to look at the lighter side for even in a war where almost the entire world has one ante, there too is a brighter side. The brighter side may be easily defined in this way, When any person undergoes a tremendous amount of hardships. The little bit of the brighter is so much more apreciated when you get it. Just like a person enjoys a drink of water when is real thirsty so much more than he does when he is not thirsty. To the doughboys the briter side was, may be a couple of days relief from the line, being able to lie down at night and know that in a couple of hours they were not going to get up and attack a hill that they knew some of them were going to be killed and wounded who it would be no one knew. Or to be back near the kitchen where they could eat a hot breakfast. To be in an "outfit" be it squad, Platoon, Co, Battallion or any unit. In which are men you like. Every single one of them, and you know that every single one of them likes you.

ORGANIZATION OF
THE 34TH RED BULL DIVISION

The 34th Division was a National Guard Division from the mid-northwest states of Minnesota, Iowa, North and South Dakota. These National Guard troops made up the nucleus and cadre of the division that shortly after the mobilization was supplemented by volunteers and selective service men. I was an under-age volunteer when I joined the outfit at that time. All of us that joined the outfit at that time were also from these mid-northwest states.

The early spring of 1941 found the 34th Division in Camp Claiborne, LA. The table of organization at that time called for an Army division to be "Square." A square division is one that consists of four infantry regiments. These regiments were divided in two, making two brigades as a complete self-contained fighting unit supported by our own field artillery, engineers, quartermasters, signal Co, medics, anti-tank units and reconnaissance.

The four infantry regiments were as follows: The 133rd and the 168th from Iowa, the 135th from Minnesota, and the 164th from North Dakota. The 133rd and 168th made up the 67th Brigade. The 135th and 164th made up the 68th Brigade. Supporting elements included the 125th, 151st, and 185th Field Artillery. The 109th Engineers, the 109th Quartermasters, 34th Signal Co, medics and recon and others from South Dakota.

In the autumn of 1941, the War Department for some reason decided to streamline all Army infantry divisions. Instead of the square division, we were converted to a triangular division, meaning we now had three infantry regiments instead of four. This reorganization resulted in the loss of our sister regiment, the 164th from North Dakota. It should be noted here that the 164th would carry on the tradition of the 34th Division by being one of the earliest arrivals in the Pacific Theater. There the famed American Division was organized, of which the 164th was an integral part compiling a splendid combat record.

At this time the Quartermaster was unable to supply these newly mobilized divisions adequately. At first our uniforms were ill-fitting left-overs from World War l. Some of our training weapons were dummies. This was before the M-1 Garand rifle was out, so we had the old Springfield .03's. The only article of clothing we had that we liked was the campaign hat that we though looked pretty sharp cocked rakishly forward atop close-cropped hair. These hats were soon declared non-uniform for enlisted men. Only commissioned officers were allowed to wear them. We always figured the reason was that the commissioned ranks thought the enlisted personnel looked too good in them.

Terminology also changes as time goes by. For example, the command car, which was sort of a roughhewn two-seat touring car with a canvass top, was known as a "jeep," which was a drawn-out version "G.P." that stood for general purpose. Later when "Willys" came out with a little puddle jumper that is commonly known today as the Jeep, we called that vehicle a "Peep." So, in this account when you hear me refer to a peep, you will know it is the same as what was later commonly known as the jeep.

On December 7, 1941, the "Day of Infamy" arrived. The U.S. Fleet at Pearl harbor was attacked by the Japanese. The very next day found the 34th Division on trucks heading for Texas City and Galveston to guard installations there. Immediately after Christmas, the 34th was aboard a train headed for Fort Dix, New Jersey. Hear the division was replenished with additional men to bring us up to combat strength. These men came from all parts of the United States and from all walks of life.

Only a short while was spent at Fort Dix. I often wonder why, but the 34th was selected over all other standing regular Army divisions to go overseas on the Atlantic side as the first American troops to set foot on European soil—the first committed to combat. The 34th compiled an incredible, almost unbelievable nearly 600 days of front-line combat that consisted of so many major engagements that it is difficult to fathom. The time the 34th spent in combat was the most of any unit in any war in the history of warfare for U.S. troops.

While compiling this monumental achievement, the 34th kept a very low profile. Other units often received much more recognition. Both our division commanders during this time, General "Red" Ryder and General Bolte, were very conservative about awarding medals and decorations to the personnel of their command. Consequently, the 34th probably is not the most decorated outfit to come out of World War ll. This didn't bother us, as we knew decorations were sometimes merited and sometimes not. There were many great American divisions in World War ll. I make no claim that the 34th was the best—only committed to the most. I think of the great divisions that fought in the same area as us, namely the 1st, 9th, 1st Armored, 3rd, 45th and the 36th. These divisions in particular certainly merit a well-earned salute. Divisions that came later also proved their stuff, such as the 88th, 85th and 91st. Spectacular achievements were made by specialized troops such as elements of the 82nd Airborne, U.S. Rangers, and the combined Canadian American 1st Special Service Force.

While the 34th was in Ireland prior to our commitment to combat, many of the original men left the outfit for various reasons, mostly for some physical disability or another. One particular very good friend of mine that I often think would have made a crackerjack had he remained in the outfit was Herb Whalen from York, North Dakota. Fortunately for Herb, he was transferred to a less hazardous unit. 🐂

ABOARD THE *AQUITANIA*

It was a cold, dreary, rainy day, the day Company K of the 335th Infantry Regiment of the 34th Division boarded the British transport ship His Majesty's *Aquitania* in New York Harbor. The U.S. had just declared war on the Aryan supermen, who were told by an ex-paper hanger with a misplaced eyebrow that they were destined to rule the world. The 34th Red Bull Division was chosen as the first to sail the Atlantic to Europe to see what it was all about.

Deep down in their hearts, the boys were pretty blue and had lumps in their throats, as big as crab apples. There was a chug from the big vessel, and we knew we were underway. We ran up on deck to see the old lady with the torch wave us goodbye and God speed. It gives a guy that had never been so far from home a peculiar feeling, but if you think there was a guy aboard that ship that would express his feelings, you are mistaken.

Phees Lars sighed and said, "Ah hell. I'm tired of these American girls anyhow." "Speed" Johnson exclaims, "Gosh, wouldn't the old man be mad if I brought back a girl with about four kids. He'd do nothin' but twist that mustache." With that, he just about wound down like an old crank phonograph getting the last bit out of a record, and murmured slowly, "I guess I'll go down and pull Curley's tail for a while." And that night, he did. As soon as Curley would get to sleep, if he didn't get a hot foot or a bucket of water in his face, it was something else. Then Speed would utter, as only a Swede from North Dakota can, "Gosh, I wish Curley had a tail, then we could all pull it."

We were all a carefree, happy bunch on the way over—always somebody playing tricks on somebody else. One night we heard the most terrific explosion that any of us heard up to that time. I was scared stiff and didn't know what to do. So, I just called over to Charley Whitworth and gave him hell for stowing away so many beans for supper. In the meantime, Curley was on top deck in a flash, clad in nothing but his B.V.D.'s screeching in his high soprano, "we're torpedoed!" After finding out it was nothing but a depth charge dropped from our own ship in case there was an enemy submarine around, we all snuggled comfortably back in the sack.

One bright morning as we clambered up on deck, we saw the most beautiful sight that we had seen in weeks—land! To us, it was a picture no artist could paint. Land that looked like a big quilt, a quilt like I believe is in every American home, a quilt that your mother made of bright strips of waste cloth, every color of the rainbow, sewn together. Well, that is what bonnie old Scotland looked like that morning. We were anchored just off Glasgow, but we never got off here. We turned back and headed for Londonderry, North Ireland (Ulster). There, we found the same scenic beauty that we viewed in Scotland. It was there we disembarked.

Heavily laden, we trudged down the gangplank and marched through the cobbled streets of "Derry." An old Irish woman was hollering, "Sure be lookin', Mrs. McGuiness, 'tis the Americans a comin'." Then a bunch of red noses stuck their heads out of the door of a pub on the corner, waving a cheery bottle of Guiness at us. As a pretty, young "Colleen" dashed across the street, everyone whistled and burst out in song, "My Wild Irish Rose."

Before you could say "Mike O'Leary," we were out at our Quonset hut camp called Camp Cromore, near Port Rush. The second night we were there, Lloyd Doe and I went in to Port Rush and took aboard a few Guiness'es. We had enough of them in us to think we saw the two most beautiful feminine creatures that mortal eyes had ever gazed upon. We got next to them and asked if we could see them home. They blushingly replied, "Sure you can, if you get us home before sundown." It seemed like sundown at that time of the year over there was about midnight. Lloyd asks them how far it was to their home. "Two miles," our beaming Colleens replied. We think, what's a couple of miles to two infantry men like us. I still can't see why in the devil American schools didn't teach us how far an Irish mile is. It seemed very long, and we were henceforth more cautious about who we escorted home.

About this time, we all assume the submarine menace in the Atlantic must be pretty bad, for it seems we don't have meals anymore, just meal times. The Limeys gave us a few clothes and a cup of tea now and then.

The Battleship[?] Malcolm was still going forward. Suddenly we came to an abrupt halt like hitting a stone wall. I knew then we had struck the submarine boom just outside "Grande Mole" The beat up Malcolm didn't have strenght enough to break it. It was getting awful hot aboard now. She was burning, the oil tanks had been hit and the mortar Ammo. was starting to burn. The Gallant Limey sailors were fighting the fire for all they were worse. The rest of us were throwing ammo over board. Thanks to the Limeys

CAMP COLEBROOK

After being stationed at Camp Cromore for some time, we get orders to move to a different camp. The Limeys load us up in lorries and wheel us to Camp Colebrook, in the vicinity of Brooksburough, Five Mile Town and Enniskillen. Here our grub gets better and our training more intense. Pressure was on officers and non-coms to exert discipline and hard knocks on the troops as a toughening-in process. Sgt. Gruenwald is our section leader. I think to myself, if I'm ever a section leader, I hope somebody kills me extremely dead if I ever become as gruesome as Gruenwald. We are getting peculiar training at this time. We never know what time are supposed to get up in the morning until the C.O. wakes us, which might be any time between midnight and 7:00 A.M.

Charley Whitworth says we are doing that to fool Hitler. He says Hitler will soon go crazy trying to figure out what we are going to do next. Charley proclaims his full title is "Sir Malcom Charles Alphonzo Alloissious Whitworth," and makes it quite clear to one and all that he desires to be referred to as such, so henceforth we just call him "Old Allah."

The first thing in the morning Sgt. Gruenwald who, in spite of being a good-looking man, somehow acquired the name the "Homely One," grabs a whistle he has hanging by his bunk blows it for all he's worth and bellers, "Get up, you lazy so-and-so's" until everyone is up but himself and Phees, who at the present time is my squad leader. Seeing Phees won't get up, the Homely One has to get up himself to get Phees up. Then it is reveille, we all fall out, and the platoon sergeant orders squad leaders report. About that time Phees comes sliding in at the head of the squad in much the same manner as "Pepper" Martin does second base, salutes and says, "Second squad all present and accounted for."

Col. Miller, our battalion commander, now has us making thirty-or forty-mile hikes with full field packs about every other day. We also have our Sundays on any day but Sunday. This is also to fool Hitler, Old Allah proclaims.

One night we desire to have a beer party in our humble abode, so we have two kegs of Bass Ale wheeled out from Five Mile Town. Bass Ale, incidentally, has kick like a mule. We soon get down to some serious drinking until everyone thinks this is a pretty rosy world to live in. The Homely One gets up on a box in the corner and starts delivering a speech. Phees, "old Tom," and Speed think this is a good time to organize a quartet, so we go over to another corner and give out with some melodious harmony. Lloyd Doe then pukes on Weigle's head, but that wasn't too bad. "P.J." Ortman obligingly gave Wiegle a Bass Ale shampoo.

Rumors get around, because Merlin Stratmoen, our platoon sergeant whom we call the "Little King," walks in to get in on the party. The Little King and the Homely One, when they are together, are jokingly known to one and all as the "Gruesome Twosome." Bob Frost, speed says, looks so much like the white gelding the old man has got at home, that from now on he will be known by one and all as "Old Tom, the White Gelding." As ad lib, "Speed" utters slowly, "I'd laugh if Old Allah was a horse and Phees was drunk and driving him in a buggy as fast as he could go."

We are staying in an old Irishman's barn in Randalstown. This man has a sick horse, of which he is very concerned. We ask him how old the horse is, to which he replies, "Sure, he's only 25, and a bloody good horse he is too. Sure, and I hate to see him go, with petrol so bloody scarce and all." There was little we could do but let the critter moan. That night when the horse was groaning, the Homely One woke up and bellowed, "For God's sake, will somebody wake Old Allah up so the rest of us can get some sleep."

The next morning the old Irishman and several of his neighbors were trying to get the poor old horse up. They got pretty mad at the poor animal too, and were cussing at him. "Ho! Be gettin' up you lazy old fool. You've been laying here for days unable to move, so up with you now, you no good so and so." Just then, Speed was coming down the street. And when he heard all the noise, he came to a screeching halt and hollered to me questioningly, "Is that Homely

One trying to get Phees up again?" We all gave the old Irishman our sympathy when old dobbin finally passed to the great beyond.

The following night the Homely One and Phees tell me that they have got two lovely damsels lined up, and one of these damsels has an even lovelier sister. They then say they already have it up for me to have a date with her. "No! No! None of these blind dates for me," I exclaim. However, I found myself defenseless. The next thing I knew, they were dragging me down the street toward our dates.

Well, I see the fair damsels and was amazed to find that Josie McKay was about the loveliest creature that mortal eyes had ever gazed upon. My heart skipped a beat, and I say, "So long Phees and Homely, Josie and I will be moving along." As we went along, I had the urge to romanticize with Josie. It wasn't long before she showed reluctance to my advances. "Why," I asked? "Sure, and I don't mind if you kiss me if you would be so kind as to remove your helmet. You see, it's nearly bashing me brains out," Josie replies. At that time, we were wearing those old-style pancake helmets left over from WW I and like the ones the Limeys now wear. Apologetically, I look at her bruised forehead and say sheepishly, "Shall we go home?"

Maneuvers are over, and we are all settled back at Camp Colebrook. We then get orders that we are on the alert. "Be ready to move with everything." We then move to Kerrick Fergus near Belfast, where we are issued a lot of supplies, ammunition and combat equipment. In place of having two machine guns in the section, we now have four. I have to lead one of the new squads, and Lloyd Doe leads the other one.

We realize now we have a job to do, but what it is, no one knows for sure. Bulldog Col. Swenson had just taken over as a battalion commander from Col. Miller. Swenson is a robust, 250-pounder, all man and can cuss like nobody else in the world. He calls us together one day and says, "Men! We've got a job to do, and it's a tough one. Our asses will probably be dribbling buttermilk before we get there, but just as sure as there's cold shit in a dead goose, we'll get there and do a good job of it." To cheer us up he added, "When we get there, we'll get a good deal." 🦌

TO AFRICA

The next morning, we board the Limey cruiser His Majesty's *Sheffield* at Belfast. Our mission and destination, still unknown. Almost the entire 3rd Battalion was aboard the *Sheffield*. We slept on the hangar deck. And if you could find a place where a couple of guys didn't lay on top of you, you were lucky. At first, we were headed almost due west. Some said we were going back to the States. There were rumors of going everywhere from Calcutta to Copenhagen. The water was at its roughest stage out in the Atlantic. The *Sheffield* seemed to buck worse than any bronc at a rodeo. Ninety percent were so seasick we didn't care whether we lived or died. Old Allah was one of the few that remained fairly healthy. He went around consoling the boys by telling them, "If you feel something hairy come up, you better swallow real quick, because that's your asshole."

After being out at sea for quite some time, we pull into Gibralter and refuel. We get a good look at the Rock. England's two biggest battleships were there, the Rodney and the Nelson. Speed never did forget the Rodney.

As we pull out to sea again, Col. Swenson calls us together to give us the dope. We are to invade the city and port of Algiers, North Africa. Each man is told in the finest detail just what his job and mission is. The battalion is to get off the *Sheffield* and board two destroyers somewhere in the Mediterranean. L Company and part of I Company are to board the destroyer Broke. K Company and a platoon from M Company are to board the destroyer, *Malcolm*. That night about 7:00 P.M. we transferred from the *Sheffield* to the *Malcolm*. The little "tin cans" were so jam packed with G.I.'s and equipment, you could hardly breathe.

The sea was as calm as a kitten. The moon resembled a ball of fire as it ascended from the eastern horizon. We are all out on the open deck, snuggling closely to one another to keep warm. Most of us fall asleep. I was asleep when Peers poked me saying, "Look, Walund, Lights. It's a city, a big city, and it ain't blacked out just like the towns back home." "Gosh!" I sighed, "must be Algiers. Ain't it pretty though."

Phees looks at his watch and says, "It's 3:30 now and H Hour is at 3:00." Just then a big beacon of light flashed on from the shore and soon was focused on the Destroyer Broke just ahead of us. Everyone is tense. We are startled as the 20 mm machine guns of the *Malcolm* start firing tracers at the light. The next moment the light is on us. We hear the shore battery fire. The projectile screeched as it passed over us and landed in the drink beyond. "Ha ha," Old Allah laughs heartily, "they missed." Evidently, the inside work that was supposed to be done by the loyal French didn't own out so good, for they were supposed to have these guns silenced for us. I had always heard the French had some of the most accurate artillery in the world, and I knew it now as I felt the concussion of a direct hit amidship bring tears to my eyes.

Then another hit and another. Machine gun fire was on us too now. I look up and see my pack is riddled with bullet holes. We are all lying flat on the open deck praying to God as we had never prayed before. The battle-torn *Malcolm* was still going forward. The British flag, the Union Jack, aboard the *Malcolm* had been replaced with the Stars and Stripes as soon as we were in proximity of Algiers. What took place in the next few moments is an epic that is so indelibly etched in my memory that I will never forget it as long as I live.

Old Glory in the spotlight from the shore batteries was radiant. Soon machine gun fire had her riddled and torn. And the more ragged and battle-torn she became, the more angrily she waved in the brisk wind. Soon the lanyard that secured her to the pole was severed and down she came, falling upon the hot deck. The flag, ragged and battle-torn, was hoisted and secured again, defiantly waving more madly than ever, and stayed as if to say "I shall prevail." To me it was a sort of omen as to how this conflagration would ultimately wind up.

Still moving forward, we suddenly came to an abrupt halt. I knew then that we had struck the submarine boom just outside of Grand Mole. The beat-up *Malcolm* didn't have strength enough to break it. It is getting awfully hot aboard now. She was burning, oil tanks had been hit and some mortar ammunition was exploding. The gallant Limey sailors were fighting the fire for all they were worth. The rest of us were throwing ammunition overboard.

Thanks to the Limeys, they got the fire out. We felt the tin can almost lay on its side. There was a heavy moan of men's voices uttering, "There she goes." Old Tom has his life belt so highly inflated it felt like a rock. Lloyd Doe asks Old Tom if he has enough air in his belt. "Not half enough," was the White Gelding's reply. But the *Malcolm* didn't sink. She was turning around heading back to sea on one boiler at a snail's pace. We knew the Broke had gotten into port, but the pressure was on us and we couldn't make it.

I was bandaging George Kaufman's leg when Major Snellman ordered every able-bodied man to help with the dead and wounded. Old Allah and I were carrying men down to Sick bay to get as much first aid as was available. Captain Bill Johnson, our battalion surgeon, was there doing the best he could with mangled bodies. The nucleus of K Company was made up of National Guard boys from Dawson, Minnesota, and Captain Bill was one of them. I could see the expression on the captain's face whenever a Dawson boy was brought in. He would shake his head in disbelief and call them by their first names.

I soon felt weak from the sight of blood and mangled bodies. They were shoveling remains of human bodies that could not be picked up by hand off into the sea with a scoop shovel. The odor of burned human flesh flung high up on the hot smokestacks added to the discomfort. It was daylight now, but thank God it was foggy.

We thought we saw a boat following us for the kill. Lloyd Doe and I look at the water simultaneously. We see a streak coming for our ship. Some swift traveling underwater object. Lloyd hollers, "Torpedo," and we both hit the deck. But I sneak a second look. As the object is a couple of yards from the side of our ship, it takes a sharp ninety degree turn to the right. We heave a sigh of relief. It may have been a shark.

The *Malcolm* manages to get us out to sea again. We pull up beside our flagship, go aboard, wash up, have a hot meal and we felt better. We then get back on the *Malcolm*, and she takes us as close to shore south of Algiers as she dared. We then get on landing barges and land unopposed on the sandy beaches of Algeria near Sidi Furuk. We all wish Col. Swenson was with us, for we had confidence in his leadership. However, he was with the party on the Broke, and all we knew of them was that they made it in and landed in Algiers. We assume any survivors are probably captured. Major Snellman is in charge of us, and makes the statement, "We got here by the grace of God." With apprehension, we dig foxholes in the sandy dunes. Not knowing what was around us, most of us stayed up on guard all night.

Next morning was the beginning of a lovely day. Here we see our first Arabs, nomads of the desert, in their long, dirty robes. We start walking towards them to make friends. They are scared at first, but Phees flashes them his Colgate smile and a friendship is born. They have big baskets full of oranges. We try to buy the oranges with English money, but nothing doing. P.J., always a shrewd dealer, pulls out his dirty handkerchief and asks how many he can get for that. He gets a whole bunch. So, we are soon trading off our old rags, and in return got more oranges than we could eat, even though it had been a good year since we had any.

The other three platoons get orders to head for Algiers and see what happened to the rest of the party. The 4th Platoon get orders to go to Sidi Faruck and take over a French fort.

That night we hit the old French fort. The nigh air was blacker than the ace of spades. None of us knew for sure what the score was, but the commander of the fort turned everything over to us with no resistance. It was an ancient calvary post overlooking the sea manned by Arab and Goum soldiers and French officers.

The Homely One put Brady and I with our machine gun up in a turret that already had a 75mm coastal gun in it. He said we would have nothing to worry about, for there would be a couple of French soldiers manning the 75 with us. Well, these so-called French soldiers were Goums with long, handle bar mustaches and daggers hanging from their belts. We were more scared of them than anything else.

Pretty soon we seen flares all over the sky, and we knew the Luftwaffe was out bombing Algiers, and they were coming close to the fort now. One whistled over our heads. We heard the bomb come down. We ducked and heard the terrific explosion. Then a big splash. They missed and dropped in the ocean, much to our relief.

In a few days we had everything under control at the fort and were beginning to feel more at ease, 'cause the Jerries weren't so accurate with their bombs anyhow. Our biggest trouble was, we were getting awfully hungry. We finally designate Lyne, our general handyman, as cook. Now we had a cook, but he had nothing to cook. So, our next problem was to get something for him to cook. We had eaten all of our C rations and were already tiring of oranges. Lt. Doty, our platoon leader at that time, finally took it upon himself to set out in search of food. He runs into a Limey kitchen and brings back some Irish stew, tea and hard tack, and we have a big feed. We got our grub from the Limeys from then on for the duration of our stay at Fort Sidi Faruk.

All this while, we had received no word from Col. Swenson and the rest of the battalion. People usually talk nice about people after they are dead. Well, we are already talking nice about everyone in the battalion—even the ones we didn't like. One morning we see a bunch of dressed-up big shots with heavy suitcases coming in the gate. They look like Palm Beach vacationers to me. But then what would Palm Beach vacationers be doing on a beach where they have to sweat out an air raid every night? Then behind them we see a couple of the boys from our battalion shooing them along with tommy guns. With them is none other than Col. Swenson. Lloyd Doe calls over to me, "Isn't that Col. Swenson coming in the gate?" "Yep," I reply. "Well, who's that behind Col. Swenson?" Doe asks. "That's still Col. Swenson," I answered. That man is so big, when he steps on a scale, it just says "one at a time, please."

The colonel then starts talking. "These people I brought here are your babies now. Take good care of them, and don't let them get away. They are members of the German and Italian Embassy. We captured them in Algiers." And he went on to tell what happened to them when they landed. The Broke go sunk completely.

"We were outnumbered. The hostile French were closing in on us, and we couldn't get out. We had no alternative but to surrender. They treated us pretty rough for a while. Yesterday, Admiral Darlan, Chief of the French Government in North Africa, ordered all colonial forces to cease resistance and join forces with the Allies. So now we are free, and the free French are fighting with." At that, we all cheered.

We took over the prisoners, and Col. Swenson goes back to Algiers. As we are putting the prisoners in their places, there is one dressed up big shot with a big, heavy suitcase that won't move. Phees, who already has a couple of snoot-fuls of vino, walks up to him and says, "What the hell's the matter with you?"

"I am a general, a German general. Who will carry my baggage?" replied the German. At that, Phees clicks the bolt on his .03, looks up in the sky as he usually does when he's a little drunk and says, "get your damned ass in gear. I am the one that's giving the orders around here." The general obeyed without further ado.

Lt. Doty calls us together one morning in his C.P. and says, "In a couple of days we are going to turn this fort back to the French, and we will join the rest of the Battalion, in Algiers. Tonight, let's all go up to the hotel at Sidi Faruck and throw a party. They have some damned good champagne up there." And of course, one and all thoroughly agrees with him.

That night everyone is present at the hotel, and we are all sipping this rare champagne till one and all are in a very cozy mood indeed. We are singing. Phees is now looking at the ceiling, cussing hell out of the guy back home who is probably out with his wife. The Homely One tears out of the hotel proclaiming he is going to knock some Limey on his ass. Old Tom likes to drink about as well as he likes to eat, and it is known quite well to one and all throughout the company that Old Tom alone eats about as much as the 3rd Squad of the 3rd Platoon altogether.

Although everyone present has a snoot full, we all look like members of the Women's Christian Temperence Union compared to Old Tom. That night when we got home, Old Tom comes in the room, kicks one leg towards the ceiling, makes a big circle in the room, puking all the while he is doing this. He finally lands on his ass at the end of the hall. One of the Arab soldiers feels sorry for him so he drags him down to the horse trough in the court yard, takes off all his clothes, throws him in the horse trough and scrubs him off with a scrub brush. Later Old Tom comes back in the nude with his belly hanging out and says, "You know, boys, that Arab is a hell of a nice guy." Next morning, we get the whole platoon on one truck, say goodbye to Fort Sidi Faruck, and head for Algiers to join the rest of our outfit.

We pull into Algiers and are surprised to see a beautiful, modern city. The bright stucco buildings with their red tiled roof were a sight for sore eyes. We pull up by a modern university building and stop. Lt. Doty says, "Boys, this is your new home." We scramble into the courtyard and see the boys from the rest of the battalion, who give us a hearty welcome. The 4th Platoon gets a nice big room, and we soon have our beds laid out on the marble floor.

That night just at dusk the air raid siren blew, and about five minutes later we knew it hadn't blown for nothing. The Luftwaffe was ruling overhead. We could hear the droll of the Dornier and Messershmidt bombers and the roar of the Stukka as it went into its power dive. We heard and felt bombs burst everywhere. We are all hugging the floor, and all who could get under the table were scared to death. It wasn't long before the raid was over with not too much damage done.

We are still getting these Limey compo-rations, fourteen men on a box, so every meal time each group gathers up their tin cans and canned heat and brew up a mulligan stew. We are wishing we could get some American cigarettes, as we are rationed seven Wild Woodbines each day. They are Limey cigarettes, and I don't know of anyone outside of a Limey who cares to smoke them. Col. Swenson says, "As soon as we can steal some more stuff, we are going to set up our regular kitchen."

The 3rd Battalion is now known all over North Africa as Col. Swenson and his 600 Thieves. Every day the colonel sends a detail down to the docks to watch the Limey boats unload. He says, "Just pretend you are working there, and when you see something good that we can use, bring the damned thing home." We soon have stolen enough stuff to have a kitchen grub and other necessities. It seems like that is the only way we are able to get anything. I guess Old Tom stole more than the rest of the battalion put together. "You gotta function around here," Old Tom would always say. Then with his belly hanging out he would nonchalantly place his hands on his hips and proudly proclaim, "Now I gotta get Brady a pair of pants." Col. Swenson went down to a French garage and picked out a bright yellow Chrysler convertible. Now Col. Swenson can be seen riding up and down Rue De Chalae most any hour of the day or night.

We have air raids every night, but I won't go into that because it is just repetition of the first night, except that we are a little braver now, and we venture out on the roof during an air raid to see how much ack-ack we are throwing up.

ALONE ON
SUGAR LOAF HILL

We are now living in many luxuries with not much to do. Part of the battalion are guarding General Ike and Allied Force headquarters, part of it is guarding the docks, part is doing M.P. duty in town, and the 4th Platoon of K and M Companies are guarding our own university building, which also billets Allied administration.

One day our top kick, who is known to one and all throughout the battalion as the "Big Assed-Bird," calls me into the C.P., coughs as he usually does and says, "P.T., I've got a job for you. You get Old Tom to steal you new pants, shirt and necktie, and dress up real good. Then you go up to Col. Swenson's C.P. and be his door man."

Col. Swenson is now quite a big shot and lives on the second floor of this building. There he has his boudoir and banquet room. Very often he has some French big wigs and high brass dine with him, including some beautiful French dolls. Well, my duties are this: The door downstairs is always automatically locked when it is shut, and it has no door knob on it to open it with. When someone wants to come in, he presses a button and it rings a bell up where I am. I in turn press a button and the door opens. That is all I do. The Big-Assed Bird always gives me soft jobs like that. It makes me feel like a doorman at the Waldorf-Astoria or someplace.

By this time, we are familiar with everything in Algiers. Down on the street below us is a bar where we spend a great deal of our time. They have champagne, wine and beer. The guy that runs the place is a big fat Frenchman whom we call Fita Lub. Every night at 5:00 he quits selling drinks. The Homely One and Phees try to get him to sell some more, but old Fita Lub just pulls out a meat cleaver, slams it on the bar and roars, "Cinque finish," and in a minute the bar room is empty. After Fita Lub closes, we go up to Spike's place on the corner. He has a waitress named Fifi. Every time we come in there, Louie Lotsahorses is chasing her over tables and spraying champagne on everyone.

Then there is the district on the other end of town where they have a place called the Sphinx and another called The Black Cat. Lloyd Doe, Speed and myself visit these places every Sunday. Speed calls this our Sunday schedule. Once in a while we wander our way to the Casbah, but as we desire to live to a ripe old age, we make our visits here rather infrequent.

Sometimes when we have nothing to do, we go over to the side door where we dump all our garbage just to watch the Arabs fight over it. There is Tin Can Charlie, a feeble old man who can't get in and fight as good as the rest of them for the garbage. His tin can is generally empty. Sometimes some of the boys feel sorry for him and make him a Barbasoll sandwich. Foaming at the mouth, he devours it eagerly. Then there is the more aggressive Hungry Hank, who always puts up a good fight and generally emerges victoriously with the prize of the day's garbage, which may probably be a moldy can of dehydrated eggs.

Hungry Hank is always garbed in a burlap bag from his waist down for the purpose of covering what is supposed to be covered, but it does this very poorly. Every time he stoops over to pick up a rotten tomato, his testicles can be seen plainly by one and all dangling to and fro. The kids throw rocks at him. And when they hit his exposed, delicate organs, he bursts into a fit of rage and afterwards laughs heartily.

Since we got our kitchen set up, Old Tom steals so much food that they have to put a guard on the kitchen with orders not to let anyone in except Louie Lotsahorses when he is drunk. Because when Louie is drunk and wants to do something, it is best just to let him do it for he will do it anyhow.

Phees now has got himself a girl. He picked her up down at Fita Lub's one night and has been with her ever since. She is extremely fat, and when she sits on a stool up to the bar, her ass resembles a pin cushion and the stool looks like a pin. Her name is Marie. Phees is always looking at the sky now. The Homely One is mad because he can't find a girl, and goes around and picks fights here and there. Old Allah has now went to the hospital on account of having an ingrown asshole.

The machine gun section is now guarding German and Italian pilots that were shot down in air raids. One of the German flyers said to me one night, "I do not think the Luftwaffe will bomb tonight." That made me feel pretty good, but that night we had the worst raid we ever had. The next day I was so mad because he had lied, I wouldn't let him go to the latrine. He had to shit in a box in his cell and smell of it all day.

Christmas day, and we had turkey for dinner. A little later on in the— we are alerted. We even set our machine guns up on the roof. The reason for this is because Admiral Darlan, Chief of the French Government of North Africa, had been assassinated. This caused a great deal of concern, excitement and confusion, but most of us G.I.'s did not know whether it was good or bad, and we sometimes wondered if the men in the higher echelon did.

New Year's Day we celebrate a little. Rumors are now that we are going to leave Algiers in a couple of days. The remainder of the division that we left in Ireland had now arrived in North Africa. We were a mad bunch as the 2nd Battalion of our sister regiment the 133rd Infantry, moved into Algiers and relieved us of our duties so that we could go back out in the sticks.

We are all saddled up in the courtyard when Col. Swenson bellers, "Okay, men, let's go." With that, the 3rd Battalion marched out of Petite Lycee, the university building, in a column of twos. The people were lined up on the streets saying goodbye to us. I thought to myself, why in the hell do we have to leave a place like this. Before we know it, we are aboard an old French train. It gave a shrill whistle and a jerk. "Well," Leo Schular of the mortars section sighs, "it was good while it lasted."

An old French train jammed packed with G.I.'s was slowly rolling west-ward. A big, fat new replacement by the name of Elmer, Old Allah, Phees and I were in one small compartment and were trying to get some sleep. As Elmer was so big and fat, we unanimously elect him to stand up all night. We get to sleep fine and dandy, but a few minutes later we woke up half frozen. We then see Elmer has the window of the old French train wide open and his belly hanging out. Phees yells. "Close the window, ya big tub-a-shit." Elmer turns around and casually replays, "I ain't got nothin' else to do, so I might as well just stand around and get cold." We then all decide to get up and let Elmer lie down, 'cause we could at least close the window and keep warm then.

Next day we stop at a little town that has a Q.M. dump in it. The train hadn't stopped more than ten seconds till Col. Swenson's 600 thieves were well deployed throughout the Q.M. dump. There were guards on the dump, but somehow—either by tact or force, I don't know which—we made a big haul. Old Tom looked like a three-ring circus as he finally got aboard with his loot. Anyhow, we had plenty of grub to last us a few days. Col. Swenson says, "You men shouldn't have taken quite so much." But there was a pleased look on the colonel's face.

Next morning, we pull into the town of Tclemson, stopped, clambered off the train, lined up in a column of threes and started marching for the hills. With our loot and heavy packs, we trudge along for about six miles till we come to a rocky side hill that was literally dotted with pup tents. Old Allah says, "This is the most gruesome sight I've seen so far, so this must be our new home." And it was.

The 3rd Battalion was the only battalion from the regiment that invaded Algiers. The 1st and 2nd Battalions had just arrived from the British Isles. We were just rejoining them now on this wind-swept hill. We pitch our pup tents on the frosty ground thinking what a come-down from our life in Algiers. Here we get down to some real intense training.

Ten percent of the company gets passes to Tclemson every day. Col. Swenson tells us before we go to town, "I want to keep this battalion in fighting condition, so when you go to town and pick up a hay bag, I don't give a damn what you do to her, but before you do it, be sure to look up a pro. Station. I don't give a damn if you have to drag her down the street by the hair before you find one, but find one. If you don't, in a couple of days you'll be as useful as tits on a boar."

Every morning at 5:00 the Homely One is up blowing his whistle for all he is worth. The Little King bellers, "Drop your cocks and grab your socks, men." Old Allah and I have our pup tents pitched together, and we have another pup tent pitched beside it to keep our barracks bags in. The Homely One and the Little King can never figure out which is our barracks bags and which is us. Most of the time they are kicking the barracks bags. One morning the Homely One did kick the right tent. Old Allah sleepily says, "It's just us barracks bags in here." Then we could hear the Homely One turn away and murmur, "I wonder where in the hell Old Allah and P.T. are. Wait a minute—barracks bags can't talk."

We weren't here very long before we get word that we are to move again. This time into combat on the Tunisian Front. The entire division, with the exception of the 168th regimental combat team who had preceded us to the front, were on trucks heading east for a showdown with General Von Arnim, Field Marshall Rommel and the African Corps. Winding through the lofty Atlas Mountains, the long convoy went through Sidi Bell Abbes, home of the French Foreign Legion, onto Algiers, Constantine, and Bone. It was starting to get awfully cold riding the back end of open six-by-sixes. Gas capes and shelterhalves helped keep the cold wind off. At first, we rode all day and bivouacked at night. Lt. Van has taken over leadership of the 4th Platoon as Lt. Doty was transferred to the 1st Platoon. Van always managed to chisel the Arabs out of enough eggs and fruit to keep the 4th Platoon chow-hounds well fed.

We are getting closer to the front now, and are riding by night and stopping during the daylight. We drive down "Messerschmidt Lane," but are not molested by the Luftwaffe. At last, we get to our final assembly area. We stay here two days and a night. It was in the woods, and we were well concealed. It is miserable weather. A cold wet snow. The last night the company crowds around the kitchen truck for their last hot meal. "Ploopie," the mess sergeant, threw some pretty good grub at us that night.

Loaded to the hilt with guns and ammunition, we loaded trucks again. They hauled us as close to the front as they dared. We then get off trucks and march silently up to Sugar Loaf Hill, or more technically known as Hill 252, where we relieve French troops who have been holding the hill.

Sugar Loaf Hill is near the town of Pichon. The hill stands alone by itself, and there is a flat valley ahead of it before the next range of mountains. It is here we relieve fighting French troops with their obsolete equipment. We live in dugouts on the rear slope of the cliff. We have our machine guns set out on the point of the hill. The Luftwaffe is going strong. We can hardly stick our heads out of our holes before a Messerschmidt or Fock-Wolf is strafing us. At night we have to carry rations and ammo from a river bed or waddy that is about two miles to our rear.

After being here a little over a week, we get orders to bring up lots of ammo and get ready to make an attack. That order wasn't out more than ten minutes before it is reversed. The Jerries are outflanking us on both sides. The French troops to the left of us had already withdrawn several miles, and we had to pull out soon or be surrounded.

The biggest share of the company is detailed to carry back all the supplies we had just brought up, leaving only a skeleton force on the hill. Out of the machine gun section there was the Homely One, Phees, Brady and myself left to hold the hill. The carrying party had been gone about an hour when they start laying a terrific mortar and artillery barrage on us. I was alone up on the machine gun and was hugging the ground for all I was worth. In between shell bursts I could hear Lt. Van barking orders.

Suddenly, I could no longer hear the voices of our own men. The artillery isn't landing so close now either. The Jerries had lifted the barrage, and it was now falling to our rear. I left the machine gun nest and run to the rear slope of the hill to try and find some of our men. I hollered to the top of my voice, but no one answered and there was nothing to be seen but scattered equipment and shell holes.

I looked at the dugout Lt. Van used as a C.P. and seen it had a direct hit. I realized then I am alone on the hill. I had failed to get the signal of withdrawl.

Reflection: As I look back at this incident, I do have some feeling of bitterness. Why wasn't I told the company was pulling out? They knew I was there on the point off the hill manning a machine gun. In some 500 more days of combat that was still facing me as I assumed responsibilities of a squad leader, section leader off and on, platoon leader, I find it inconceivable that I would leave any of my men in such a position as they left me. At that time, I was the youngest man in the company, a naïve farm boy, wanting to be a friend to all my fellow soldiers. I knew if I made an issue of this incident, it would bring discredit to some people that I basically liked.

The irony of the situation is that being everyone else had pulled out, there was no one else to witness what I went through. Only me alone. When I related my experience to the troops, I sensed an aura of repression of the story. No one wanted to look bad. I am only thankful it turned out as it did. I feel that God was by my side as he was in the many battles yet to come. And I swear to God that this account is true.

I find forgiveness in my heart for these people whom I liked, for it was their first battle as well as mine.

Half panicky, I dashed back up to the machine gun. It is dusk now, and I am unable to see very far. I look cautiously at the flat ground in front of me. Then not more than a hundred yards in front of me I see a skirmish line of Jerries advancing slowly and cautiously on the hill. Some of them are silhouetted on the skyline now.

I then let out a burst of about fifty rounds aimed wildly at the skirmish line. I seen the Jerries hit the ground. Without wasting any more time, I hastily jerked the back plate of the machine gun and threw it as far as I could. I had to make a decision: Stay on the hill and be captured or take a chance of running through the barrage to seek safety in the rear. I gambled on the barrage.

Armed only with my 45, I started running down the rear slope of the hill. Half running, half falling, I couldn't stop now if I had to. Shells were bursting on either side of me, but somehow missing me. Gasping for breath, I finally reached the river bed. I had no idea which route or direction the company took on the withdrawal. I did, however, know that the carrying party that left earlier had went along this river bed.

I follow the river around the bend, I come to where our ammo dump had been, but there was no one to be seen. Nothing but a few boxes of motor and machine gun ammo and a spool of communication wire. They must of kept right on following the river to the rear, I think to myself. So, I keep on following the shallow stream. I am dog tired now after that long run and am walking right up the middle of the stream, splashing water with each step.

I suddenly look to the ridge above me. There I seen the silhouettes of two men in the pale moonlight. They had spotted me first. They could hear me splash in the water. "Are they Germans or Americans?" I ask myself. Well, it makes no difference who they are, they got the drop on me anyhow, I decides, so I walk towards them. I then hear the bolt of an M-1 click.

In a low but firm voice I hear, "Halt, Boston." I felt like giving out with a joyous war whoop, but just replied equally as low, "Red Sox." At that, the two men came running towards me. I then recognize them as the Little King and P.J. I don't believe I was ever more glad to see anyone.

"Are you okay, P.T.?" was the first thing P.J. asked. "Where are the rest of them?" the Little King asks. "Aren't they here?" I answered. "No," was the Little King's reply. I then tell them what happened. Just then Capt. Thayler, our company commander, comes up and says, "The rest of the company withdrew around to the left. They got a good start on us. We'll have to get going and withdraw to the right as fast as we can and take everything along that we can carry 'cause we're going to need it." He went on to say, "The Germans have broken through all around, and they're coming with armor now. We've got to withdraw about twenty miles and fast, so let's go."

We start our long walk. I was glad to be back with at least part of the company again. There were only a few weapons carriers to haul equipment, so most of us were pretty heavily loaded. We had left all our food to the Germans and there was no water fit to drink. We get far enough to the rear, we come to an assembly are. There we see the rest of the company. The Homely One and Phees came a-running. "Thank God you're here," the Homely One says. Phees says, "We thought sure you were captured." Lloyd Doe, Speed, Old Tom, Old Allah and Leo Schular were popping questions at me faster than I could answer them. Even the Big-Assed Bird is asking questions.

We then get on six-by-sixes and travel several more miles. At daybreak, we start walking again. Capt. Thayler says Ploopie will bring us some grub by tonight, but unfortunately the Jerry Tiger Tanks were travelling too fast. Ploopie's stew wagon got caught between a mark six and a General Sherman tank. I guess Ploopie and the cooks had their stock pots and frying pans at high port and ready for action, but finally go out of it by leaving our nice hot supper for the conquering Germans. So, we go another 24 hours without grub.

It is pitch dark and raining when we get to a position to set up a defense for the night. We are cold, wet, tired and hungry when Ploopie finally comes with some hot chow. I think that was one of the best meals I have ever eaten. Afterwards those who were not on guard curled up in the cold mud and dropped off in deep slumber till they awoke to take their turn on guard. While I was on the gun it was so dark, aided by the cold rain, I don't think I could have seen a Jerry till he was on top of me.

Next day it is still cold and rainy. We stood around, huddled up in bunches like a herd of cattle in a storm. No one seemed to know for sure where we were. We don't know where our friendly units to the left or right of us are. We are sending out patrols all day. The Homely One takes a patrol out at a 50-degree azimuth and comes back reporting they seen no Germans, no Americans. "Bean Pole" of the mortar section takes out the next patrol at a 250-degree azimuth. They return with the same report as the Homely One's patrol had brought back. Bean Pole is exceptionally good for his patrol work, as he has a physique just made for it as he is so tall and thin. That man is so thin that when he steps on a scale, all he gets is his fortune. When we were getting fed so poorly back in Ireland, the rumor was going around that Bean Pole swallowed a walnut to keep his pants up. But I myself never really believed that. Although it is awfully hard to distinguish Bean pole's foxhole from a straddle trench, and very often one does mistake his foxhole for the straddle trench, that is why he gets shit on so much. Old Allah says, "Bean Pole hasn't anything to worry about. All he has to do is turn sideways when things get rough and it will be impossible for the Jerries to hit him."

It's getting towards evening now, and time to send out another patrol. "Big Stoop," a Sergeant from the 1st Platoon, is designated to lead this patrol. As I didn't have to go on any patrols during the day, I get hooked for this one along with Speed and Jack Plumber from the 4th Platoon. Lt. Van gave us orders. "Strike out at a 280-degree azimuth, and don't be afraid to go a couple of miles. If you don't run into anything, stop and set up an outpost for the night. Turn your 536 radio for communication, and don't come back till you hear from me."

With that, the patrol strikes out at 280 degrees. We had covered a good distance when we reach a cactus patch out in the wide-open spaces. Big Stoop says, "This is where we will have out outpost." We then dig in in the cactus patch. Nothing happens that night except that it is still raining. In the morning the sun comes out, shining brightly. We turn on the 536, but get nothing but static. Big Stoop would say, "Able to King, Able to King, over," but we could hear nothing in return but a lot of strange noises. Personally, the only time I did hear a 536 work worth a damn was when all you would have to do is raise your voice a little and the other party could hear you anyhow.

With no communications with the company, Big Stoop decides to send a party back to the company that night to find out the score and get some food and water, as we are getting pretty dry and hungry by this time. The party comes back some hours later, reporting that the company had apparently moved out of their old positions, for there wasn't any sign of them anywhere around. Now we are all beginning to worry a little out alone somewhere in no-man's land with no food or water, not knowing where to go or what to do.

Next morning, we had company—an old Arab and his camel. Arabs generally had eggs, so we all flock around him to try to get some eggs out of him. The difficulty of making him understand what we wanted now arose. We make faces, crow like roosters, to no avail. The Old Arab just murmured, "No compreh." We are thinking seriously of slaughtering the old camel for camel burgers when Speed emerges with a bright idea for making Mohammed understand we wanted eggs. With his bayonet, he draws in the sand a picture of a hen, and right under the hen's ass he draws an egg. Mohammed then jumps on his camel saying, "Compreh," motioning he will return with the merchandise.

A few minutes later he comes back with about the biggest and oldest rooster in all Tunisia. Well, that was better than nothing, so we take up a collection and give the Arab about $10 worth of francs for the aged rooster. The meat from this bird filled three helmets, and we soon have three helmets full of chicken boiling over a brush fire. It boiled half the day and still was not done. Finally, our impatience overwhelmed us.

Jack Plumber and I think we see a truck off in the distance so we take off for it. We walk a good distance before we see it is a British lorry. The Limeys greet us cheerfully. One of them yelled, "Hey you bloody Yanks, get out of the open or the Luftwaffe will be on all of us." Just about then a flock of ME. 109's roared overhead and dropped some eggs on their anti-tank guns. After they fly away, we tell the Limeys our trouble. "We are the Coldstream Guards, the King's Royal Troops. Anything we have is yours. Come in and have a spot of tea," the Limeys hospitably say.

They feed us Irish stew till I thought we would burst. We then carry a five gallon can of stew back for the boys. When we finally get back to the outpost, the chicken is done. Big Stoop had found the company and brought back several cans of sardines, so now we flourish in grub. Big Stoop says, "I found the company. They are back a couple of miles on that big mountain you see. As soon as you finish eating, we are going to rejoin them." Everybody is full now and hates to move. It is surprising how good an old rooster can taste cooked in nothing but dirty creek water without even any salt and pepper to season it with.

We walk several miles before we reach the peak of the mountain and join our company. The Homely One and Phees are shining a new machine gun. They say it's a present for me, a replacement for the one I abandoned on Sugar Loaf Hill.

We aren't settled here more than an hour when we get orders to move again. We are all tired and blow our tops, but pack up and start moving again. Apparently, we had withdrawn far enough, for we are moving ahead again now.

It is in the wee hours of the morning when we finally reach our destination. There we are told this would be our final defensive position. We dig elaborate defensive positions with lots of mines and barbed wire in front of us. We are told here is where we will turn back the Jerries. We work here about a week and had what we thought was a perfect defensive position. The we get orders to move ahead further and dig in and hold another defense line. We had with-drawn about 40 miles from Sugar Loaf Hill, and now we had moved ahead again about 20 miles and hadn't encountered any German opposition.

We get to our new positions and find the terrain is a group of small rolling hills overlooking a flat valley to our front that would be a perfect approach for the Germans on the attack. The 4th Platoon is split up. The mortar section is to the rear. They have their "Sixties" set up in a defalate position behind the hill. The machine gun section is on the extreme right flank of the company. We have our "Thirties" dug in at the base of the hill with a perfect field of fire across the valley in front of us. We have our range cards made out perfectly. Directly in front of us we have a mine field, so we feel pretty secure. The 1st, 2nd and 3rd Platoons extend to the left of us in that order.

After having our front-line positions dug, we dig living quarters on the rear slope of the hill. P.J. and I dig a big, deep hole and pitch a pup tent over it. I guess P.J. and I have the most super deluxe foxhole in the section. The Homely One makes Old Allah hole up with him as he says Old Allah is his runner now. Old Tom and Lloyd Doe have a hole almost as good as ours. Speed and Brady have a big one, so Phees moves in with them to save himself the trouble of digging.

I guess we are still quite a ways from the Jerries, as everything is nice and peaceful. Just once in a while a Jerry plane flies over, and he is on nothing but a reconnaissance mission. We send motorized and foot patrols out every day and night, but seldom run into anything. The 34th Recon sent out patrol on halftracks. They went about ten miles and only run into a similar patrol of the Germans, had a little scrap returned.

The only casualties we have had so far in this position are caused by our own mine field. There has already been a six-by-six, a weapons carrier and two camels blown up. One day we see one of our peeps coming hell bent for the mine field. Seeing it come, we all jump up and wave and holler to try to stop them, but they pay us no never mind. They keep right on coming till suddenly there was a bang and the peep went about ten feet straight in the air. The four passengers all flew in different directions. We then run out to the wreck and find Lt. Smith, our battalion adjutant, in pretty bad shape. A French officer is gasping for his last breath of air, the other two are uninjured. Lt. Smith recovered okay, but the Frenchman could not be saved. After that, we guard the mine field closely so that no more of our own men would be blown up.

By now, we are beginning to enjoy being in this position as our lines and the Jerry lines seem to be a good distance apart. Ploopie brings us hot stew every morning before daylight for breakfast. We have Limey tea and hardtack for dinner. After dark Ploopie brings us more hot stew for supper. Some of the fellers from the mortar section would even get the grub off the weapons carrier and carry it to us, then they would eat with us.

Those who generally carried chow from the motor were Bean Pole, Leo Schular, Danny Howagner, Jack Plumber and Big Barnsmell. Big Barnsmell comes over mostly to discuss the price of rice in China with Old Allah. The Homely One and Old Tom get into some pretty hot arguments over the grub. One day Old Tom had been functioning and got himself a couple of eggs from an Arab. He lays the eggs gently on the ground while he makes preparation to boil them. Just then, Speed comes and sits tight smack down on the rare hen fruit. "Speed, you dumb asshole! Now look what you've done," Old Tom burst out angrily. "Oh, that's alright. I'll buy you a dozen when we get back to the states," Speed murmurs slowly.

We are beginning to wonder when we are going to start pushing. Lt. Van, who is always optimistic, says "We aren't going so good now, but the British 8th Army is going hell bent for election. They jumped off from El Alamain and came a thousand miles. They're up to the Mareth Line now." That makes us all feel much better.

One day we get orders to pull a raid. Guinie Pig deals—we always call them—and it seems to us that Col. Swenson's 3rd Battalion generally gets hooked for these deals. The Berdache 8th Army had come a long way—all the way from El Alemain on through Mersa Matruh, Bengahzi Tobruk and Tripoli. They were now up to Mareth. General Montgomery's great army had come the 1300 miles in record time, but the Germans had them stopped now by their powerful defensive position called the Mareth Line. Apparently, generals Ike,

Montgomery, Alexander, Anderson and Patton got their heads together and decided to use part of Patton's 2nd Corps to pull a fake attack on the weaker part of the German lines from the southwest. Col. Swenson's 3rd Battalion is the part of the American 2nd Corps to pull the raid. Col. War, who is our regimental commander, leads the raid himself.

That night we get on trucks. We take our bed rolls along. We ride a good distance, then start walking. We are in the approach march formation. With us were some General Grant and Sherman tanks and tank destroyers. Out T.D.'s at that stage of the war were nothing but halftracks mounted with a 75mm rifle. We also had a battery of field artillery with us. Our artillery at that time used the British 25-pounder.

Col. Swenson said we would have a squadron of fighter planes to support us, but we just laugh at that, for we know the only fighter planes in North Africa are Fock-Wolffs, Stukkas or Messershmidts. American planes were just something in a defense plant back home to keep people employed. We figure it is something like a P.W.A. project.

We keep walking till all of a sudden, we hear the rapid fire of a German (Shmitzer) machine pistol. It cut the cactus right over our heads. In a split second everyone hit the dirt, start to deploy and shootin' at everything in general. Pretty soon one of the boys bring an Arab out of the cactus patch at the point of a tommy gun. They bring the squawking Arab back to Col. Ward. Col. Ward then urges the Arab to come with him behind a big cactus. It wasn't long before Col. Ward came back alone, jamming his smoking .45 in his holster, and we continue on our mission. We don't do much farther before the battalion splits up. I Company goes to the left; L Company goes to the right and K Company goes straight ahead in the broad-assed open. After going about 400 yards, we hear the droll of planes. We look to our rear and see a flock of them flying gracefully through the blue sky dotted with white clouds.

"Oh goodie!" the Homely One exclaims joyfully. "Here comes our air support. I told you we had some planes." Old Allah then squints skyward and hastily looks back at the Homely One saying, "If them's our planes, some asshole has painted black crosses and Swastikas all over the damned things."

31

He no more gets the words out of his mouth and they are down on us. They were strafing, but we deployed so quickly and retaliated with rifle fire that they soon flew off to the wild blue yonder with no casualties inflicted in either side.

Shortly after the Luftwaffe left, we see tanks coming at us in good numbers. We then reverse about 500 yards and cut to the left. We hastily set up our machine guns. Jerry machine guns were racking the flat ground with vicious grazing fire. P.J. and I dig our gun in. We can't pick out any Jerries, so we run through a couple of hundred rounds just for the hell of it, then went behind a cactus and brew us a canteen cup of mud. Our artillery is now going over our heads and landing in German territory at a rapid pace. Leo Schular and Danny Howagner are plucking away with their mortars as fast as they can.

After a brief but fiery skirmish, Col. Swenson bellers, "Let's get our ass a bobbin' to the rear." Without further question, we are on our way getting out of the hot spot as fast as we can. M Company had several casualties, and the I Company had several men captured.

It is getting dark now and starting to rain and raining hard. After walking quite some distance, we stop. None of the enlisted men know the score, but we hope that somebody does. Most of us curl up in the mud and go to sleep. We are all soaked and beginning to feel pretty chilly. An hour or so later, Col. Ward issues the order for all vehicles to turn on their lights and head back towards the Germans, as the Jerries were advancing on us.

We all think the colonel must be crazy to do a thing like that. We don't go ahead very far when the lights are turned off again, and we cut to the right and head back to our old defensive position as fast a darkness and terrain would permit us to travel. One reconnaissance car went over an embankment and mired itself deeply in the clay-like mud. We are forced to abandon that vehicle. The men were riding anything that moved from hang-on to the safety belt of the tail end of a six-by-six to riding straddling the barrel of a 37mm anti-tank gun.

We are glad when we finally make it back to Pinochle Hill, which is the name we hung on our defensive position, as the mortar section played so much pinochle there. Ploopie comes with hot chow, and we are soon settled back to our old routine on Pinochle Hill. We hear later that our raid was highly successful. We hit the Jerries from the southwest.

Thinking we had a large force; they pulled a lot of their troops and equipment from the Mereth Line to stop and counter attack us. When Col. Ward ordered the vehicles to turn on their lights, it apparently must have confused the Jerries, for their counter attack never materialized to any serious extent and gave us adequate time to withdraw to our old positions. Whie that was going on, the British 8th Army smashed through the Mereth Line and are now heading for Sfax and Soose.

Everything is back to normal on Pinochle Hill now. As we don't get any coffee, we always have a 5-gallon can of Limey tea boiling over a suety gas fire. By now we are beginning to understand why the Limeys are so fond of their bloody tea. There are rumors going around that we are soon going to be getting American rations instead of Limey compo rations. Ploopie says service company already has a can of Spam, but we understand that it is for display purposes only.

We get a bulletin down from Old Blood 'N Guts that there will be a $30 fine for anyone caught not wearing a helmet. The officers are even supposed to wear ties, the bulletin states. But as we figures Old Blood 'N Guts will never come to Pinochle Hill, no one adheres to this order.

It is about a week after the Al Allah Raid when we get attack orders. This is to be the start of the big push. The British 8th and 1st Armies and the American 2nd Corps commanded by Old Blood 'N Guts make up the Allied forces in North Africa. The American 2nd Corps is made up of the 1st, 9th and 34th Infantry Divisions and the 1st Armored Division.

Just at dusk, loaded with packs, ammo and rations, we get on trucks. Our mission is to break the German stronghold and take Fondouk Pass, sometimes known as Karawan Pass. After riding a good distance, we get to an assembly area, get off trucks, sprawl on the ground and try to grab a couple of hours sleep.

At 2:00 we are up again. We start a 14-mile march from this assembly area to Fondouk Pass, carrying our mortars and machine guns. Each ammo carrier had to pack four boxes of machine gun ammo. The truck P.J. was on got wrecked, so Old Allah is my assistant gunner. We had gone a good distance when it started getting daylight. We now deploy in a skirmish line. We are entering a flat plain as lever as a pool table. At the end of the plains stood the mountains where the Germans were looking down our throats. I looked to the right, then to the left, and as far as I could see across the flat land in either direction were doughboys of the 34th Division in perfect scattered formation, walking into HELL. Walking into one of the most gruesome, bloodiest, terrorizing battles of this war.

We encountered the "Jerry" outposts, had brief fire fights before they withdraw to their main line of resistance. Our artillery has been silent. We all hit the ground as the first German shell comes in. From then on it was hell. They were coming in fast now and landing right amongst us. Between the terrific shell bursts, I could hear the anguished cry of pain call, "medics, medics." We couldn't stop here we had to push on. So, running and flopping we advance slowly, leaving our dead and wounded buddies behind. If possible, the rifles of the fallen men were jammed bayonet first into the ground to signify their position to the medics. The high velocity fire from the deadly German 88's are coming in on us now and our manpower is rapidly depleting.

We finally reached a shallow ditch that afforded us some protection. No one from the machine gun section had been hit yet, but not far from me I heard "Beanpole" beg Wassen to speak to him, but Wassen spoke no more. Danny Howagner called for the medics to come quickly to save Dave Montgomery. When the medic managed to crawl up to where Danny and Dave were, he said it was too late, but Danny wouldn't give up. He worked on Dave and later Dave came to and asked for a drink of water. Danny then carried Dave to the aid station and Dave lived to come back and get even with the "Jerries." Danny is one of the outstanding heroes of K Co. That man is super.

The mortar section was hit hard, and didn't have many men left. It is getting dark now and "The Homely One" tells us to make a mad dash across the open and set up our guns. It was quite a long run raked with vicious machine gun fire. I hesitated at first, then grabbed the tripod and ran zig zagging crazily as I heard the spay of bullets fall around me. In utter fatigue, I finally reach a defilade spot that protected me from M.G. fire. I flopped on the ground panting, a shell came in, I didn't even move as I was so pooped I didn't much care whether I was hit or not.

Then Old Allah comes in behind me with the gun, which he just throws ahead of him as he flops beside me. I thanked God that Old Allah got through okay and felt better as I seen him beside me. It's plumb dark now. The 1st platoon is on a little knoll to our left fighting it out with the Jerries. A good many of the boys were coming down wounded, others were carrying the dead.

Our parched throats were so dry we could hardly talk. Old Allah and I finally grab up a bunch of canteens and go back about a mile to a muddy creek to get some water. The water tasted like frog piss—and it probably was—but it satisfied us anyhow. It was getting towards morning when we got back. Capt. Thayler was trying desperately to contact L Company on the 536, but as usual was unable to do so. Col. Swenson then decides this is no place to spend another day so we withdraw a couple of hundred yards. We dig in a cactus patch that keeps us fairly well concealed.

The next day we just sit, sweating it out in our fox holes. Every time our artillery opens up, the Luftwaffe flies over and silences them. As soon as it began to get dark, P.J. comes back. I was glad to have him help out on guard. Next night we move over to the right rear and dig in on a small knoll. The ground was so rocky that we scarcely have time to get our holes dug before daylight.

P.J.'s and my hole was so small that one guy would have a hard time squeezing into it, but somehow we both manage to get in and sweat it out until darkness came again. One Fock-Wolff almost dove right into our fox hole, but outside of that the Jerries didn't molest us much. But we were pinned down all day. We couldn't stick our heads out of our holes. Our latrine was in a C ration can. Speed and Brady have their hole right next to ours. Speed fills up a C ration can, and as he dumps it out, the wind blows the contents all back in Brady's face. Brady just grits his teeth and says painfully, "Cripes, Speed, your piss is salty."

When darkness finally comes, we are so stiff from being cramped up in our tiny holes all day that it takes us about an hour to limber up. Col. Swenson says we are pulling back to a wadi tonight and rest up a bit, which makes us all feel much better. So, under the cover of darkness, we withdraw. On the withdrawal, Col. Swenson fell in a well. And when close to 300 pounds falls on one bent ankle, something had to give—and Col. Swenson's ankle gave. He was taken to the hospital that night leaving Major Snellman in charge of the battalion. We get to the wadi and Ploopie brings us some hot chow. "Pugly," the supply sergeant had even gotten in some new clothes. I managed to get new pants that my ass had been so badly in need of for the past few months. Most of the boys needed shoes, but Pugly only had a few of them.

While we are in this position, the 2nd Platoon gets hooked for an outpost that is a good 1,000 yards in front of us. So, Staff Sergeant Bennie Hill takes his 2nd Platoon out. His sawed-off right guide, likable little "Cutsie" Mickalson, brought up the rear as they took off. They were out there a night and a day when Cutsie came back to ask Capt. Thayler something. Then Capt. Thayler, a new lieutenant, and Cutsie climb into a Jeep driven by "Ginger" Holte and take off. That's the last time we seen any of them. They got a little too far out in Jerryland and tangled with a Jerry armored car. Capt. Thayler was reported killed, but the other three were taken alive.

The next night the machine gun section moves out to help the 2nd Platoon hold their outpost. We labor all night, digging positions in almost solid rock ground. We are here for a couple of days when all noncoms are called back to the C.P. to meet out new company commander. His name is Capt. Skaliky.

The Homely One, who is the machine gun, section leader, and the two squad leaders who are Phees and Old Tom, return from the company C.P. with very long faces. We ask them what is bothering them. "Nothing," they reply, but we knew they were lying.

Next day we are told we are going to Fondouck Pass again. We are told we would accomplish what we failed to do the first time, and do it or else. They tell us we will be supported by Limey tanks this time. This time was even worse for us than the last one, because now we knew what a death trap we were walking into.

That night we start the approach march back to the deadly Fondouck Pass. When it broke daylight, we immediately fan out into a skirmish line the very same way we did the first time. We all knew just as sure as there is cold shit in a dead goose what would happen in a few minutes, and it did.

The Jerries were even more prepared for us this time than they were the first time. We are getting fairly close to the base of the mountain when they start pouring it on us with all kinds of artillery and mortars. The deadly 88's were coming in so fast they already exploded before we could hear them. We were also close enough so that their grazing interlocking machine gun fire had us pinned down right in the broad open unable to move. It was there we were forced to stay flat on the ground until darkness.

There, I believe, we put in the most horrible day of the war. I could hear the familiar voices of my wounded buddies; cry painfully for help that they were unable to get. Many voices died out entirely. There was hardly a let up in the barrage all day. Hugging the ground, I tried to light a cigarette. But every time I raised my arm, I was forced to hug the ground again.

Speed managed to crawl close to me and says calmly, "Say, them 88's are dangerous, ain't they?" Suddenly we heard the rumble of tanks. I looked up and seen some tanks maneuvering around to the left of us. They were coming towards us now. Old Tom was just ahead of me. He looks back at me and says, "If them are German tanks, we're done for." We were pinned so we couldn't even dig any fox holes.

As the tanks came closer, I recognized them to be British Crusader and Matilda tanks. That made us feel better, but even though they were friendly, they were unable to see the doughboys lying on the ground. We tried to steer them away from them, but some of our boys were crushed by the armor. One tank pulled up fairly close to us, and right away it got a direct hit from an 88 and started to burn.

The Limey crew crawled out of the turret and under the tank and nonchalantly start brewing a spot of tea. The Luftwaffe flew over and bombed and strafed us at regular intervals throughout the day to add to the terrorization. When darkness finally came, we were very much relieved.

We now had to gather up the dead and wounded. K Company was much smaller that night. So many of the fellows that we had lived with for the past two years, known each other like brothers, were gone and we missed them. The Homely One was wounded and had to be evacuated. Phees had gone back to the medics. Old Tom was the only non-com left in the section.

Very much disorganized, we moved a couple of hundred yards to the rear. Speed, Lloyd Doe, "Miss Polda," Old Allah, P.J. and myself dig us some super deluxe fox holes in a somewhat concealed area. It was beginning to get daylight when we pull our necks in our holes to sweat out another day.

My hole was a good five feet deep. More of our tanks were approaching now. They drive right up to our holes and stop. It wasn't long before the heaviest artillery the Germans had zeroed in on them. I heard one particular one fire. It sounded like it might be coming all the way from Munich. The sickening whistling sound kept coming closer and closer by the second as I hug the bottom of my hole and shudder.

As I hear the last sizzle, I think to myself, this is it. Then BANG! She hit. I was completely covered with the walls of my foxhole. I got my head free, and after some time I managed to get the rest of my body out. I could feel the effects of concussion. Lloyd Doe and P.J. come a-running. I guess they thought I got it. I look at my pack and jacket that was lying on the ground beside my hole and see they look like so many pounds of confetti.

P.J. then says, "It's going to be like this all day here now that they got us spotted. Let's make a run for it." Lloyd Doe and I second the motion, but Old Allah, Speed, and Miss Polda seem to think it is safer where they are, so the choose to stay. P.J., Lloyd and I then run madly, zig zagging and flopping to the rear, till we reach a wadi. There we dug us some holes and have a much more peaceful day. As my pack blew up, I didn't have any rations. But P.J. is such a big eater, that he always carries extra rations, so we have plenty of chow anyhow.

When darkness came again, we went up forward to go into a night attack, but it was like bumping our heads against a stone wall. Our attack was once again a failure, and we were forced to withdraw. P.J. and I dig us a subterranean fox hole after we withdraw. We get a few hours' sleep, then wake up suddenly as the sun was shining brightly down on us. As we gaze out of our hole, the first person we see is none other than a Limey. "What's going on here?" we ask him.

To which the Limey calmly replies, "The bloody Sherman tanks have broken through and are going faster than the London-Glasgow Express."

P.J. and I look at each other for a moment and I finally say, "Let's get to diggen' this hole. Ain't half deep enough." "Damned good idea." P.J. replies. We had dug down another foot when another Limey comes by. We ask how far the German tanks are from us now. "You're mistaken, Yanks, it isn't German tanks at all, but it is our Sherman tanks that have broken through. We should have Karawan in a few hours," the limey replies. With a sigh of relief, we quit digging immediately. P.J. Says, "to think we done all that digging just because we mistook the word "Sherman" for "German."

We then get out of our hole and see nothing but a long string of British armor pouring through Fondouck Pass. To us it was the nicest thing we could see at that particular time. Fondouck Pass line had been cracked thanks to the aid of the British 6th Armored Division. We now went rounding up Jerries, the first big bunch we had ever captured. They were well equipped, well dressed, big, ignorant Nazis. The pride of Field Marshal Rommel's Afrika Korps.

We explore their elaborate defensive positions along the base of the hills at the Pass. Big swastikas laid in stone decorated the interior of their positions. Here we capture a lot of material and equipment as well as troops. Nearly all of us had a Luger, P-38 or a machine pistol (Smitzer) along with lots of other stuff. We also captured several of the long-barreled 88's that had been shooting at us for so long.

This battle was equally as bloody and gruesome as the first attack. However, this time we emerged victorious. With the aid of the British 6th Armored Division, we broke through Bloody Fondouck Pass.

The morale of the company took a sudden surge upward. After taking a terrific beating, we had finally broken the German lines. That night we were relieved as the British 6th Armored Division moved through us. Major Hall was transferred in to replace Col. Swenson as battalion commander, Col. Swenson will be confined to the hospital for quite some time with his injured leg.

After reorganizing somewhat, we get on trucks and head for a rear area. For once the trucks weren't crowded. There were only seven or eight men on each six-by-six. Old Allah remarks, "You can always tell if we are going up or coming back from the front. When we go up, we have so many men we can't get the company on ten trucks. And when we come back, we can nearly get them all on one."

After riding a good distance, we pull into a wooded area and bivouac. Here we get intense training for the next two weeks, with a very meager supply of rations. We get so hungry here that we understand why Hungry Hank back in Algiers fought so bitterly over the contents of a garbage can. Ploopie is so desperate, he is thinking seriously of butchering a camel for us.

Here we get to know our new company commander, Capt. Skaliky, and find he is a regular Joe. We all call him Capt. Sky. Old Blood 'N Guts is no longer in command of the 2nd Corps. We now have a new corps commander, some lieutenant general by the name of Omar N. Bradley. Little did we know at that time what an important part of this new general would play in the overall victory of the allies.

It is here we get our replacements. We watch them as they as they come marching into the company area. All of K Company, after the beating it got at Fondouck Pass, was no bigger than a good size platoon, so we welcomed our replacements whole-heartedly. The group included a wide variety of men from all parts of the United States—tall, short, fat and thin. The four platoon sergeants of the company were making remarks as they passed by. "Thor," 1st Platoon Sergeant, wanted one little fellow for the first scout. "Bennie," 2nd Platoon Officer, wanted a big one for a B.A.R. man. George, 3rd Platoon Sergeant and the Little King, 4th Platoon Sergeant, decide they all look pretty good.

One of the replacements we get in the 4th Platoon is a straight-as-an-arrow West Virginian who is known as John L. Sullivan. We ask John L. what he done in civilian life. "Oh, I work around the still most of the time," John L. sputters quickly. When we ask his pal Southerland what he done, he coolly replies, "Oh, I was drunk most of the time." On the more serious type were Henry Thibadaue and quite a few others.

We were here about ten days when we got orders to move. Where to, we weren't told. This move seemed hard for us enlisted men to comprehend.

We crowded everything we had on trucks and climbed aboard. We traveled for miles and miles on rough, dusty roads and trails, sometimes traveling east, other times west, but we were making our way generally north.

To add to the confusion, we met convoy after convoy of desert-painted British vehicles of either the British 1st or 8th Armies. Despite these traffic hazards, the two huge convoys going in opposite directions managed to pass through each other undetected by the enemy and reach their destination at the designated time. Later, this journey was to be known as one of the most brilliant non-combat maneuvers of this war. When we finally reach an assembly area and detruck, we find we are many miles north of the section we had previously fought in. Here we organize for an all-out attack.

ON TO HILL 609

A little after noon we once again get on trucks, which take us up as close to our jumping off spot as they dared. On our way up, we pass an evacuation hospital. P.J. calls to the medics at the hospital, "I'll be seeing you in a day or two," and he wasn't lying. After detrucking, we march single file along the best concealment we could find. Just at dusk we reach a rocky cliff. The entire company hugs closely to the sheer rock wall for protection, while Capt. Sky gets final attack orders from Major Hall. Col. Ward, our regimental commander, was also there.

It is plumb dark when Capt. Sky returns and says, "Did you see that hill out in front of us about a mile? That hill is known on the map as Hill 490, and that's where the Jerries are. In about an hour we're going to pull a night attack on that hill." Then he goes on to say, "The 1st platoon will be on the right, the 2nd platoon on the left, and the 3rd platoon will be in reserve. The weapons platoon will set up their machine guns and mortars on a little knoll just before Hill 490. And if necessary, give us supporting fire."

Capt. Sky turns to the Little King, who is the weapons platoon sergeant, and says, "Now, don't fire till you get a signal from the assaulting platoon. The signal for you to fire will be one red flare fired from a vary pistol. We don't want to fire any sooner than we have to, for this is a surprise attack and we want to sneak up on them. If you see two green flares, go up, dash up to the hill quickly. That's the signal that we've secured the hill, and we'll need those machine guns and mortars right away to beat off an almost certain counter attack."

As the grim-faced riflemen with fixed bayonets lead off heavily loaded with hand grenades, I felt for them, but I was glad I was a machine gunner. When we reach the little knoll, we quickly set up our guns. After establishing a safety zone for our own troops in our overhead fire concentration area, as we await action and flare signals.

The first noise we hear to break the silence of the up-to-now calm, peaceful, chilly night was the popping of hand grenades popping like popcorn. Then concentrated fanatical bursts from the rapid firing Jerry machine guns. Our M-1's were barking a steady and deadly tune. We were watching for a flare signal. We were expecting a red one, but the firing died down and soon two emerald green flares went up. The hill was ours, so we rapidly take our guns out of action and start up Hill 490.

It was getting daylight as we pull up to the rear slope of Hill 490. Capt. Sky was hollering, "Get them damned machine guns up to the point of this hill and beat off this counter attack." The Jerries already were lying a terrific barrage on us and coming in more and more by the minute. P.J. is hit now, Phees is too. Old Allah is missing. While the boys are getting knocked off and wounded, Old Tom hollers to Lloyd Doe and I that we'll have to take our squads, set up and start firing as soon as we can.

I find that in my squad I have nothing but two new replacements who are not wounded. The two replacements and I struggle to the point of Hill 490, passing our fallen and wounded buddies. We finally reach the point and set up quickly. I spotted Jerry skirmishers coming up the rear slope of the hill to my left front, and zeroed in on them. I let go with a long burst of about 50 rounds. They all hit the dirt. The beaten zone of that burst must have done some damage. Heavy artillery and mortar shells are bursting all around us increasingly by the moment, and we are in the broad open and very vulnerable to all of it.

I see some of the Jerries running and flopping to the rear. I encourage their departure with another hail of machine gun fire. In a moment I was almost sorry I made the Jerries mad at me, for now the concentrated barrage was almost unbearable. But none of the three of us had been hit yet. I decide it's too hot to stick, so I tell the two replacements not to get up and run, but to roll down the hill.

We manage to roll off the point okay, but we rolled off to the right and were now on an exposed side of Hill 490. For what looked like about a mile or two to our right front stood a mammoth mountain. The Jerries had a fortress on it almost as impregnable the British have Gibraltar. It was a perfect artillery O.P. They could see every move we made. Not only us could they observe, but everything for miles and miles around.

The hill was as full of 88's and machine guns as a hive of bees. We know now that nothing can be done in all North Africa till this hill is taken. The few remaining of us laid on the exposed side of Hill 490 all day listening to whispering death come at us unceasingly with never a let-up. In places, scarlet blood could be seen trickling down through the jagged grey rocks on Hill 490.

I think most everyone was saying some kind of prayer. It seemed like every shell had my name, rank and serial number on it. They were all landing incredibly close. I could feel the effects of concussion, but somehow the shrapnel was missing me. Our artillery observer was below me. In between shell bursts, I could hear him call frantically on his radio back to the 155 Long Toms. I heard him give a fire order regarding Hill 609. A second later, he was killed instantly by artillery just like a Jerry might have been near enough to hear his fire order on Hill 609 and killed him for it. Hill 609, I think to myself and wonder how we can take it. There is only about $^1/_3$ of the company left now. It's bound to be rough.

Now I see the 2nd battalion going out in a skirmish line in the flat valley below and to the right of us, heading for Hill 609. I shuddered to think of what they were walking into. The Jerries see them too, and quickly pour it on. The shells hit E Company like a fly swatter might hit a group of flies grouped around a lump of sugar. The anguished cry of pain and the scream for medics could be heard between shell bursts.

The 2nd Battalion was forced to withdraw to cover. As it begins to get dusk, me and my two-man squad rush to the rear of Hill 490 for more adequate protection. We no more than get back there before the riflemen holler counter attack. We hurriedly set the machine gun up on the right flank, but the fighting 1st Platoon already had them driven back in a gallant struggle. That was the last attempt the Jerries made to regain Hill 490.

When darkness finally came, we were very much relieved as then we could move around without being seen. At that stage of the war, the Jerries fired very little artillery at night as they didn't want to give away their positions with gun flashes. So, the nights were comparatively peaceful. The company and the entire battalion had taken another terrific beating that day. We took Hill 490 and held it, but the cost was high. It was just as bad, if not worse, than either of the Fondouck attacks. We had lost about ²/₃ of our men. I was glad to see Old Allah back. In the confusion he had wound up fighting with the 2ⁿᵈ Platoon.

We now were getting hungry. A ration-carrying detail is organized to go back and find the ration dump and bring back food, water and ammunition. After getting the carrying party organized, we take off and walk and walk for miles, searching for the ration dump all in vain. As it grew towards morning, we were forced to return to Hill 490 without food, water or ammunition. Tired, thirsty and hungry, we finally pulled back up to Hill 490. The boys that stayed on the hill while we were searching for the dump dropped their chins as they see us come up empty handed.

A battalion from the 133ʳᵈ Infantry Regiment moved up on Hill 490 and relieved us as we moved over to the right of Hill 490 in a draw just below Hill 609. It was dawn when the company got completely concealed in the draw. We dig holes along the bank and sweat out another day with no food or water. Major Hall called Capt. Sky to proceed with the attack on Hill 609. "We're not going to attack anything until we get food, water and ammunition," Capt. Sky replies angrily.

I was tired and tried desperately to sleep, but somehow couldn't. Suddenly we hear a roar of planes. Oh-oh, we all think, here is where we get another pasting from the Luftwaffe, as we turn our faces skyward. "Look," Old Tom exclaims excitedly, "there are some planes that have no black crosses or swastikas on them. They have a bull's eye." "British Spitfire," the Little King says. "Well, whattya' know. We've got planes on our side too," Old Allah says with a relieved tone in his voice.

Yes, that was the beginning of the rise of the Allied Air Force. Later on, that day we also saw about a squadron of American P-38's with their twin fuselage glide gracefully through the air. The white star in the blue circle looked mighty good to us, for the Jerries had superiority in the air. And when you've seen a friendly plane, it was something to shout about.

When darkness finally came, it was time to go hunt for rations again. It took a big carrying party to bring back all the food, water and ammunition. By the time we get back to the draw and distribute the food, water and ammo it is midnight. Tired from no sleep in over 50 hours, I lie down and try to catch a few winks before we start the attack on Hill 609 at 400 hours

I no more than get lied down when Old Tom comes over and says, "P.T., you and Danny Howagner have to go on a reconnaissance patrol. Contact L Company, who are up ahead, and pick out a route of approach for the company to take on the attack at 4:00." "Why in the hell do you pick on me for all this shit?" I complain, getting up bitching about everything in general. I tie a few extra grenades on my belt and contact Danny, who tells me him and I will make the patrol alone.

Danny leads off and I follow about ten feet behind. I don't mind doing something like this when I'm with a man like Danny. After winding our way through some wadis, we run into L Company and talk to their company commander, who is known to one and all throughout the Battalion as Capt. Ichabod Crane, who was a most exemplary combat officer. Through towering Capt. Ichabod's shaggy beard, signs were visible of his deep concern for his company and the other companies of the battalion.

He didn't have to say anything. We could sort of read the expression on his strong but gentle face. He was thinking 609 would be tougher than hell for a depleted battalion such as ours to take. After some thought, Capt. Ichabod finally says, "When K Company attacks, L Company will be to your right, but don't expect too much of us. I've only got about ten men to platoon left now, and the company is really too weak to do much wholesale attacking."

Danny and I then pick out the most likely route of approach and make our way back to the company. It is just 4:00 when we get back to the company, and they're waiting all saddled up for us to show them the route we picked.

As we advance on Hill 609, we watch the big mountain fortress closely. We could see it clearly now, silhouetted against the pink eastern sky. It was dawn now. The jagged hill cast long, dark shadows down on us as it hid the early rising sun. From where we were now, Hill 609 appeared sort of flat at the summit to give it an almost mesa-like look and somewhat haunted in appearance to match its naively-known name of Djebel Tahent.

I looked back to the left and rear and see bloody Hill 490, the costly stepping stone to Hill 609. I could see our tanks maneuvering on this side of Hill 490. They were tactfully heading for the left flank of Hill 609 when the 88's opened up on them. We had just reached the base of 609 when machine guns and mortars opened up on us from all over.

We were fortunate to be as near the top of the hill as we were before they opened up on us too strongly. We picked our way up the hill through a veritable hail of bullets. Going through an olive orchard, we would run and flop quickly from one olive tree to another. At last, we come to the terracing of the hill. Hugging closely behind a ledge for safety, we take our second wind. Here we talk it over for a while. If we can only take this hill, it will eliminate the greatest barrier in all Tunisia.

Once we take Hill 609, opposition would quickly deteriorate. We should be able to march right into Mature, 12 miles away. On to Ferryville, Bizerta and Tunis. It can be taken, but we all know it will mean more casualties, blood and death. We know that after the eventual capture of Hill 609, the outfit will be even smaller than it is now, and that's really small.

The 1st and 3rd Platoons were already assaulting the hill. The spray of Jerry machine gun fire was going everywhere. Hand grenades, M-1's, B.A.R.'s and tommy guns were the answers of the Yankee dough foot. Old Tom led the machine gun section up the hill at a rapid speed. As we neared the crest, we took a quick inventory, and not a man from the section had been hit.

The Jerries were already pretty well routed, and for the moment at least, hostile fire had almost died down completely. There wasn't a Jerry in sight—nothing but their abandoned mortars, machine guns and other equipment. We hurriedly set up our guns at the cliff of the right flank of the hill.

We had taken Djebel Tahent. Hill 609 was ours. We rule King's Hill now, and intend to hold it. We quickly take advantage of our new ownership of the great fortress mountain. On a smaller hill to our right and slightly to our rear, the 1st Battalion was attacking. From our position we were looking downward to the rear slope of the hill. We had perfect observation of the battle as we watched the Jerries fight desperately to beat off the ferocious attack of the 1st Battalion.

We then commence firing our machine guns and mortars at the Jerries from the rear. It was too much for them to take and they begin to withdraw. When they start to retreat, from the view we have on 609, they show up like a three-ring circus, and we really pour it to them.

Lloyd Doe and I were behind our machine guns, and we already had them sizzling hot. Danny Howagner fired all the mortar ammo of his own and then proceeded to fire the Jerries' own mortar at them. The 1st Battalion was coming up from the front, and we were giving them from their right rear. What a spot they were in. It was about as bad for them to go one way as it was the other. It gave us a good feeling after taking beatings from them. We now were slaughtering them, giving them probably the worst whipping they ever had. Through field glasses we could see them drop like flies as the 2nd Battalion took final possession of their hill.

Shortly after we had secured Hill 609, our sister regiment, the 168th Infantry, were moving in echelon from the left rear toward the rearward slopes of Hill 609. At that time in that sector, a dense fog was lying low in the valley. The Jerries apparently thought due to the fog it would be a good time to sneak up the rear slopes of Hill 609 and reconquer the prize hill they had lost.

Unfortunately for them, however, the 168th had themselves aligned in a very good position just as the fog lifted. The veterans of Faid Pass opened up on them, and the potential counter attack soon deteriorated into a mass slaughter of Jerries.

Major Hall radioed Capt. Sky that the 133rd infantry, our sister regiment, had moved up on our left flank, which was a high, flat rock edge that protruded outward to the left of 609, so by now we were beginning to feel fairly secure. Hill 609 is fringed at the top by a sort of horseshoe rock rim. We have our outposts on this rim, except for the part the 133rd is supposed to take care of. The remainder of the battalion stays in the inner part of this horseshoe.

Just as it begins to get dusk, Capt. Sky comes up to look over the positions and is walking around as big as you please when "Brrrrr," machine gun fire lands all around him. I look to the left and can plainly see the muzzle blast from the gun that fired, which was in the 133rd sector. Capt. Sky seen the gun too, and stands up waving his arms and yelling, "Hey! You crazy bastards in the 133rd, quit that damned shootin'. This is the 135th down here."

He no more than gets the words out of his mouth when they open up on him again. He repeats his call back to them. They fire again. This time, they get son close to him that they have him pinned down behind a rock. After being pinned down in silence for a few moments, he hollers again, "Hey! Lt. Doty, open up on them birds. They got me pinned down. If that's the 133rd up there, we're the Martians from Mars."

By now there was Jerry machine gun fire coming from several different places in the rocky walls of Hill 609. We then pour everything we have at them and start pursuing them with hand grenades. The Jerry firing stops suddenly, and all we can hear now is the Jerries calling frantically for one another so they can get out of there. One Jerry we could hear plainly call, "Herman! Herman! Come arouse, come arouse."

Old Allah hollers back at him, "Yeah, if I find Herman before, he'll have a Bangalore Torpedo up his ass," and periods it with a shot from his .3. Speed could never forget about Herman. He muttered slowly, "Gosh! I would like to get Herman's ears and take them home to Tillie for a souvenir. I should get her something like that cause she always wants me to send her souvenirs." We evidently hadn't screened the rim of the 609 quite thoroughly enough, for these Jerries had been holed up in the rocks all day, not daring to move. When darkness finally come, they opened up on Capt. Sky in a desperate attempt to withdraw. We hear later that the battalion from the 133rd captured most of them. Later on that night it was time to go for water rations and ammo. Lt. Doty tells me to stay on the hill and put out some outposts with the men that didn't go for rations.

John L. Sullivan, the new replacement, was one of the men they left me. So, I put them on guard in a fairly safe place. Two minutes after I had posted him, he comes back. I look at him and say, "What in the hell are you doing back here, John? You're supposed to be on guard." "I ain't gone out dere no mo. Dem

Germans, dey kill a guy if he stan out dere." I put him out there three times, but he wouldn't stay. He told me, "Man, you ain't got no mo sense den a rat turd, puttin' me out dere like dat. Don't you know dats dangerous?" I realize then that he is right. For the safety of everyone concerned, it is best not to have him on guard. So, I tell him to go to bed. He just replies, "Dem Germans, dey smart people, ain't dey?" and curls up on the open ground and goes to sleep.

When the ration party come back, I finally got to sleep. We slept in an old Arab shack, and I didn't wake up until 11:00 the next day. Everything was peaceful this morning. The sun was shining brightly and the Jerries had taken off. The rations they brought up the night before were something new. Instead of the usual C ration, we had the new K ration. The change seemed good. We devoured the cheese and ham and eggs like nobody's business.

We were sitting around the slope of 609 lazily sunning ourselves and talking over the things that took place the last few days. Lt. Doty was passing the time by filing notched on the stock of his .03. "I got eight for sure, but the notches on Betsy are just for the dead ones. The others were only crippled," he drawls out slowly.

Capt. Sky comes up and has a big smile on his face and says, "We're going to get relieved tonight. And when we get back, the battalion commander is going to set up wine for the battalion. He just got promoted to lieutenant colonel so from now on, you address him as Col. Hall instead of Major," and he continues to say, "I think this outfit needs a good party anyhow."

One thing the Jerries left on Hill 609 was a flock of chickens, so we are running all over the hill hunting chickens like they were pheasants. Old Allah and Big Barnsmell got the most. The company had about 40 chickens all together. When Ploopie came up, he took them back to the kitchen so tomorrow we'll have chicken for dinner.

That night the entire battalion is assembled below Hill 609 We have a good meal, and everyone is happy. The moon was just coming over the summit of Hill 609 and resembled a ball of fire as it ascended skywards, and we started to march to the rear. The order of march was Battalion Headquarters, I Company, K Company, L Company and M Company. As we march along, the 4th platoon of K Company starts singing as they usually do whenever a tactical situation doesn't prevail:

Company I is full of shit, parley voo
Company I is full of shit, parley voo
Oh! Company I is full of shit
And so are the non-coms running it
Hinky Dinky parley voo

Company L is always late, parley voo
Company L is always late, parley voo
Oh! Company L is always late
They lie in their bunks and masturbate
Hinky Dinky parley voo

Company M, they won the war, parley voo
Company M, they won the war, parley voo
Oh! Company M, they won the war
Shootin' crap on a whorehouse floor
Hinky Dinky parley voo

We finally get to an assembly area and lie down and get some sleep. Next day we lay around most of the day in whatever shade we can find to get away from the hot sun. Ploopie brought the chickens we bagged on 609. They were roasted and had dressing to go with it, so we had quite a feast.

We can now actually notice an increase in our air power. That day we seen several bunches of P-40's fly over and also big numbers of B-25 Mitchel's, B-26 Marauders and A-20 Boston's fly over on longer range bombing missions. It was a pretty sight to have our own planes fly over instead of the Jerries. ⚜

SURRENDER IN NORTH AFRICA

It was mid-afternoon when we get on trucks. We move to the right and forward again. Our trucks get mixed up with a convoy of Limey lorries, but finally make it to our destination where we relieve the 1st Armored Division. We stay in this position one day. Then we get on trucks again and head for the Tebourba area. Here we send out motorized patrols that do nothing but round up defenseless, beaten remanent of Marshall Rommel's once elite Afrika Korps. They come surrendering in large groups. All you could hear from the kraut-eaters was "Komrade, Komrade." At last, we were herding them to the rear like a cowboy does to his herd on roundup day.

When we get all the Jerries cleaned up in our sector, we started having some fun. We captured a lot of equipment from the Jerries. Practically everyone had some kind of Jerrie gun and was a-shooting things up. We also captured a bunch of long, white nightgowns that we found in an evacuated Jerry field hospital. Everyone in the company had one on that night. Captain Sky brought in two barrels of wine, so the personnel of the company varied in moods from slightly high to dead drunk. Singing and dancing in the moonlight, garbed only in our white nightgowns, K Company looked like a revival in a cemetery.

By now Tunis had fell. After we had taken Hill 609, the war in Africa was practically over. Now there was only resistance on Cape Bon Peninsula, and later that afternoon we got word that all Germans and Italians in North Africa had surrendered. Field Marshall Rommel got away, but we got General Von Arnim, whom he left to command the remanent of the Africa Corps. It was a great day for us and meant we should get a little break out of it. So, one and all were happy as we head for a bivouac area for a rest.

Right in the middle of a big wheat field was our bivouac area. Almost as far as you could see, this wheat field was literally dotted with pup tents. The hot Africa sun was beating down on us, and as the days rolled by the boys that were able to come back from the hospital were slowly stringing back. P.J. came back, and his arm is as good as ever. We then get in a big batch of replacements. Pretty good-looking bunch of boys too. This filled beat up old K Company to capacity again like we were back in Ireland.

Some of the replacements we get in the 4th Platoon are: Oscar Kotz from Chicago; Fred Hays from Cleveland; Kreible from Philadelphia, and many others. The company also got a new shavetail of Italian descent by the name of Frank Foto from Brooklyn. This new shavetail goes merrily running tirelessly from place to place like he has a torpedo up his ass, uttering chin music all the while. Old Allah calmly remarks, "Most of 'em tame down in a week or two, but it may take a month before we get him under control." These dynamic shavetails fresh from the states are known to one and all in this outfit as F.B.I. men (Fort Benning Idiots.)

Ploopie is getting some pretty good rations now, and we are eating better than we have for quite some time. We get everything cleaned up and are lying around beating our gums about this and that. Suddenly we see Ole Evans of the 2nd Platoon come bounding out of his pup tent with an old Saturday Evening Post in hand. He was running so fast when he came by our tent, it just made a swish. We think he might be training for a race with Gunder Haag or something.

Pretty soon Big Jake of the 1st Platoon comes sprinting by also. Before long we could see guys running from every direction. They seemed to be heading in the general direction of the straddle trench. A couple of minutes later, Leo Schular and I both get up and race for the straddle trench. Before night came, I don't believe there was a man in the company that didn't have an acute case of the drizzling shits. "Hoky," our company first aid man, was kept busy running back and forth from the battalion aid station bringing paregoric to us, but it didn't do much good. A good many of the boys had to be evacuated to a hospital.

Today we are supposed to go on a victory parade in Tunis to be reviewed by General Ike, General Giraud and General DeGaule and some more brass. K Company took 25 men, all that were able to go. When the boys came back filled with vino and cognac, we enviously wished we had been able to go on the parade too.

Capt. Sky tells us, "Tomorrow we are going up the beach by Bizerta and have a whole weeks' vacation just lying around doing nothing." While we were up there Old Allah remarks "This would be a damned good time to commit suicide, cause things are bound to get worse. We'll never have it any better than we have right now." After our vacation we come back to the wheat field again. A couple of days later we move to Ferryville to do M.P. and guard duty.

We pull into Ferryville and bivouac in Stade De La Marine, the French name for Navel Stadium. It isn't anything like Yankee Stadium. It's just a plot of ground dotted with a few olive trees with an iron fence around it. As soon as we get to Ferryville, everyone runs uptown before someone tells us we can't. P.J., Old Allah and myself take out together and explore the town. Before long we find ourselves in front of a building with a dome on it and another big square building.

There are already several G.I.'s in front of each building. A line is formed. We get in. The line grew very rapidly. We went in the big square building. When we come out, the first guy we see in line is Speed, grinning like a skunk eating shit. Speed raises his left eyebrow and utters slowly, "Say! Ain't this good though." He then jumps in the air and clicks his heels, which is always a sign that Speed is happy. Lloyd Doe is also in line, and right behind Speed and Lloyd is none other than Old Tom. Old Tom is already very drunk. With his belly thrust outward he yelled, "Yippee," and then in broken French he adds, *"Ferryville tri bon, beaucoup cognac, beaucoup mademoiselles."*

Next day we are put to work. Part of the company are guarding the docks, some are doing M.P. duty, and others are doing as little as they can. The big square house and the dome are put out of bounds immediately, so they put K Company M.P.'s on guard down there, and that's like setting a bushel of corn in front of a hog and telling her not to eat it.

Old Tom is corporal of the guard down at the docks, and comes back every evening with a good-sized loot. One night he comes back with a six-by-six, backs it up to the kitchen tent and unloads a cargo of stolen rations for Ploopie to feed the company on. "Ya gotta function around here," Old Tom nonchalantly states. "I went up to an old base section colonel from a Q.M. outfit with tears in my eyes as big as horse turds and told him our outfit was starvin' to death. Look what he gave me." With thumbs hooked in his pistol belt, Old Tom proudly displayed the merchandise. Ploopie just grunted a little, but was well pleased with the loot.

Phees just returned from being over the hill for two weeks. He gets busted and gets put in the guard house at Bizerta along with John L. Sullivan. Lloyd Doe becomes corporal in Phees' place. The Homely One just returned from the hospital. He brought a home-made distillery back with him and is busy brewing "white lightning," a sort of an alcohol distilled from wine.

Our top kick, who is known to one and all as the "Big-Assed Bird," puts me on M.P. duty in Tindja along with Brady and Jimmy Smith. Tindja is a small town about three miles straight west of Ferryville. Tindja is a quaint little Tunisian village not so different from many of our small towns in the States. The French town folks treat us as if we were some local boys and they'd known us all of their life.

As we make our rounds through the residential district, we learn to know each family by name. At almost every home we are invited in for *en po vino* (French for a little wine). Considering it a social obligation—plus our natural fondness for the tempting liquid—we find it very difficult to refuse. By the time we complete our round and return to our starting point, we are in a very jovial mood indeed. Upon returning from our second round one morning, Brady complained that he had a very peculiar limp. As I can tell he has a snootful, I look at him limping along side of me. I say, "No wonder you're limpin', you dumb asshole, you got one foot in the gutter."

We sort of make our headquarters at an old French couples' place that we just call Momma and Papa. And to us they were the next thing to a mamma and papa. She would bawl the hell out of us when she seen we were getting a little too much wine.

We soon became so fond of Tindja that we are out there when we are off duty as well as when we are on. By now we can speak French quite fluently (we think). Brady and I spend much of our evenings sitting on Monsieur Boudiar's terrace of his lovely home with his two charming daughters Dunice and Annette Boudiar. As we sit in the pale moonlight that is partially screened by overhanging vines, Old Man Boudiar draws up a fresh supply of his varied assortment of wines that he has cooling in his rock-curbed well for us. I see Brady gazing at Annette with that pup tent look in his eye, so we say, *"Bon swa,"* and head back to Ferryville thinking we never had it so good.

The rumor is going around now that we will soon leave Ferryville. That rumor is undoubtedly true, because that is a bad rumor. Bad rumors generally come true. The good ones don't. 🦌

OUT OF UNIFORM

Today Sicily was invaded. We felt pretty good about it to think there was some fighting being done somewhere that we didn't have to do. We can't figure out how we got out of it. The 1st and 9th Divisions who had fought in Africa with us were in the invasion, along with the 3rd Division, a semi-amphibious division who were in on the initial landings in Noth Africa but were not in combat on the Tunisian Front, and the 45th Thunderbird Division that came directly from the States. As the days go by the war in Sicily progresses very well, but we know the boys in these divisions will have a tough job to do. However, we also know that these crack outfits are just the ones that can handle a tough job plenty good.

Our last day on M.P. duty in Tindja made us feel pretty blue as we bid all our newly made friends goodbye. Mamma and Papa both cried and made us promise we would come back and see them sometime.

Every time we have to leave a good place, we get pretty disgusted so half the company was drunk as we left Ferryville. We wound up in an olive orchard about ten miles out of Ferryville where we bivouac. Here we practice for a parade for none other than Prime Minister Winston Churchill and Foreign Secretary Anthony Eden. The 3rd Battalion of the 135th Infantry is supposed to be the honor guard of the division, so we get hooked for this Churchill-Eden deal.

We parade up to the big castle, stand at attention while the band plays "God Save The King" as Churchill and Eden drive up in a big limousine escorted by a convoy of motorcycles. The Prime Minister says a few words, but no one knew what he said as we were too far back and he didn't speak very loudly. We then march back to camp where we are told that we will soon move back to the vicinity of Oran for more intensive training at General Mark Clark's battle school. From Tunis to Oran is a good-sized trip.

A couple of days later we mount trucks and head for Tunis where we get aboard a troop train that takes us back to Oran. We crowd into these little 40-and-8 boxcars. 40-and-8 means it will hold 40 men or 8 mules. It was towards evening when the old train gave a chug and slowly started rolling westward. Old Allah hollers over to me, "Is your journey really necessary?" We roll through Medjez El Bab that night. Next day is hot as the torrid African sun beats down on the slowly moving boxcars. The crowded cars are contaminated from the disagreeable odor of C ration farts.

At the next stop P.J., Old Allah, Miss Polda and myself crawl into a refriger-ator car that still has some ice in it. There we find it comfortably cool. Towards evening we stop in some small Africa town. Old Allah, Miss Polda, P.J. and I run uptown, drink some wine, talk to some "Mamzells." The train was moving when we got back, and we had to run like the devil to catch it.

The next days of traveling grew kinda boresome. The only thing that relieved the monotony of the journey were the Arab kids running alongside the train begging "chocolate, bon bon, bisquite." So, we would throw them C ration candy and watch them scramble for it.

We figure we must be getting close to Algiers now, and we are wondering if the train will stop there. "If it does," P.J. says, "I kinda think I'll stay awhile." Old Allah, Miss Polda and I agree that it is a very pleasant thought indeed. Next morning when we wake up, the train is standing still. P.J. then pops his nearly bald head out from under the blanket and looks out the door. His ugly scowl suddenly turns into a bright, pleasant smile and says, "Do you see what I see?"

I look out the door, and sure enough, there she was, Algiers. It was some-thing like coming home after being gone for a while. "Well, what are we waiting for?" P.J. says as he wakes up Old Allah and Miss Polda. We can hear the colonel bellering for no one to leave the train. Old Allah murmurs, "He talks like a man with a paper ass." With that, the four of us make a mad dash for uptown Algiers in our dirty, ragged uniforms. It made us feel almost like we were back in our old home town as we passed familiar faces and places on our way to our first stop, which naturally was Fita Lub's bar.

When we get into Fita Lubs place, we are greeted by none other than the Little king, the Homely One, Phees and Bean Pole, who are already sipping the watery French beer. Fita Lub bellers gruffly, "Bon Jur, comrade. Entreevous veneer Algeree mio donnay vous beaucoup vino." In English that means, "Hello friends, you come back to Algiers so I give you lots of wine." Phees is lookin' for Marie, the big fat girl he left behind. The Little King and the Homely One want to get back on the train. As they leave, the Little King barks, "Make damned sure you guys get back on that train before it leaves or there will be hell to pay."

After they leave, we go up to Spike's place on the corner. As soon as we come in the door, Spike opens his arms, runs towards us and in old French tradition, kisses us on each cheek and is very much excited as he sets up wine for us. Then with significant gesture he says, "Fifi marry," very sadly in much the same manner one might announce the death of a friend. Old Allah then tells Spike, "Don't tell Louie Lotsahorses or it will break his heart."

We then leave Spike's place to go down to Petite Lycee, the university building where we used to be billeted. As we barge into the guard at the door of the U building, we are stopped by a white legged M.P. who is on guard at the door. He asks us for passes. As the M.P. was one of the boys out of the 133rd Infantry Regiment that took our place on M.P. duty in Algiers, he let us in. we then go down to the kitchen and talk the cooks of the 133rd out of some chow.

We then go over to the side door and watch Tin Can Charley and Hungry Hank fight over a can of rotten tomatoes. P.J. slaps Hungry Hank on his bare ass as Old Allah splits the moldy can of tomatoes equally between them. The two old Arabs just grin sort of sheepishly and say, *"Merci beaucoup."* We then continue on our way up the street as little Arab kids beg us to have our shoes shined.

We felt pretty crummy in our ragged, dirty and even blood-stained uniforms. Just then we run right smack into two shavetail base section M.P.'s in their immaculately-clean uniforms with razor-sharp creases in their trousers, as they beckon for us to stop and say, "May we see your passes? Why are you out of uniform? You are a disgrace to the American Army."

I guess that got the ire out of all of us up at once. Disregarding all military courtesy we say, "We're just the guys that took this town so you guys could have a nice place to live while we were up fighting on the Tunisian Front. Now that the campaigning is over, we intend to pay our respects to some of our friends in this town." The two shavetails calmed down a little and said, "Okay, boys, but don't make yourselves too conspicuous." We were naturally going down Rue De Chalaue heading east in the general direction of the Sphinx and The Black Cat. When we get there, all we see is white legged M.P.'s and out-of-bounds signs. So much to our disliking, we wander towards the Casbah district.

That night we went back to the railroad yard and slept in a boxcar. The next day we loaf around Algiers as we did the preceding day. At dusk that night, we grab a handful of boxcars that were heading west. The train was already traveling pretty fast, and we had quite a time getting aboard, but finally made it okay.

Next morning at our first stop we buy a loaf of that long narrow French bread, a sack of onions and about four bottles of red wine, so our menu for the day was onion sandwiches and red wine. This train had a good number of flat cars with Sherman tanks on them. Each of the four of us got into the driver's seat of four tanks and rode the steam-propelled tanks the rest of the way. We were turning and pointing the barrel of the 75's at almost everything we seen.

Later on, that day we stop at a small town where there was a canteen right near the tracks that sold wine and onion sandwiches. I run up to the woman at the counter, and in sloppy French say, "Av ay vous vin blanche?" she turns and replies in perfect English, "Yes, we have some very good white wine." Old Allah says, "Say! Where did you pick up that Brooklyn accent?" "I'm not from Brooklyn, I'm from the Bronx. I married a French sailor from the last war, and this is where I wound up."

Next morning as we wake up, we are pulling into Oran. We hurriedly get off the train and rush uptown to explore the city we are in for the first time. Once again, the first thing we run into is a couple of white legged M.P.'s. They ask us for the dog tags and passes that, of course, none of us have. So, they take our name, rank, serial number and organization. Somehow none of us were quick enough thinkers to think up phony names, numbers and organizations right then, so we gave them the real McCoy. The M.P.'s then say our C.O. will hear from them.

We leisurely explore Oran all day and decide that Algiers is a much nicer place. Towards evening we spot a 34th six-by-six. We run it down and find it's from the 109th Engineers. The guys on the truck say the 135th are bivouacked only a few miles from them, so we get in the back of the six-by-six and head for our outfit, sort of wondering what the C.O. and head for our outfit, sort of wondering what the C.O has in store for us.

When we finally get to the 109th Engineer bivouac area, the boys there point out a group of small, rocky knolls about two miles away and say, "The 135th are scattered about there somewhere." We then start walking up the trail. Soon, a weapons carrier from M Company comes along and takes us up to the 3rd Battalion bivouac area. As we sheepishly walk up to K Company area, we see a long line in front of the kitchen tent. As it is about 9:00 P.M. we know it is too late for chow, it isn't pay day and we just had short-arm before we left Tunisia so we can't figure out what the line is for.

As we get closer, we see "Paper Ass" behind a stockpot with a big dipper. Paper Ass is one of the three brothers in K Company. The other two, of course, are the Little King, 4th Platoon Sergeant, and "Black Rufe," the mortar section leader. Paper ass is a sergeant in the 2nd Platoon. We generally call him Pape. Pape's favorite hobby seems to be dishing out grub or drinks whenever there's a special occasion in the company.

Just as we fall in line, the Little King comes up, scowls and bellers, "Well, you guys really got your peckers under the gate this time. The Old Man is so mad he thinks murder is too good for you." Then the Homely One come up and says to me "You shouldn't have done that. Now I can't make you corporal." I then tell the Homely One, "Tell the Old Man he can shove them corporal stripes up his ass."

P.J. and I then pitch our pup tents as far away from the company and platoon C.P. as possible. Old Allah and Miss Polda also pitch their tent out there. Next morning at 5:00 I hear the C.O.'s whistle blow hard. P.J. and I both scrunch down and pull the covers over our heads. The Little King comes barking for us to get up. We're still in the sack when we hear the bugle blow reveille and hear the platoon sergeant's report. The 1st, 2nd, and 3rd Platoon Sergeants all report their platoons present and accounted for. Then the top-kick, who is known as the Big-Assed Bird, looks toward the 4th Platoon and says, "4th Platoon REPORT!" The Little King then barks back, "Five men missing."

After reveille, the Little King comes back to our tents fairly foaming at the mouth saying we will pay dearly for this. None of us say anything back except Old Allah, who just rolls over and lets a ripping fart. Shortly after we get up, we are called up to the platoon C.P. for our first stop where the Little King and our platoon leader, who at that time was Lt. North, give us a third degree. That was just the preliminaries.

From there we are sent up to the Company C.P. to have it out with the Old Man. We enter the orderly tent, take off our head gear, stand at attention and salute Capt. Sky, who is sitting behind his desk gritting his teeth. The first thing Capt. Sky says is "All right, have any of you guys got alibis?" "No, sir," we all reply. Capt. Sky then commences to chew ass.

"I don't know what to do with you men. I can't think of anything bad enough for you. By going AWOL while the company was right in the middle of a big move was one of the worst things you could do. You men are all a black eye to the K Company. Will you accept a company punishment, or do you want a court martial?"

We all agree to take company punishment. Capt. Sky was trying awfully hard to look gruff, but I think he was chuckling to himself all along. Capt. Sky then says, "All right, you are all busted to the lowest degree. It's going to cost you $3 a day for every day you were gone. You'll get no passes until I give you permission. The company has beer every night, but you'll get none of it. Now, go get on your fatigues and start carrying rocks over the hill."

We then salute, do an about face and go back to our pup tents where we meet the Little King, who gives us orders to move our tents over close to his and the company C.P. so that all the big operators can keep their eyes on us. We then proceed to carry rocks on the project known as Capt. Sky's rock garden. We just pick up all the rocks in K Company's area and throw them over to L

Company's area. We get intensive training from 5:00 A.M. to 5:00 P.M. every day. After training hours, we carry rocks for Capt. Sky's rock garden 'til midnight. Capt. Sky has his tent pitched on a high knoll and can see the minute we aren't working. As soon as we sit down, he calls the orderly tent and bellers to the C.O., "Get them guys back to work."

Our bivouac area is close to the village of Beau Sfer, and in spite of Capt. Sky's restrictions we manage to sneak down for a sip of wine every so often. Just when we're getting to where Capt. Sky is beginning to talk a little friendly to us, he gets that letter from the M.P.'s in Oran, so now we're back in the dog house worse than ever. Capt. Sky says, "I don't give a damn what a man does if he don't get caught at it, but if he's dumb enough to get caught he should suffer for it. And believe me, you guys are going to suffer." So, we continue to work on Capt. Sky's rock garden more aggressively than ever.

The Big-Assed Bird has an ailment, a sore ass. Old Allah says, "You would have a sore ass too if you had it sucked as much as he has." The Big-Assed Bird is preparing to go to the hospital where he'll be confined for at least three months. The Little King feels pretty good about this, as the Big-Assed Bird is giving him some pointers around the orderly tent, as the Little King is the one who will succeed the Big-Assed Bird as top kick.

The Little King is very happy indeed over the prospect of being promoted to the first soldier of K Company. This puts the Homely One in a good mood. Also, as he'll succeed the Little King as 4th Platoon Sergeant. That left an opening for Machine Gun Section Leader, which naturally would be Old Tom. But Old Tom went over the hill when we were up around Tunis, and the Old Man never did anything about it until we went over the hill in Algiers. Capt. Sky told the Homely One, "Old Tom is the best damn corporal in the company. There's nobody that can function like Old Tom. I'd like to make him sergeant and put him in command of the machine gun section, but I can't do it on account of them and other screwballs that went over the hill in Algiers. I had to bust and punish them, and Old Tom done the same thing in Tunis. So as much as I hate to, I'm going to have to bust Old Tom down to a private too."

When Old Tom heard this, he took it pretty hard and right away went to the medics with a sore back and got reclassified to limited service. That left only one non-com left in the machine gun section, and that was newly-made Corporal Lloyd Doe. Phees got busted back in Ferryville. Lloyd takes over the section for the time being. P.J. takes over Lloyd's squad, and I once again take over the 2nd squad. The only ones that are happy about this are the Little King and the Homely One, for they are sure of being promoted. P.J. and I are still on the shit list.

Next day we go to Ain El Turk, a town by the sea, and get aboard a ship, the USS Lyon. We weren't going any place, we were just to spend a week aboard this ship doing amphibious training. The Lyon was the first American ship we had ever been on, and they sure do throw the grub to us. Every night we get in landing barges and assimilate an assault on the beach. We then drive ahead, capture a group of hills, then go back and do it all over again.

My squad is attached to the 3rd Platoon for these problems. The 3rd Platoon has a new platoon leader, 2nd Lt. Knox, who has a long handlebar mustache. Every night I get my orders from Lt. Knox. The last day aboard the Lyon we prepare for our final beach assault. That night we make our assimilated amphibious assault, then pick out the roughest terrain possible and start hiking the 12 miles back to our bivouac area over sandy hills with heavy packs, machine guns, mortars and ammo. It was about 7:00 the next morning when we hit the old bivouac area. Ploopie and the cooks had a good hot breakfast for us, after which we flop down and go to sleep.

Back in the old bivouac area we get a new shavetail who is assigned to the 4th Platoon whom we call Lt. "Sad Sack." Lt. North is still 4th Platoon Leader, but this Sad Sack is just sort of a spare tire. Waldo, who used to be a sergeant in the 2nd Platoon before he was severely wounded at the first Fondouk attack, just returned from the hospital. Waldo takes command of the machine gun section and Lloyd Doe takes back his old squad. P.J. and Brady are Lloyd's gunners, Miss Polda and Old Allah are my gunners.

Although we all wanted Lloyd Doe for section leader, we are also glad to get a guy like Waldo. Waldo is 100 percent. He likes to have a lot of fun, and really knows his stuff about soldiering. The Little King and the Homely One now have their promotions and are heavily laden with stripes and are very happy about it indeed. P.J., Old Allah, Miss Polda and I are still buck privates. Capt. Sky still won't give us any passes; however we are no longer working on Capt. Sky's rock garden.

A few days after we get off the good ship Lyon, we get on trucks which take us south to French Morocco. We move through Sidi Bell Abbes, home of the French Foreign Legion, and bivouac in a nice wooded area near a small Arab village by the name of Slisson. We now weren't so very far from our first training area after we left Algiers and before we went to the Tunisian front, which was close to the town of T'clemson. Here we get more intensive training.

We have reveille long before daylight, and the Homely One is out with his flashlight seeing that everyone has their leggings on. We're now in a strictly Arab community. You can see them dashing madly in every direction on their little donkeys. Contrary to the way most people ride horses or mules, the Arabs sit way back on the donkey's ass and flop their legs in and out as fast as they can, hollering, "Hubba hubba, brrrrr, brrrrr," urging their donkeys to go faster. Later years when I returned to the States, I was somewhat surprised to hear hubba hubba to be a byword to teenagers and oldsters alike. No one seemed to know for sure the origin of this slang, although there were rumors of many places where it originated. But the men in North Africa who heard the words hubba hubba there for the first time, know where it originated.

Here, we go on night patrol almost every night. One night we have scouting and patrolling. The 4th Platoon is divided into two sections. Lt. North takes the mortar section and the Sad Sack takes the machine gun section. Capt. Sky is there as we take off. Col. Swenson, who just came back from the hospital and who is now our regimental executive officer, was also there.

The Sad Sack strides up to me and asks, "Give me two good scouts." I pick out two mischievous for him, namely Speed and Oscar Kotz. Lt. Sad Sack then says, "Say! I got a good idea. We'll just walk up the road and then they'll think we're part of the road." Capt. Sky and Col. Swenson bust out laughing. Col. Swenson then making a joke out of it, bellers, "Take off barracks bags at the trail." Waldo then tells Lt Sad Sack that he better take some route other than the road. Speed and Oscar then lead off crawling on their hands and knees through thick, messy brush followed closely by Lt. Sad Sack. The rest of us just stay where we are and await the outcome. Pretty soon Speed and Oscar come back reporting the Sad Sack lost in the brush. After the problem is over, we have to search for the Sad Sack.

Waldo talked Capt. Sky into finally giving us a pass. So P.J., Old Allah, Miss Polda and I go into Sidi Bell Abbes. Big Barnsmell also goes along. The lines in Sidi Bel Abbes are worse to sweat out than anyplace we'd been yet, but Speed still went through four times.

We were here about two weeks when we move back to the place we were before we came to the Slisson area. Only this time we bivouac closer to the town of Ain El Turk. Here, our training slackens up and we get 20 percent passes to Oran every day.

The Little King tells me I've now been promoted to corporal. One Sunday, Lloyd Doe, Old Allah and I go to Ain El Turk, where there is a convalescent hospital in which Old Tom is confined. When we see Old Tom, he shows us his living quarters saying, "There's only one window in this building with two windows and an electric light bulb, and of course, I've got that." He then shows us all the stuff he's accumulated, which looks like a small Q.M. depot. Old Tom says, "Take anything you want, boys, you know me. I can always function and get some more." So, we go back to camp well supplied.

One night when the Homely One was in Oran, he got in a fight. The Homely One hit the bar rail with his head, and it paralyzed half of his face. Next day the Homely One went to the hospital where he got transferred to limited service and has a good chance of returning to the states soon. This, of course, once again left an opening for 4th Platoon Sergeant. Naturally, Black Rufe, who is the mortar section leader, takes command of the 4th Platoon and is promoted to staff sergeant. Black Rufe is a brother to the Little King and Pape, but is more easy going.

Good news just came that the campaign in Sicily has just come to a victorious end for the Allies. A little later there was more good news. MUSSOLINI QUITS AS HEAD OF THE ITALIAN GOVERNMENT.

ON TO ITALY

We all know now that we're about to go on a long trip. We are pretty sure where we're going, but we don't discuss it much once we get aboard a transport ship in Oran Harbor. It's a British troopship His Majesty's *Durbin Castle*. After we are out at sea a few days we get word that Italy had been invaded in two places: The British 8th Army had invaded way down at the toe, and the American 36th Division along with British units had invaded at Selarno and Pasteum.

After hearing this, we are pretty well assured that we won't make a beach assault as we had expected. News now came that Italy has surrendered to the Allies, but that meant very little, for the country of Italy was full of crack German troops, and the Nazis took control of everything.

As we near the Italian mainland we meet a convoy of small Italian ships who had turned themselves over to the Allies. According to official communiques, we get aboard ship, the 8th Army was moving right along from the south. However, opposition was much more stubborn in the Selarno beachhead area and fierce battles were raging there. Determined German counter attacks were made in an effort to push the Allies back to the east, but the Yanks and tommies were equally as stubborn.

The American 36th Division was a new outfit in combat, but they fought like experienced veterans. The 36th Division was a National Guard outfit made up with men greatly from Texas. The 36th fought gallantly along with their British allies to gain ground and hold it against bitter opposition while reinforcements were coming in. American reinforcements were the 3rd, 45th, and, of course, the 34th Divisions.

It was getting dusk as we first sighted land, and it was dark when we got on landing barges and made for the shores of Italy. We could hear the heavy guns booming as we rapidly neared the beach. Most of us were glad that the beachhead had been pretty well secured. When we hit the beach, it was peaceful enough, but in the darkness all we could see was the scarlet blare of gun flashes not far away.

Carrying all our equipment, we start marching to an assembly area. After walking most of the night, daybreak found us at our destination. Next day was nice any sunny. We talk to a few Italian farmers who were shy and didn't seem to know whether to treat us as friends or enemies. That night we have a terrific rain and wind storm. Next morning Capt. Sky orders all non-coms up to the C.P., and we know what for.

The first thing Capt. Sky says is, "Alert your men and be ready to move by 9:00. We're going into the line near a small Italian village by the name of Montefusco." Then he goes on to say, "Most of the resistance has broken and the Germans are beginning to slowly withdraw, as the 8th Army is moving up fast. At the rate they're going, we should join forces in a few days."

As we move up to the front, we go through the town of Pattibagalia where some of the initial battles took place. It was nothing but a mass of rubble and debris. We then went through Pasteum, where we could still see the remains of the ancient Greek temples of the Gods. We hit below Montefusco. There was only a small amount of sporadic machine gun fire that soon ceased. We put out outposts. There was every indication that the Germans were withdrawing. The next day we were able to pitch pup tents on yesterday's battlefield.

The village of Montefusco was built high up on a lofty mountain. We labor our way up the mountain to explore the town. We find the Italian people sort of indifferent and don't seem to care to have much to do with us. To the right or to the east of us, other units of our division captured the industrial city of Benevento, the first city of any large size to be captured in Italy.

We get a division G-2 report in saying that General Montgomery's 8th Army has now joined forces with General Mark Clark's 5th Army. Not long after that, the British 8th Army captured the great air base at Foggia. We are moving right along now. We advance during daylight, meeting only scattered resistance and rear-guard action. Two days after the 8th Army took Foggia, units of the 82nd Airborne Division moved in and took Naples, while we bypassed it and were several miles north of the great port city.

Right now, we think this is a much easier war than the African Campaign was. We think these Jerries have a lot of guts as so far as they have no solid line, just a few scattered machine guns, mortars, and mobile artillery. Some days we may advance several miles, then we'd get in a hot spot and be pinned down for the remainder of the day. And when night comes, they would fire on us steadily all night until about 4:00 in the morning. Then everything would be quiet and peaceful. They had withdrawn to another position where they could hold us up for another 12 or 24 hours. This is typical rear-guard action. All the bridges and crossings are blown up before we get to them.

The Italian people we run into as we advance further north are poor, hungry peasants and are much more friendly than they were at first. A good many of them had at one time or another been in the United States and could speak English with a high accent. The withdrawing Germans had taken everything they could use from these poor peasants. When we asked one old Dago where the Germans went, he replied, *Tediski tuta via,* meaning the Germans have all left. Then in broken English he says, "Tediski dirty son-of-a-bitch. He taka my cow, he taka my pig, he taka my daughter. I wish the dirty son-of-a-bitch bring my cow back. She was a vera nice cow." Oscar Kotz always got a good chuckle out of the way these Italians talked.

One thing we have now that we value almost more than anything else—unless it's our shooting iron or entrenching tool—and that is a little gas stove that we can heat our rations and boil coffee on. Each squad has one. The minute we stop, somebody is cooking up and it doesn't stop until we are on the go again. It's the fall of the year, and the Italian gardens are full of fresh onions, red and green peppers and onions, and that's a good deal for us as it highly flavors the distasteful C ration stew. Waldo and Speed are the greatest for cooking spicy concoctions, although P.J. and Old Allah don't do bad either.

Lt. Doty, who has been our company's executive officer, has went to the hospital, so Lt. North is now company exec. That left the Sad Sack as 4th Platoon

Leader. Lt. Sad Sack says, "I get a lot of good ideas, but when I tell them to Capt. Sky, he just laughs. So, I'm not going to tell him any more of my good ideas." Lt. Hennel is transferred in and takes over as 4th Platoon Leader, so Lt. Sad Sack is once more a spare tire. Lt. Hennel is a regular feller.

Lt. Sad Sack comes to Waldo one day and says, "I don't know why I'm carrying this rifle, there's no bolt in it." "Did you lose it?" Waldo asks. "I lost it about a month ago," the Sad Sack replies. Waldo laughs, gives him a bayonet saying, "Well, I guess you'll have to do your fighting with this." Now during his spare time, Lt. Sad Sack can be seen practicing the long thrust, short jab and vertical butt stroke with every ounce of energy he has.

We are now in a position overlooking a big river. The Germans presumably have a strong defense line immediately behind that river. The river is called the Volturno, and we're to make the initial crossing tonight. It's about midnight when we saddle up and start the attack. We walk a good distance, winding our way around the lofty Italian mountains before we come to the banks of the river. The 3rd Platoon starts fording the mad stream. The current is very swift, and the assault squad has a difficult time fording the violent Volturno, but finally make it okay without a shot being fired.

Then they throw a rope across, which is tied to a tree at each bank of the river, so that the rest of the company can cross the mad river more easily. Soon the entire company is across and begin to fan out and advance in the jet-black darkness when we hear a couple of explosions. We had forded the river in the right place, for there were no mines there. But on the north bank of the Volturno is where we hit the mine fields.

After three or four men had been wounded by mines, we shift to the right. There, we run into a thick mass of brush and start pushing through it as we run into booby traps and trip wires that are strung from one tree to another. The booby traps inflict several more casualties on the company, but we finally make it through the booby trap area.

Here we receive our first fire from the enemy. They were throwing mortar and artillery fire on us. There was a small amount of machine gun fire. We keep advancing in the darkness and get through the mortar and artillery impact area and assault the machine gun positions. The Jerries withdrew, and by morning we had a sizeable bridgehead secured on the enemy's side of the Volturno. The only casualties we had on the attack were those inflicted by mines and booby traps. The next day we are pretty satisfied that we made the crossing as easily as we did and are glad that the job is done.

We then get orders to pull back across the river, as another unit moved in to relieve us and hold the ground. We're happy as we march back across the pontoon bridge the engineers had already erected across the Volturno, thinking we were getting relieved. As usual, we got fooled. We just get to an assembly area and saw a fresh supply of C rations and ammo. We then get orders to cross the Volturno again at a different place, which once again causes the morale barometer to drop to a low degree.

We make our second crossing of the Volturno just at dusk. This attack is comparatively easy and even more successful than the first one, as we suffered no casualties. We only run into a few machine guns that soon withdrew. The Volturno zig-zags and runs crazily around mountains like spaghetti in a bowl, which is one reason it has to be crossed so many times. And I guess altogether we crossed the violent Volturno five times before we could finally say it was rear echelon. In fact, to this day when a doughboy of this 34th Division sees a stream, he heaves a sigh of disgust and says, "What the hell! The Volturno again?"

The 5th Army at this stage of the war is composed of the 3rd, 36th, 45th, and 34th Infantry Divisions, the 1st Armored Division and one regiment from the 82nd Airborne Division along with supporting elements. We also have the British 10th Corps which take care of the west coastal sector.

On the hour of 300 we start marching for another attack. It is just breaking day as we come out of the brushy hills and see a clearing in front of us, and what a clearing it is. Nothing but swamp land with water hip deep in places and at least a mile across. We deploy in a skirmish line and advance across the swampy marshlands. Lloyd Doe's squad is on the left, mine is on the right. Waldo is up ahead leading us. With him is Phees, who at this time is our section runner. Phees follows Waldo closely, and as we splash along, I can hear him say to

Waldo, "Just another Fondouk, that's all it is. We'll all be wiped out. This will make Fondouk look like a Sunday school picnic."

I then see Waldo turn back to Phees and say, "For gosh sake, will you shut up. It's bad enough without you painting such a black picture." Fortunately, it is foggy and we are well concealed in our advance. As the fog begins to lift, we are just about 600 yards from a small town that is situated right at the base of a huge mountain.

This town has a rock wall about eight feet high all the way around it. We run madly for the south wall as it offered us good protection and concealment. When we get there, things seem peaceful enough so we stop and cook up. This day the 2nd Platoon happens to be the assaulting platoon, of which the dynamic shavetail from Brooklyn, Lt. Foto, is in charge.

As Lt. Foto is a comparatively new officer to this outfit, he still has that aggressive let-me-at-em attitude, so he leads the 2nd Platoon through the town and half way up the mountain. Lt. Foto being of Italian descent, immediately makes friends with all the natives of this community and very often gets some vital information out of them. They were gone about three hours before they come back to where the rest of the company was hugging closely to the rock wall. Talking like a tobacco auctioneer, Lt. Foto says he contacted no Jerries. And from what the Italians had told him, they had *"tuta via'd,"* meaning they had pulled out. Lt. Foto and a good share of the 2nd Platoon were half buzzed up on dago red wine when they returned. With this information we feel better and spend the rest of the day sunning ourselves on the sunny side of the rock wall, drinking mud. The name of this town we are in now is Alief.

That night, when darkness came, we saddle up and start the long trudge up the lofty mountain north of Alief. It was even more of a climb than it looked to be. K Company was the leading company that night, so Capt. Sky led the battalion. When we finally reach the top, Capt. Sky orders to set up a defense for the night. Col. Hall, the battalion commander, had some controversy over this, but Capt. Sky seemed to have won out.

The next day is nice and sunny, and the best part of it is there were no Jerries around. That night Ploopie brought hot chow to the base of the mountain.

We were in this position two days. The third day Capt. Moody, our battalion S-3, got killed by artillery. Col. Hall then calls Capt. Sky, telling him leave the company, although he'll still be in the battalion. Capt. Sky says so long to us and introduces us to our new C.O., who is Lt. Hall—no relation to Col. Hall— transferred in from L Company.

From this high mountain perch, we can plainly see the air raids over Naples every night. It was quite a sight to see the amber tracers spray the jet-black sky as they rake the midnight atmosphere for the bombing Luftwaffe.

Next day we start on the attack again. Single file we wind our way around the mountains for several miles, then stop and dig in. Just as we get comfortably settled in our holes, we can hear the footsteps of our platoon runner approaching. When a platoon runner comes around at such an hour, you know he brings nothing but bad news. Soon we hear him call, "Sgt. Black Rufe, alert your platoon and be ready to move in a half hour." Black Rufe then calls for all squad leaders.

We in turn awaken our men. I go over to wake Speed. Drowsily Speed mumbles, "Gosh, I wish I was the old black tom cat the old man has got at home. He never has to anything like this." As he feels around in the darkness in search of his equipment, he feels something soft and says, "What's this?" After some pause, he says, "It's warm," as he lifts it up in his hands. Just then someone stumbles over him in the darkness, pushing the contents of his hands into his face. "Ohhhh," I hear Speed moan as I ask, "What is it, Speed?"

"Shit," was Speed's melancholy answer. "What kinda shit, Speed?" I ask. "Person shit. That's what it is, person shit. I'd like to catch the dirty SOB that shit by my hole. Gosh, it stinks awful." By the time Speed got all the shit off his face we were organized and on the march. As we march along, I can hear Speed mumble in the rear of the squad. "Gosh! The old man will be glad when he gets that check. He always wanted a combine, and he'll get it sooner or later if this war don't end pretty soon." "What check is that?" I hear Oscar Kotz ask. "The insurance check when I get bumped off," Speed replies. Every time we go on the attack, he tries to think of all the things his old man will spend his insurance check on.

We keep steadily advancing for the next few days, meeting only a small amount of scattered rear-guard action. The rainy season in Italy has now begun. When the sun comes out these days, we really appreciate it. If there's anything that makes a man's morale drop, it's marching for an attack in the pitch-black darkness driving against blinding rain soaking wet from head to toe.

Well, that's just what we were doing this particular night. On top of this, we had a river to cross. We crossed where the remains of a steel bridge once stood, but now was nothing but a mass of tangled steel. Half of it was under water. The other half was mangled steel girders pointing crazily skyward. This destroyed bridge was a perfect example of the efficiency of Nazi demolition. Hanging desperately to steel girders, letting themselves drop to where they hoped there was something solid to land on (sometimes there was, sometimes there wasn't), the doughboys done acrobatics across the river.

Several men from the company were seriously injured in the crossing, but after quite a struggle we get across. Dawn found us entering a small village at the base of a big mountain. It had quit raining now and was a little foggy. As we marched through the ancient streets, we see the name Montequalla printed on some of the buildings, and we know that's the name of the town.

We march through most of the town and are just at the northern edge of it when the Jerries start laying in a terrific barrage concentrated on all parts of the town. Everyone seeks protection. The ancient buildings make nothing but a cloud of dust when they receive a direct hit from the heavy shells. Between shell bursts I could hear the frantic cry of Italian civilians, particularly women and children.

I sneak a quick glance at the open street to the left of me. The first thing I see is the scarlet flow of blood trickling down through the cobbled street. Later I see an Italian woman come running and screaming frantically with a bleeding, mortally wounded Italian child in her arms. It sort of made a feller think a little what if this was happening back home? Seeing kids play gaily on the streets yesterday and being slaughtered in the same streets today. It made a feller thankful to know the war was being fought here instead of back home.

Yet these people were good, God-fearing people, never wanting to do harm to anyone, just live and let live. Was it right that they should be slaughtered in their own homes for a few power-hungry maniacs? The Italian populace of this town had suffered more from this barrage than we did.

When the firing ceased somewhat, we started attacking the mountain above Montequalla. Lt. Foto's 2nd Platoon once again was the assaulting platoon. We get to the top of the first hill. The machine gun section set up there to give supporting overhead fire for the assaulting 2nd Platoon, who were now fanning out in a skirmish line in the valley below.

Waldo, Lloyd Doe and I were watching them through our field glasses as they advanced slowly up the next slope. Lt. Foto is leading and Sgt. Pete, a squad leader from the 2nd Platoon, is just to the right of him. Just then Lieutenant grabs toward the ground and pulls up a tarp. We hear a frantic scream from a Jerry. "Hands up," Lt. Foto demands. The Jerry raises his hands and drops them again. He does this several times. Each time, Lt. Foto repeats his command. The fanatical Nazi does not want to adhere to Lt. Foto's order and finally makes a dash for a Lugar he has lying in his hole.

Just then Pete comes up. We hear Brrrrr Brrrrr as he empties a clip into the head of each Jerry with his tommy gun. The rest of the Jerries were aroused by this commotion and start opening up on the now-exposed 2nd Platoon with everything they had, and the 2nd Platoon was forced to withdraw.

When they get back, Lt. Foto and Pete are pretty excited. Pete says, "I made two good Germans out of them two birds. I put a clip into the head of each one of them." He then proudly shows us the Lugars he took from the two extremely dead Jerries. Lt. Foto brought back a bunch of maps and papers he took off of them, which proved they were artillery observers and were the ones that directed the barrage on us in Montequalla. So, we feel pretty good to get partly even with them anyhow.

It starts raining again. We're all shivering as we set up a hasty defense on the hill. Capt. Sky, who is now our battalion S-3 and seems to have almost taken complete charge of the battalion, is up there with us. He's trying to read his maps, which are all soaked up by the rain, and is talking to Col. Hall, the battalion commander, who has his C.P. some distance to the rear.

We could detect harsh words in that radio conversation between the battalion S-3 and the battalion commander. A little later, Col. Ward, our regimental commander, was up talking things over with Capt. Sky. As darkness drew closer, we start to prepare a more stable defense for the night. I have my machine gun squad on the extreme right flank of the company with no support whatsoever from the rifle platoons, who had all they could do to take care of their own immediate sector. I was somewhat skeptical about my position.

As soon as darkness comes, the Jerries start counter-attacking. They would counter attack violently as we would desperately beat them off with small arms fire and hand grenades. They would attempt and fail and attempt again. This went on all night long. We were all glad when daylight finally came and the Jerries finally pulled back to their own lines. However, they didn't all pull back off the hill. There were some good ones lying on the forward slope. Yes, as we looked to our front the next morning, we see several good Jerries lying prone harmlessly dead in front of our position. A dead Jerry, incidentally, is what we called a good one.

Later that morning there once again was enemy movement out in front. We called for artillery fire on the determined counter-attacking kraut eater. Our artillery responded almost immediately, but their range was considerably short of the target and was landing all around us. It hit the 1st Platoon sector particularly hard. Before we could get the barrage lifted, three men from the 1st Platoon were killed by our own artillery. Together with artillery and small arms fire, once again the enemy was repulsed in their last vain attempt to regain the ground they were so reluctant to yield.

The remainder of the day is comparatively peaceful. The sun is shining and we begin to relax. Waldo comes over to the squad. He has a grin on his face as he says, "I bring good news. The company sent the first man home on a new rotation system. The lucky guy is none other than Bean Pole." Bean Pole has been the mortar section leader ever since Black Rufe took over as 4th Platoon Sergeant. Danny will succeed Bean Pole as mortar section leader. Then Waldo goes on to say, "We can send one man from the section on a five-day pass plus travel time to Naples under a new pass system the 5th Army has just put out." We decide to put the name of every man from the section in a helmet. The name of the man that is drawn out of the helmet is the one that will get the pass.

Every man hopes his name will be drawn, but Speed is the lucky man whose name is drawn, and he certainly deserved it. Speed jumps up, clicking his heels saying, "Now I'll find out what these Italian women are like."

That night Lloyd Doe moves his squad over next to mine to stabilize our defense, and it makes us all feel more secure. This night is much more peaceful, and we are not molested by the Jerries at all. Next morning was nice and sunny. We lie around reading the *Stars and Stripes* and letters that were brought up the night before. We are now able to move around quite freely without being observed by the enemy. Lt. Foto comes over and talks to us for a while. He drags out his maps and shows us that we're through fighting rear guard action and are now just beginning to run into the strong outposts of their heavily fortified Winter Line, which is known as the Gustave Line, which is hinged on the stronghold of Cassino. From now on, things are going to be tough.

P.J. went down to Montequalla and brought back a small mule or burrow, which comes in mighty handy for carrying feed, water and ammo up the hill. We're in this position several days just holding when we are relieved by the 1st Battalion. We then pull back to a wooded area just outside Montequalla and bivouac.

Here we hear that Col. Hall has been transferred. Next day all non-coms are called up to the battalion C.P. to meet our new battalion commander. He's a great big tall man, fairly young for a Lieutenant Col. He has a very deep voice. His name is Lt. Col. Mearns, a West Pointer. He gives us a very nice talk.

The Sad Sack says, "The 4th Platoon doesn't seem to care if I'm with them or not, so from now on I'm just going to stay with company headquarters." So, from now on, Lt. Sad Sack follows company headquarters around. We're here about five days when we get orders to go out as a screening force for the 2nd Battalion while they dig in on a hill. We'll then return to this same area while the 2nd Battalion holds the hill.

Col. Mearns, our new battalion commander, leads the battalion up the long, steep mountain. We wind our way along the narrow rocky trails, advancing single file. We hadn't gone far before someone opens up on us from the left. As that is supposed to be friendly territory, we examine the terrain closely. When they fire again, we can distinguish the fire as that coming from a water-cooled heavy .30 caliber American machine gun. It's the 168th Infantry, our sister regiment, who are on our left flank. But before we can make them recognize who we are, they shoot the Little King right smack in the ass.

Litter bearers carry the Little King back to the aid station where he'll be evacuated to a hospital. We then continue on our mission. We get quite a ways out in no-man's land, patrol the area quite thoroughly, keeping concealed all the while as the 2nd Battalion digs in. To our good fortune a misty fog prevailed in that area, keeping enemy observation to a minimum. It's just getting dusk as we start our long journey back to Montequalla. When we get about half way back, they lay a pretty heavy barrage on us. But as we're headed for the rear, we don't even stop but speed up all the faster.

It's plum dark now, and we have a difficult time walking over the rough terrain. But when we're going to the rear, it doesn't seem to matter so much. We get to Montequalla and find some old houses and barns to sleep in that night. P.J., who is one of the best men to snoop around that I've ever seen, locates a deserted Italian house. The downstairs is full of wood, so we take quarters upstairs, and the 2nd machine gun squad has a dry, warm place to sleep tonight.

Next day is raining again, of course. Kotz and I made the mistake of both going out and standing on our porch at the same time. The old rotten timbers cracked beneath us, and we drop to the ground in much the same manner as an elevator with a broken cable might drop. When we hit the ground with a bang I ask Oscar, "Are ya hurt?" "Not yet" was Oscar's reply as he lies kicking around in the broken timbers trying to break a leg so that he could be evacuated to a hospital.

That night Lloyd Doe moves his squad up with us. Waldo and Phees also moved in, so now the entire machine gun section is in this house, and we're all very comfortable indeed. We then get orders to move out of Montequalla and back to our old bivouac area in the woods as regimental headquarters were moving into Montequalla, and we had to make room for them. We're now back in our old bivouac area out in the woods keeping busy ditching around our pup tents to keep from getting flooded out.

Bennie, former 2nd Platoon sergeant, has now taken over as top kick succeeding the Little King, who got shot in the ass by the 168th and is now in the hospital and will remain there for quite some time.

One night Lt. Hennel comes over to where we're all huddled around a brush fire shootin' the bull. He says, "Waldo, you'll have to leave the 4th Platoon and take over as 2nd Platoon Sergeant succeeding Benny, who is now top kick." In spite of the promotion, Waldo isn't too overly enthused to go back to the 2nd Platoon as platoon sergeant. We all hate to see Waldo go. We hope Lloyd Doe will take his place, but the 2nd Platoon gives us Sgt. Pete in exchange of Waldo. Pete is also a good egg. Pete likes most of all to drink mud and talk, among other things. P.J. and I are also very fond of mud, so we have something in common. Pete talks so much that all we can do is listen.

Next day we prepare to move out and relieve the 2nd Battalion, who are in a defensive position. We take the same trail we did on the day we went out as a screening force for the 2nd Battalion. Just as we get about half way to our destination they lay a barrage in on us. We were coming around the bend of a terraced hill. We were apparently observed by the enemy. The shells were bursting very close to us as we all hit the dirt. One particular shell sounded like it was coming all the way from Munich and straight for me and Kotz, who is a couple yards behind me.

We are both lying prone, hugging the ground and shuddering, thinking sure this is the one. It bursts not more than two feet to the left of us. Fortunately for us the hill was terraced, for just a matter of inches to the left of us the ground dropped to another five-foot level, and that was all that saved us. The barrage finally ended, and we continued on our journey.

We relieve the 2nd Battalion at dusk. The machine gun section, as usual, was placed covering a draw which was a natural route of approach for the enemy. The 2nd Platoon was to the left of us, the 3rd Platoon to the right, and the 1st Platoon in reserve. It rains every day we're here. We haven't seen dry ground and clear skies for so long that a lot of the boys are beginning to quack like ducks. Our holes are so full of water that one man is detailed at all times to bail out water.

Old Allah, Pete and I are in one hole. As we lie in the mud, Pete keeps up his constant chatter. We brew mud all day and most of the night. It's here we spend our second Thanksgiving overseas. Although it's cold, wet and miserable in this position, it's comparatively peaceful. We're here about ten days when the 1ˢᵗ Battalion comes up to relieve us. As it's a misty day, we make the relief during daylight without being observed.

As we march back to Montequalla, Old Allah is bitching, "It'll be dark when we get there and nobody will know where to go." I then bet him we'll get there before dark. They lay another small barrage on us at the usual place, but that just hastened us along as we were going to the rear. We get to Montequalla about a half hour before dark. The machine gun section finds and old barn with clean, dry straw in it, which makes very comfortable quarters for us for the duration of our stay here.

Its pitch dark when we get everything in order and set out in search for the kitchen tent. After stumbling over half of Montequalla we finally find the kitchen. Ploopie and the cooks have a good meal for us. We then go back to the old barn, make a light out of a hand grenade, read our mail, brew mud and bat the breeze. One of the few fine things about warfare is how happy you can be with so little. The whole outfit was like a bunch of kids with new toys by just having a dry place to sleep for a few nights without being tensely alert as they are at the front.

Just to have a few hot meals with no one shooting a them, I believe they were happier than many people with a million dollars and all the luxuries in the world. Everybody was in a very jovial mood that night. John L. Sullivan talked till 3:00 in the morning about his still back in Virginia. A good many of the heavy artillery guns are dug in next to a bank just below us. And every time they fire, we almost hit the roof of the old barn. Next morning the sun is shining brightly for the first time in a mighty long time. Although it's quite some time after Thanksgiving, Ploopie, with his Yankee ingenuity, improvised a good Thanksgiving dinner for us. Phees goes to the hospital with a severe case of boils.

We get some new machine guns here and take them out to zero them in. As we're firing away, Capt. Sky comes out and orders us to quit firing and go back to our company area, as we're alerted to move out. When we get back, Lt. Hennel says, "There's no definite time set for us to move. We're just supposed to be ready to move at a moment's notice." It may be tonight, or it may not be for a week yet. It all depends on whether the 133rd Infantry Regiment gets attacked or not. If they do, it's up to us to counter attack the enemy in the 133rd sector.

We relax in this position several days before we get word to move. The expected counter attack in the 133rd sector evidently didn't come off, for as we started for the front, we take the same trail we had taken several times before up to where the 2nd Battalion is holding. When we get about 200 yards to the rear of the 2nd Battalion's position, we disperse in defilade areas and wait. None of us seem to know for sure what we are waiting for. Shortly before dusk we get word that the 168th Infantry had taken Mt. Pantano in a fierce battle suffering heavy casualties. The Jerries had been counter-attacking strongly to regain the hill. The 168th have very few men left, so it's up to us to go up and relieve them. Once again, it's cold and drizzly as we start to march single file along a steep, rocky mountain trail. About every 200 yards we're forced to hit the dirt by incoming artillery. This harassing fire slows up our march somewhat. It's dark as we get to the small Italian village, but in the darkness, we can see most of the buildings are nothing but a mass of rubble and debris. The Germans have really concentrated their mortars and artillery on this town.

As we march through the battered streets, we can see the village is jammed with jeeps, weapons carriers and ambulances. Right in the middle of this village is a large church with just a few shell holes in it. As we get closer to this church, we see a lot of activity. Ambulances are dashing madly from the church to the rear. Litter bearers, tired and worn out, are going up the hill above the village. Other litter squads were coming down carrying patients. Some were moaning in pain; others were so mangled and weak they couldn't utter a sound.

Near the church were several stacks of equipment such as helmets, packs, cartridge belts and rifles. The O.D. equipment seemed to have turned a sort of purple as it appeared literally soaked with blood. Empty plasma cans were piled high at the side door of the church. Yes, this was evidence enough of what our sister regiment has been up against. They were badly in need of relief. But with the enemy at every advantage, the gallant men of the 168th weren't budging a bit and were still repelling the ferocious German counter attacks in spite of their terrific loss in manpower and equipment.

The terrain up Mt. Pantano was almost impossible. In fact, in places it was even too rugged for mules to travel. It took an immense amount of ammunition to hold Mt. Pantano, and several times the 168th was caught short of ammo. But even then, they out fought the Jerries. The cold rain was making the jagged trail sloppy as we slowly marched up the steep mountain. We were walking up the mountain in a sort of gully. The men were stumbling and falling all up and down the line. As I stumble over a soft object, I put my hand forward to stop the fall. My hand lands on the face of a dead doughboy. There were many soldiers lying dead along this trail. It was way past midnight before we had completely relieved the 168th.

It's raining harder and getting colder by the hour. Mt. Pantano is solid rock, and we are unable to dig foxholes so we just build up rock barricades to ward off incoming shrapnel. Next morning is still cold and rainy as the Jerries throw a barrage of mortar and artillery fire in on us. Old Allah, Kotz and I get caught in the open. And before we can make it back to our small barricades, Kotz gets hit in the leg and thigh, and hit hard. He was trying to drag himself to a safer place by pulling his wounded body over the jagged rocks with his hands.

P.J. and I run out and carry him over to a rock precipice where we get a medical first aid to tend his wound and give him a shot of morphine. Oscar is in very much pain and is losing a lot of blood in spite of the tourniquet on his leg. It may be hours before the extremely busy litter bearers will be able to carry Oscar back to the aid station, so P.J. and I decide to carry him back ourselves as he must have medical attention very soon.

We put Oscar's arms around our necks and half drag, half carry him down the hill. After we get about 500 yards down the hill, we meet a litter squad and talk them out of their stretcher so it was somewhat easier to carry him the rest of the way. We pass many dead bodies on our way down the hill. When we finally reach the church in the village that is used as an aid station, we find the medics swamped in work. The floor of the church was covered with critically wounded litter patients.

The men with yellow jaundice, trench foot and lighter wounds stood back so that the more severe cases could be taken care of. Oscar's wound being quite severe, received attention almost right away. We say so long to Oscar, borrow a stove from the medics, brew a cup of mud that was so strong that it almost bent a mess spoon when we stirred it, but it was delicious to the last drop. "Well, shall we head back?" P.J. asks. "I suppose," I reply somewhat reluctantly, and we start trudging back up the hill

On our way back up the hill we meet many soldiers on their way back to the aid station—some with bloody wounds, some were hobbling down the hill with trench foot, others were throwing up and dead sick with yellow jaundice. One particular scene that will be marked in my memory forever was a dough-boy with a severe case of trench foot and yellow jaundice at the same time. This soldier was crawling on his hands and knees over the dead bodies of his fallen buddies that were literally strewn from the village to the peak of Mt. Pantano, pausing every now and then to heave his guts out. P.J. and I stop and ask if he wants some help. "I'll make 'er now boys. I haven't much further to go," the doughboy managed to say. So P.J. and I continue to make our way up the costly mountain.

When we finally get back to our positions, Speed comes out from behind his rock barricade saying, "Ya know, the old man damn near got his combine a little while ago. A big son-of-a-bitch lit right beside me. Gosh, the old man would be mad if he knew he come that close to getting the insurance money, yet not." "What the hell are you limping around for, Speed?" I ask. "Oh, gosh! I can't hardly stand on my feet, and I can't get my shoes off unless I cut them off. Gosh, they hurt awful."

Just then Pete comes up and says, "For God's sake, Speed, go back to the medics and have that trench foot taken care of." In spite of his misery, Speed seemed sort of happy as he limped down the hill towards the aid station. That night was a son-of-a-gun for misery. Our rain and mud-soaked clothing was freezing and they cracked like brittle boards as we moved around.

When morning finally came, I was sick, along with many others. Many more go back to the medics, and K Company and the whole 3rd Battalion was now very weak from the loss of manpower. I would have went back to the medics myself, but a rumor came out that we would be relieved in a day or two by French Moroccan forces. So, I think to myself this would be a hell of a time to get sick and sent to the hospital, just as we are about to be relieved, so I stay on the hill.

Later on, that day we get orders to move to the right and push forward a couple of hundred yards. All of K Company, when they got assembled, didn't look any bigger than a good-sized platoon. We didn't go so very far, but to me it seemed like miles. Every step I took I hurt. Then I started puking. I puked until I couldn't throw up any more, but still wanted to. We get to our new positions without meeting any determined resistance. Pete gives me orders to set my gun in some brush covering an opening in the middle of the 2nd Platoon sector. I'm glad that I have good, capable gunners like Old Allah and Miss Polda, for I know they can take care of everything. After we get set up, Pete and P.J. come over to our position. Pete says to me, "I brought P.J. over from Lloyd Doe's squad to take over your squad, cause you're going to the medics." "Okay," I replied, and was glad Pete had said that for I was about to ask him if I could go back anyhow. "Old Allah will give you all the dope about the position," I tell P.J. as I start down the hill.

I felt sort of cheap as I walked down the hill. I was glad to get away from it all, but I kept thinking of the boys who had to stay on the hill. This was the first time I had ever went to the medics in the 2 ½ years of Army service. When I finally reach the church in the village, which is our aid station, I see the medics are still very busy caring for the sick and wounded. The church was filled with mangled bodies of severely wounded soldiers. I suddenly feel ashamed of myself for being here unwounded, just a little sick, trying to get medical aid when there were so many men that needed the aid so very much more than I did.

I then leave and go over to an old barn. There I find Speed soaking his feet in a helmet full of hot water. Speed felt the same as I did. "Gosh," Speed says, "I hate to go to the medics with sore feet when they're so busy taking care of guys that are almost dead." We brew a cup of mud after which I puke all up. Speed and I sleep in the old barn that night along with several other soldiers.

Next morning Speed's trench foot is worse, and I don't feel any better, so we go to the aid station.

The medics weren't so busy this morning. Speed gets evacuated right away. When I come up the doc asks, "What's the matter with you?" "I don't know. All I know is puke and piss and feel like hell," I reply. "What color is your piss?" Doc asks. "Black," I reply. The doc then looks at the thermometer, calls over, "Evacuate this man. Diagnosis—yellow jaundice." It wasn't long before I was on an ambulance heading for an evacuation hospital. My battered old helmet was half full of puke by the time we reached the 94th Evacuation Hospital.

It was about 3:00 and still cold and rainy. The hospital tents were warm. The little gas heaters were red with heat. I absorbed all of the heat I could, then take off my shoes and flop on a canvas bunk and sleep till they call us for chow. When I try to put my shoes back on, I find they no longer fit as my feet are swelled up with trench foot too. When I tried to walk, I understood why so many soldiers had crawled on their hands and knees down Mt. Pantano.

Next day we are loaded on a train that heads for Naples to a station hospital. When we arrive at the Naples railroad yards, trucks pick us up and take us to a big, swell building that formerly was a Roman art institute, but now is used as the 70th Station Hospital. When we get into the reception room, the first one I see is none other than Speed, grinning like a skunk eating shit. "Say, ain't this a good deal though? In where it's nice and warm, good grub and nobody shooting at ya' and our pay goes on just the same," was the first thing Speed said.

Lt. North is also here all yellowed up with yellow jaundice and other fellers from K Company with shrapnel and machine gun wounds. We're sent to different wards. These wards have honest-to-goodness beds with clean, white sheets and everything. The nurse tells me I'll be here for quite some time, so I figure it's safe to take off my shoes and even my pants before going to bed. This was the first time I had been in a bed since we left our canvas bunks back in Ireland in November 1942.

I get my meals served in bed at first. Later on, I get to go down to the mess hall for chow. The grub is wonderful. Speed and I spend a couple of hours at each meal. The mess hall is decorated with huge naked Roman statues. All of the male statues had their genital organs shot off—all but one, and that was an enormous statue of Hercules or somebody. Speed would look at it enviously and say, "Gosh, what I could do with that."

We get word that our outfit was relieved two days after we left. I was here two weeks when I was released and sent out to the 29th replacement center, which is located just outside of Naples on the fair grounds. The particular area we go to is situated right on the racetrack. When I get out there, I again run into Speed, who already has been there two days. As we know, our outfit is enjoying relief. Now we are anxious to get back. Fortunately, there was a shipment of 34th Division men going out the next day. We get aboard trucks that take us up to the vicinity of Piedmont D'Alief where the outfit is camped for the duration of the relief.

It's about 10:00 in the evening when we get to K Company's area. Speed and I stop first at the kitchen tent and bum the cooks for a cup of mud before going to the 4th Platoon area. This was Christmas Eve, and as we enter the first machine gun tent, Lloyd Doe, Brady, P.J., Old Allah, Miss Polda and Leo Schular from the mortar section are eagerly devouring the contents of a gallon of cognac.

There also were a lot of other men in the tent that I had never seen before. They were young-looking guys, singing something about a pistol packin' mama that none of us had heard before. I had been the youngest guy in the company ever since we organized, but after looking at these kids, I suddenly felt like an old man. Lloyd Doe then says, "We got a bunch of new replacements in the section. Meet Macky, Bartlett, Lauro, Lange and Monahan. Lange, Lauro and Monahan are in your squad. The other two are in mine." The new men are a great bunch of fellers. They're happy-go-lucky and seem to have some of the pep that us old war dogs suddenly realized we lost more than somewhat.

Next morning was the beginning of Christmas Day. Speed was sicker than ever, so he went to the medics and got evacuated to a hospital again. Some of the guys went to Piedmont D'Alief last night on a six-by-six that rolled over several times. Pete was on the truck and injured his leg so he gets evacuated to a hospital too. Lloyd Doe finally takes permanent charge of the machine gun section, P.J. takes over Lloyd's old squad.

This was Christmas Day, but we had little time to enjoy it as everything was a hustle-bustle, for we were preparing to move up to the front again. We had to draw a lot of new equipment for the new replacements. We also get the new carbines that we'd waited two years for, and we were busy cleaning the cosmoline of them. The carbines are nice to handle compared to the old .03 that the weapons platoon previously had to carry on top of their already too heavy load.

We get trucks the next afternoon. It's just getting dusk as we pull through Venafro, and it's dark when we reach battered, recently captured San Fietro. It's there we detruck and start marching up a winding trail. We get to our destination, we relieve the 36th Texas Division. Next day we can see what kind of position we're in. There is a village right below the hill we're on. It's about one mile from us. The name of this village is San Vattore. About four or five miles beyond San Vattore is another village by the name of Cevero. To the left of these two villages is a flat valley.

The table-top flatness of this valley is broken up only by two comparatively small mountains, which only resemble small knolls relative to the lofty peaks that flank each side of the broad valley. The first mountain is called Mt. Lungo. Parallel to Mt. Lungo and further down the valley rises the second bulge, which is known as Mt. Porchia. Down the middle of this valley just to the right of Mt. Lungo and Porchia runs Highway 6, the ultimate road to Rome.

Across the wide expanse of this valley, opposite the town of Cevero, is an enormous mountain known as Mt. Trocchio. The gigantic Mt. Trocchio is dwarfed in size by only one more visible mountain, and that can be seen only faintly in the distance. But on a clear day we can see a very large building atop this mountain. They tell us our artillery will not be allowed to fire on this building as it is the sacred home and study of Benedictine Monks. They also say this building is immediately above and overlooking the German-held fortress town of Cassino, which we were told was the anchor of the formidable Gustave Line way back when we were in the Montequalla area. But from where we are now, Cassino is hidden from our view by the gigantic Mt. Trocchio.

While we're in this position, we are sending out patrols day and night to the German-held town of San Vattore. These patrols come back with the information that there are lots of Jerries in San Vattore. Lt. Foto returns from one of these reconnaissance missions talking a blue streak. "There's Beaucoup down there, but I've got their strong points spotted," proclaims the dynamic shavetail.

We are waiting in this position to accumulate all the information we can concerning San Vattore before we attack, for we are quite sure it will be a plenty rough deal. Meanwhile, we are taking it easy, waiting for the time to attack, eating 10-in-1 rations and keeping amused by the antics of the replacement Mack. As it has been comparatively peaceful, we learn to know the new men better. They're a bunch of good guys. We are still here on New Year's Day when we get a lot of snow, then it turns cold and very windy. Hidden from view of the enemy, we pitch pup tents over our holes for shelter from the miserable weather.

After being here a little over a week we get attack orders. It's to be a night attack on San Vattore. Lt. Hall, our company commander, gives us the dope. The 3rd Battalion is to assault San Vattore itself as the 1st Battalion flanks us on the high ground to the north. K Company is to be the assault company. The 1st Platoon is to move in from the right as the 2nd Platoon moves in from the left. P.J.'s machine gun squad is to be attached to the 1st Platoon; my machine gun squad is to be attached to the 2nd Platoon. The 3rd Platoon is to be in reserve awaiting immediate call. The mortar section is set up in a gully just before San Vattore and await fire orders. I Company is on our left flank and is to skirt the outer edge of San Vattore. L Company is to be in reserve.

As we are rolling up, preparing for the attack, Black Rufe, our platoon sergeant, comes up and says, "We're allowed one man to go to Naples on a five-day pass." Black Rufe then looks at me and goes on to say, "All the old men in the platoon had their pass while you were in the hospital, so that leaves only you left, ya lucky pup. You can ride back to the kitchen with Ploopie tonight when he brings up the rations." "Yippee," I yell, jumping up clicking my heels.

Then I suddenly felt ashamed of myself. This is a hell of a time to leave the boys with this rough deal coming up. "Maybe I better stay, Rufe. I will if you want me to," I say. "You'd be a damned fool to do that," was Black Rufe's reply. I then turn to Lloyd Doe and say, "That puts you in a hell of a spot, Lloyd."

"No, it doesn't, as long as the section is going to be split up anyhow, I'll take your squad myself," Lloyd says. "Gee, thanks Lloyd." I then look at the new replacements who were going on their first attack. They had a kind of sad look on their faces. I swallowed and said, "So long, fellows. I don't think it's going to be so tough anyhow." I knew I'd lied, but I had to say something.

On my way to the Company C.P. I meet "Gordie," the 3rd Platoon Sergeant and one of my very best friends in the company. He'd been my squad leader when I was a rookie taking training back in Camp Clairborne, and we'd been very close buddies ever since. "Where do ya think you're going P.T.?" P.T. was the nickname Gordie had originated for me, and now most of the company knew me by nothing else. "Things are going to get rough tonight, so I'm a leavin'," I say. "Are you really going on pass? Where do you keep that rabbit's foot? But I'm glad to see you go. You sure as hell deserve it." "Gee thanks Gordie, but I wish you were going too," I say as we shake hands.

We shook hands hard. I had a lump in my throat as big as a horse turd, and Gordie had a look in his eyes, a look of premonition, I think it was, and I turned and went down the hill. Ploopie didn't come with the rations till quite late, as one of the jeeps got blown up by a mine. It's about midnight when we get back to the kitchen area. "Ducky" makes us some sandwiches so we eat, drink mud and talk till about 3:00. Next morning before daylight we are on trucks heading for Naples. We drive down Via Roma, the main drag of Naples, and turn to the right up the hill to an old Italian garrison by the name of Caserma Victor Emanuel. That's where the 5th Army rest camp is located. Here we are assigned quarters, take showers and get clean clothes, then a big supper and we're ready to go out and see what Naples is like. As we walk up Via Roma, Italian kids are tugging at our clothes saying, *"Una bottilia cognac diece cento lira, vino cento lira,"* trying to sell us cognac and wine. Then they'd say, "Mongarie," meaning "ya wanna eat, Joe?" Finally, they say, *"Signorina."* We wind up at a café eating spaghetti and drinking champagne. Although I was enjoying myself very much, I couldn't help thinking how the company was making out on the attack on San Vattore.

Next morning the first thing I do, is get the morning edition of the *Stars and Stripes*. The headlines were "YANKS ENTER SAN VATORE, FIERCE

BATTLE RAGING." As I read further, I can see the boys are having a rough time, meeting overwhelming opposition and suffering many casualties. I appreciated the fact that I had gotten out of the attack, but the idea of me being in Naples having a good time gave me a sort of inferior feeling. Next day the headlines were "YANKS MAKE SLIGHT GAINS; SAVAGE FIGHTING CONTINUES IN SAN VATORE." The third day the headlines were "YANKS TAKE SAN VATORE AFTER THREE DAY BITTER BATTLE." I was glad San Vatore was finally taken, but was wondering about the casualties. The fourth day the *Stars and Stripes* comes out with a dramatized story entitled, "In K Co. they were all heroes". In this story, I read how Waldo and Lt. Foto led the 2nd platoon in a fierce house to house campaign, many other men's names in the Co. were not revealed as the *Stars and Stripes* stated, they were killed in action. I was wondering now who these men were.

The fifth day we leave Naples and head back to our Co's. It is just dusk as we get to the kitchen area. The first man I see is "Jeep" our Co. articifer. "Jeep" looks kind of down in the dumps and the first thing is. Gordie got it. When "Jeep" said that, my morale dropped to a new low. I remembered the look in Gordie's eyes as we shook hands before I left. It was a look of premonition all right. "Jeep" then tells who the other men were that were killed or wounded, many of them were new replacements. The following night, I go up to the Co. with Ploopie and "Swanee." "Swanee" was driving the peep, as he is the transportation corporal and we call him the "Fleet Commander." His fleet consists of two peeps and a weapons carrier. We drive through San Vatore which is now a battered mass of rubble. About a mile beyond San Vatore, the terrain turns into a mass of rolling knobs with several buildings along the knolls. We stop at the battalion C.P. Louie Lostsahorses, our battalion runner is there, so I follow Louie to the Co.'s positions.

The boys in the section seem pretty happy as I join them. The section had only two casualties in the battle of San Vatore. Our position was in an old Italian house, we have our machine guns set up to fire out of the windows. We get word from Co. C.P. that L Co. will have a patrol out in front of us tonight. A couple of hours after that, we see the patrol coming for the house. As they get closer "P.J." calls out "Halt, French." We were expecting the patrol to call back "Fries", which was the parole to our password, but instead they open up on us with tommy guns, B.A.R.'s and M-1s. After some contemplation, we decide that it is not a jerry patrol which can easily be detected by the sound of automatic fire weapons, unless it was such a thing that the krauts were using some captured American weapons for this patrol. We finally holler back at them, "This is K Co., in here, quit your damned firing." We then hear someone call to the men. "Cease firing, that's K Co. in there." The firing dies down and we begin to move around again, when someone from the patrol calls out "Commence firing again, that ain't K Co. in there that that house is full of jerries, I just seen one," and they cut loose again. We plead to quit firing but they pay us no never mind. Next thing we hear is a bazooka shell explode right near one of the machine guns. We then decide to fire back at them so they could recognize our fire as they were attempting to (unreadable) grenades in the windows. In the windows. L Co. suddenly ceases their aggressive (unreadable) is about a minute of silence. Lloyd Doe again called out the first part of the password. "French." Someone from the patrol called back "Fries." "Advance to be recognized" Lloyd replies. When they get close enough, we recognize them as L Co. "So, this is K Co. after all" The Sgt. Of the patrol sighs. "You catch on real quick" was old Allah's reply. L Co.'s patrol leaves and we spend the rest of the night peacefully.

Next afternoon we move up to the next ridge of small knolls and dig in. The jerries send several patrols at us this night. One particular hit the 2nd platoon sector right where Pete Housler was hiding behind a B.A.R. Pete killed three jerries and wounded another. We spend the next day behind a bank where we can move around without being seen. The battle of San Vattore had made K. Co. pretty small again, particularly the 1st platoon who had many casualties. That night we dig new positions for our machine guns. As we are digging, they throw a mortar barrage in on us. "Miss" Polda gets hit in the head with a chunk of shrapnel that went right through his helmet. When the barrage ended, we got "Miss Polda" back to the medics. "Miss Polda" lived but we never seen him again as he got put in limited and sent back to the states. "Old Allah" didn't seem quite the same after "Miss Polda" got hit.

The town of Cevero is not far from us, it is to our right front, and our sister regiment the 168th was attacking it tonight. There was an immense amount of small arms fire that went on all night, so we assume the 168th is having a pretty tough battle. Next day we learn that our next mission is to take Mt. Trocchio, the huge mountain to the left and across the valley from us. That night the battle in Cevero rages again until the wee hours of the morning when the 168th capture all of the disputed village. Next day we prepare to attack Mt. Trocchio. By the looks of the terrain, we have to cover and considering the stubborn opposition we have run into lately, Mt. Trocchio looks like it may be a tough deal. As we start attacking across the valley, each man takes about a ten-yard interval between men. The artillery has laid down a smoke screen for us. The 2nd battalion is attacking with us on our left flank. Under the cover of smoke, we lose no time in crossing the valley and we rapidly approach the enemy's last apparent stronghold before the Rapido River. We get to the base of the mountain without a shot being fired. We set up our machine guns to deliver overhead fire as the riflemen tactfully advance in skirmishes up the steep rugged slopes of the giant mountain. Much to our surprise, there isn't a jerry on Mt. Trocchio. We then shift more to the left where there are several farm buildings. The Co. stops here, while Waldo takes a patrol quite a ways out in front where he contacts units of the 36th Division who are coming in from the left. When Waldo returns, he says, "We're damn near cut off right now by the 36th Division who are partially out in front of us. They are continuing their advance as they are not meeting any opposition." We are all pretty jubilant to be on the ground the jerries not only yielded but refused to defend. From all indications the enemy had withdrawn all forces across the Rapido River. As we are now automatically in sort of a semi-reserve, we billet ourselves in these farm houses and once again are relaxed and at ease.

Next day is nice and clear. Artillery guns are moving in close to where we are now and we feel pretty good about that, for when a dough-boy gets as far back as heavy artillery he figures he is pretty much in rear echelon. It was real heavy artillery that was digging in here. 155 long toms, 8-inch howitzers and a little further back there were some 240s. We get word that the 2nd battalion is occupying ground in front of Mt. Trocchio so that puts us in complete reserve.

Not a great distance on the other side of Mt. Trocchio runs the Rapido River, almost immediately across the Rapido lies the German stronghold city of Cassino, and that is the general picture as we sit around a cozy fire place watching the glowing embers in the dark. We form a ring big for everyone in the section to sit in around the fire place. Waldo comes over to visit with us. Here we sit talking and brewing mud, talking about almost everything but war. About the girls back home, good things to eat and arguing which kind of car is the best. The replacements are singing songs that are a couple of years old but are new to us. One good thing about these Italian houses, almost everyone has a fireplace and we really make whenever the situation permits. I miss "Speed" these days, he was always good for a chuckle or two. Now "Old Allah" with the aid of "Big Barnsmell" Slink produce most of the laughs, the replacement Macky gets his two bits worth in too. The second day we are here, we get some new replacements. We get two in the machine gun section, whose names are Jim Fenstemaker and Dick Jewitt. I get Jim in my squad, P.J. gets Jewitt in his. Jim is very fond of wine, and we have a whole barrel of Dago red that we found in the wine cellar. Jim keeps himself in a very good mood by sipping the sour brew. P.J. finally gets told he is now officially a corporal.

That night we get orders to go on a combat patrol in force. The entire Co. with the exception of the mortar section was to go. Our mission was to go to the Rapido River, send scattered patrols across, feel out the enemy on the other side, then return to this same position. As we push off single file many of us wish we were in the mortar section so we would not have to go on this mission. It is quite moonlight and as we silently march, along we can view the terrain quite clearly. As we draw nearer the Rapido we see the tall man with the silver leaf on his collar is along on this mission. Yes, Col. Mearns our battalion commander who has won the deepest admiration of his command was always right in there with the men, particularly on rough deals and precarious missions. Here we fan out somewhat and pick our way along more cautiously. Suddenly BANG BANG. A cloud of smoke arose in the moonlight air, followed by the anguished cry of pain from a screaming "Medics medics." Everyone wanted to help this man and the men went towards him. Then BANG BANG there were explosions everywhere. Yes, K Co. was caught right in the middle of a mine field. Men were lying with their legs blown off painfully crying for help. We are trying to figure out a way to get these men without getting blown up ourselves. Col. Mearns somehow had gotten a big heavy door off some building; he slams it on the ground in front of himself. If it hit a mine, it would explode it and at the same time keep it from injuring anybody. Soon a path is cleared so we can carry the wounded out. Two men are already dead, we take the bodies back with us. Col. Mearns has won the respect of his battalion by many deeds such as this. As we change off carrying the wounded men back, I hear a man call out. "Has anybody got their left foot blown off?" "Ya right here," I hear another man call back. "Well let's get together, I've got my right one blown off," replied the other man.

Lt. North also has both legs badly wounded. It's just getting dawn as we finally get back to the rear of Mt. Trocchio to our old houses. We are mighty glad to get back and soon are cooking up ten-in-one rations. Old Allah chirps up, "Who in the hell is the guy that's always borrowing my mess spoon and not licking it off good before he brings it back?" In this outfit it's the standing law never to return a dirty spoon, but always lick it off so that it's nice and clean. So Old Allah has very good grounds for his complaints.

Next day we are told to be ready to move at a moment's notice, although no particular time has been set for us to move. When we bed down at night we shudder every time we hear the footsteps of a man approaching the house, thinking it's a runner with the message to pack up and move. Old Allah says, "We should declare an open season on all runners, as they never bring us anything but bad news anyhow." We sweat it out like this for a couple of nights before we really get orders to move. The orders are that we are to move out in front of Mt. Trocchio and relieve the 2nd Battalion, who are holding ground there.

We start out just as it gets good and dark. The nights are pitch black now, and we find it difficult to walk in the rough terrain with our heavy loads of weapons and ammo. When we reach our destination, Lt. Hennel points out on a map to Lloyd Doe where he wants to set up our machine guns. S-2 had the information that there still was a great deal of enemy activity on this side of the Rapido River, consisting mostly of reconnaissance and combat patrols in force.

The 2nd Battalion reconnaissance patrols could find nothing that indicated the Germans had a main line of resistance this side of the Rapido, however it was known that they had many heavily manned and fortified outposts that were mobile enough not to remain in any one place for any length of time.

The mission Lts. Hall and Hennel assigned to Lloyd Doe for the machine gun section was to go way out in front of the company into no-man's land as close to the banks of the Rapido as feasible terrain and logical reasoning would permit to combat any aggression of the enemy and seek out any information we could get. To us, it sounded like a screwy mission for just a machine gun section, as somewhat reluctantly we take off into no-man's land.

Lloyd Doe leads the section and tells me to bring up the rear. We talk as silently as possible following every reasonable terrain feature that aided our concealment in spite of the jet-black darkness. Now we could hear the rippling of the Rapido. We stop and listen and look. Then night was exceptionally silent, aside from the gurgling of the river. There was hardly another sound.

We start moving again. As we get almost to the banks of the river, we turn to the left, traveling almost parallel to the rustling river. Suddenly there was a splash of water, a rustle of brush, the spray of Jerry machine gun bullets going over our heads. We all hit the dirt and lie silently for a moment. In between the rapid firing machine gun bursts, I could hear faint murmurs of the Jerries from several directions.

I could see gun flashes from three different positions, but there were many more that I didn't see. I think to myself that the place is full of Krauts. I decide to crawl up to the head of the column and talk the situation over with Lloyd Doe. Just then I hear a low, deep voice from the head of the column say calmly, "Turn back. Keep on going. Go silently, but quickly." There was a slight trace of a German accent in this man's voice.

For a moment I think this is it, we're captured. Then again, I think that voice sounded a awful lot like Danny's, who was of German descent. But what would Danny be doing out here with the machine gun section? He would be back with his mortar section of which he is in charge. Now that the column had been reversed, I was at the head of it and leading it at a rapid but silent pace. I proceed to retrack the ground we had just come over. Soon I look back and see the silhouette of a big man come running up to the head of the column. I heave a sigh of relief. Sure enough it's none other than Danny.

Quite confident that we had now given the kraut eaters the slip, I say, "How come you out here, Danny?" "Oh, I had to know where you guys were so that I would be able to bring your rations and ammo at night so I just come along out. I was kinda scared something like this would happen. We damned near got ambushed good and proper. That place is full of Germans," Danny replies. I was glad that Danny was along that night. Yet Danny didn't have to go out with us. It was a little more than his regular duty. But being second in command of the platoon, he figured he better go along as he sensed danger and wanted to be there with us.

Danny is probably the best soldier in the company, and I've seen colonels and majors take advice from him. We make it back to where the 3rd Platoon is occupying some houses. Lloyd Doe, who is disgusted anyhow for being set out on a mission like this, tells P.J. and I to find places for our squads to get some rest. So, we take up places in some houses with the 3rd Platoon. Next morning, we get up and are cooking our K ration breakfast when a Jerry patrol comes up. It's about a 20-man patrol and are already very close to the house. We hadn't discovered them a minute too soon as they were already firing rifle grenades at the windows, but they fortunately do no on any harm. We open up on them with everything we have, and they soon withdraw leaving three of their comrades behind extremely dead.

Later on, that day we move over to the left flank of the company and set up covering a draw that would be a likely route of approach for the enemy. Here we get full view of Monte Abby Cassino, the monastery perched high on the lofty peak of what we call the Monastery Hill. It's the dominating ground for miles around. Right below it is the stronghold city of Cassino. We can see it plainly. It isn't far off, just across the river. It was a picturesque scene in a weird sort of way. To the left of us the 36th Division had a bridgehead across the Rapido River and were pinned down in the marshlands to the left of Cassino. The hard luck 36th Division was taking a terrific beating there, and after holding their bridgehead three days they were forced to withdraw.

Early one morning we are alerted for a counter attack. Well, this forecasted counter attack comes in a sort of a raid or a large scale combat patrol. Unfortunately for Der Fuhrer's supermen, we were prepared for them. We let them get close before we opened up on them. When we did open up, we done plenty of damage. We kept our machine guns sizzling hot. The Jerries soon became disorganized, and when the skirmish ended many Jerries were behind our lines. Others were lying out in front of our positions, dead and wounded. Between the 1st Battalion, who are on our right flank and us, we killed, wounded and captured an outlandish number of enemy troops. The damage we inflicted on this raiding party must have been pretty much of a crippling blow to the enemy. To us it was just that many more enemy troops have to be eliminated.

We were in this position several days before we pack up and move. It's a very dark night as we stumble our way along in the rough terrain, making our way back to the slopes of Mt. Trocchio. Near the base of Mt. Trocchio where the gradual slopes begin to rise more steeply toward the rocky summit, we turn to the left. We march quite some distance before we come to a cluster of old farm buildings. Here we stop and bed down for the night.

These barns had dry hay in them so we had a nice place to spend the night. Black Rufe, Danny, Lloyd Doe, Leo Schular and I were cooking mud in an old gallon can when Lt. Hennel comes back from the company C.P. where he has been conferring with Lt. Hall and battalion officers. After some pause, Lt. Hennel says, "Tomorrow were going to cross the Rapido and start the long battle for our final objective, which is the monastery on the hill." With a sort of a frown on his face, Lt. Hennel goes on to say, "Just between us guys here, I'll bet this will be one of the bloodiest battles of this war."

Next morning as we move out in the predawn darkness, we get word that there has been an amphibious landing up north at a place called Anzio and Nettuno. There had been rumors of a landing for quite some time, but it was officially announced this morning. The initial landings were made by Ranger Battalions, the 3rd Division and British units. They met no opposition whatsoever in the beachhead assault, as they caught the Germans by surprise. However, after they had secured their beachhead and started moving inland, Smilin' Albert Kesselring, the German commander in Italy, had time to bring down reserve forces from the north in overwhelming numbers.

Soon the limited Allied forces on the beachhead were stopped as the enemy outnumbered them with the aid of having every possible terrain feature in their favor, geographically the enemy had every advantage. Allied troops on the newly established beachhead were now fighting bitterly to hold their ground. But right now, we on the southern front are concerned with the crossing of the Rapido River, Monastery Hill and Cassino.

Our sister regiment, the 168th Infantry, was to make the initial crossing. We of the 135th are to push through them and take the ground beyond. We move to right parallel to the Rapido for a good distance, then stop along a sort of ditch-like ravine where we could not be observed by the enemy. Here we wait for the 168th to secure their bridgehead across the river. Later on, that day, the 168th accomplished their mission as they always do.

As we had tank battalions in support of us, they managed to get some armor across the river. At dark we ford the Rapido in a shallow place. We are cold and wet when we get across the river. We fan out somewhat and push forward. Some scattered artillery was landing in the area, but we hadn't run into any concentrated barrage as yet. We go quite a ways as we route out the Jerry outposts, and they withdraw to their mountain retreat.

We are right below Monastery Hill on perfectly flat ground, and the Jerries are up there looking down our throats. There are several buildings on this flat land. Here we stop and build up a defense. The machine gun section is put out forward on an outpost covering a perfectly flat strip of terrain. Here we hastily dig foxholes and camouflage them perfectly before daylight.

We spend the next day pinned down in our foxholes. Old Allah and I share the same hole together. I can see the marks of war are beginning to show on Old Allah's bearded face. He has been a little bit nervous ever since Miss Polda got hit. Our holes are quite shallow, and we have a difficult time pissing in a C ration can without being seen. The Jerries keep harassing us with artillery and mortar fire all day long.

We are glad when darkness finally came and are able to get out of our holes, stretch and move around a bit, but we had to be very much on the alert for a counter attack or enemy patrols. That night Lloyd Doe goes back to the company C.P. and asks the C.O. if we can move back to some of these buildings during the hours of daylight so that we wouldn't have to remain cramped in our holes all day. If we were attacked during daylight, we could fight them off from there just as well as we can from here. The C.O. tells Lloyd it's all right as long as we're out there during the hours of darkness, so at the first peep of dawn next morning we withdraw about 500 yards to a pretty fair building. Here we make ourselves comfortable, start brewing mud and get some rest.

We don't know for sure when we'll make the assault on Monastery Hill, but we all have a feeling it won't be long and sort of dread the thought of it. Later on, that day Danny picks his way over to where we were. Danny is right guide of the 4th Platoon, so he brought some rations over to us and made sure we had plenty of chow. Danny visits with us quite a while, laughing and joking most of the time. I was glad he had come over. And when he left, I little realized that that was the last time I would ever see him. We all stay in the house with the exception of Brady, who digs himself a hole beside the house and stays in that. Brady says, "You guys ain't going to get me in that house, them Jerries are going to knock it flat one of these days."

That night I take my squad out to the outpost. P.J.'s squad stays in the house, as we figure one squad can take care of the outpost. Tomorrow night if we are still here P.J. will take his squad out to the outpost and my squad will stay in the house. That night half the squad stays awake half the night, the other half stays awake the remainder of the night. The nights are getting quite moonlight now, making visibility relatively good. During the time I was asleep, Lange crawls over to my hole, wakes me up saying he has spotted a Jerry patrol out in front.

I tell Lange to awaken the rest of the squad as I crawl over to the machine gun as silently as possible. After scanning the terrain in front of me for quite some time, I am unable to see anything visually. However, I do know there is a Kraut patrol out in front not so far off as I can hear the crack of dry vegetation crinkle under their feet. After some contemplation I decide to remain silent, as we could not see them, neither could they see us. If we opened fire on them, we would be unable to do them any damage as we could not see them, and our firing would give them the information they were seeking. They then could go back to their lines and spot our positions on their artillery data. Then we would be in a hot spot. We remain very much on the alert for the remainder of the night. And as early dawn approaches, we are quite confident that the patrol returned to their lines mission unaccomplished, as we know they found out absolutely nothing in our sector.

At the first sight of dawn, we withdraw back to the house that the rest of the machine gun section is occupying. We were about half way to the house when we hear the hiss of an incoming artillery shell. As soon as the shell left the gun, we knew it was going to come close by the sound. You can somehow always tell when them kind are going to be close. We all hit the dirt as it bursts on the trail ahead of us not more than ten yards away. That first shell was followed by a heavy barrage in the general area. I figure they have this trail on their firing data, so I tell the boys to follow me and we shift to the left.

It wasn't long after we left the trail that a terrific barrage landed right where we were a few minutes earlier. Shells were bursting close to us again now. A heavy mortar shell came down silently. My ears caught the barely audible hiss before it lands, and we all flop to the ground. There was an explosion. And even before I hit the dirt, I know I am hit. There was a lapse of several minutes before the air around us cleared enough to see ahead.

The sickening odor of powder hung heavy over us. A matter of yards in front of me the ugly crater left by the exploding shell was staring me in the face. The warm blood running down my neck reminded me that I had been hit. I was hit in the jaw, but it was only a slight wound and was giving me very little pain. The barrage ends, and I call back, "Anyone hurt?" They call back, "No." Old Allah is about 20 feet behind me, and he calls out, "That one was pretty close. Let's get going before they lay in some more."

I open my first aid packet and tie it around my neck to stop the bleeding, then say, "Let's go." Lloyd Doe is up when we get back to the house. It's now almost plum daylight. Lange looks at me and says, "Hey, you're wounded." It is beginning to hurt a little now, and I found it hard to talk. "Yeah, and it's a million dollar one too," I reply. "By gosh, it's a good one all right. Ya wanna sell it?" Lloyd Doe asks. A million-dollar wound is what we call a wound that's bad enough to take you back to a hospital and not bad enough to leave you permanently injured or give you much pain. "You better go up to the company C.P. and have the first aid man fix it up," Lloyd Doe tells me. So, I take off picking my way over to the company C.P.

When I reach the company C.P., Col. Mearns, Lt. Hall and Lt. Hennel are drinking mud. "Why did you let them kraut eaters hit you, Corporal?" Col. Mearns asks good naturedly. Lt. Hennel pours me a cup of mud as the medics put some more bandages on my jaw. Bruce Leasman from the Commo Section at company headquarters was also wounded, so we make our way back to the battalion aid station together.

When we get there, the doc redresses our wounds, loads us in a Peep, which takes us back to the 109th collecting station which is now located in San Vattore. From there we're put on an ambulance and taken to the 94th Evacuation Hospital. When we get off at the receiving ward, the tall, lead man was standing in front of the tent. That was the first time I had seen General Mark Clark, our Army commander.

"Things are pretty rough up there, aren't they, man?" The General asks. "Yes, sir," we all reply. I can barely open my mouth now as my jaw is fractured. It wasn't long before they put me on a stretcher and carry me to the operating tent. There the nurse tells me to look at the wall as she jabs a needle into my arm. She then tells me to count to ten. I counted to three, and that's the last thing I remember. 🐂

THINGS THAT KEEP THEM GOING

When I come to again it's the following day. I was in a ward with a lot of other wounded men. I feel of my face and I can feel nothing but a mass of bandages, only my mouth, nose and eyes were in the open. I look around and see that almost every other patient had their faces covered with bandages, but most of them were much worse off than I was. A nurse comes up to my bed and shows me a piece of shrapnel about the size of her thumb nail and says pleasantly, "See what they took out of your jaw?"

I found it hard to talk, so I didn't say much. I get soup for breakfast, dinner and supper as that was all I was able to eat. The patient in the bed next to me is a tank man who had been severely burned. We both had our faced bandaged up, so we couldn't tell what the other fellow looked like. But we enjoyed each other's company anyhow. The patients that are unable to walk keep the nurses and ward boys busy carrying urinals and bed pans back and forth. Here we call a urinal a P-38 and a bed pan a "flying fort." One patient yells in a hurry, "Quick, nurse, send out a B-17 with a fighter escort. I've got two missions to make at one time." The tank man next to me calls for a flying fort. The nurse hurriedly places it under him. The tank man heaves a sigh and says, "oh, oh, nurse, I hate to tell you this, but I missed her completely."

Next day I'm put on a train and head for Naples where they take us to the 45th General Hospital. I spend my time here convalescing and consider myself very lucky not to be up at the front as one of the bloodiest battles of the war was being fought now. My outfit was struggling to take Monastery Hill and Cassino, while up at the Anzio beachhead other forces were fighting their hearts out with the odds against them to hold the beachhead. But in spite of almost impregnable opposition, our forces were still able to make slight gains.

The hospitals are now filled to over capacity as the casualties were coming in very fast. The first thing I do every morning is to get a *Stars and Stripes* and see what the latest developments are. I always hoped to see Monastery Hill and Cassino taken or breakthrough at Anzio, but there was nothing in the news but bitter fighting. They finally decide to blast the Monastery on the Hill with bombs and artillery fire. They blow it to pieces, but the Jerries still hang on as tough as ever, fighting from the very debris that was knocked down on them.

I was in the hospital three weeks before I was released. I then go out to the 29th Replacement Center by the race track again. I was fortunate to get sent back to the outfit the following day. By fortunate I mean that most combat soldiers have a mutual dislike for replacement centers, and for very good reasons too numerous to mention. To the old "doggies" who knew the horrors of war, it was plain rotten and chicken shit. For the new replacements fresh from the States, it was bad enough for them knowing they would soon be up fighting for their lives without first getting dumped in a place like that.

Of other replacement centers in Italy, I never heard any complaint, only the 29th was spoken of in utter disrespect. To go into detail in what way this center was the way it was would probably only bring embarrassment and shame to certain ranking officers in charge of the center. Trucks take us up to division C.P. where we pitch pup tents and stay overnight. Here we learn that the whole division had been relieved by New Zealand forces after being beaten down to almost nothing. Once again it made me wonder who all the casualties in the company were.

I look up the hill and see a man jump up and click his heels, and I know in a moment it must be Speed. As I walk up the hill, I holler, "Did you just get out of the hospital now, Speed?" "Oh, this is the second time I've been out. After I got out the first time I went uptown in Naples and got wounded by a blonde. So, I had to go back to the hospital again. I'm just on my way back to the outfit now." I was glad to see Speed again, as he had been gone for quite a while.

Next day we rejoin the company. They're camped at the same place they were during the last divisional relief, near Piedmont D'Alief. As we walk up to the company area, they had just finished putting up pyramidal tents and were now cleaning their weapons and equipment. But there weren't many of them around, as the company come off the Monastery Hill with a total of 30 men. We had 200 when we started.

I finally ask Lloyd Doe, "Who were all the casualties?" Lloyd looks up from the new platoon roster he has written in his book and says, "They got Danny after he got about a dozen of them. Lt. Hall got it as well as L Company's Commander, Capt. Ichabod Crane and many more." Lloyd goes on to say, "P.J. got wounded pretty bad again. So did Leo Schular, Big Barnsmell, Waldo and Col. Mearns. Many others went to the hospital with general sickness and trench foot, including Brady, Lange and others."

Old Allah was still here though. He was singing his favorite song, Ole' San Antone, he was taking a bath in his helmet. We got our tents rigged up pretty comfortable, and some of the men are gradually stringing back from the hospital including Brady, Leo, Big Barnsmell and even Phees comes back after being gone for a very long time. Brady takes over P.J.'s squad and is promoted to Corporal right away, as P.J. will be gone for quite some time. While we're hear each man gets promoted on grade under a new infantry order, so I'm now a Buck Sergeant. Leo Schular takes over the mortar section succeeding Galant Danny.

The have increased the percentage of passes while we are here, so we have about ten men from the company in Naples at all times. Lt. Hennel gets transferred to England, and Lt. Foto gets promoted to company executive officer. Lt. Dots is back after being gone for a long time, and takes over as our new company commander, succeeding Lt. Hall. As we all know Lt. Doty so well, we're glad to have him for company commander. Capt. Sky, who has been in charge of the battalion since Col. Mearns was wounded, gets to go home on rotation.

We're here about two weeks when we move way down south near Benevento. As we go that far south, we are all pretty sure we will never fight on the Cassino front again. But in all probability, we'll sail for Anzio. Here we get some pretty stiff training. My turn comes up for a five-day pass while we are here. This time we go to Caserta, as Naples is declared out of bounds for all American troops.

"Lennie" Holtegaard. "Wild Bill" Keller and Herr from company headquarters were also on pass. Even though Naples is out of bounds, we slip down there a couple of times from Caserta till the M.P.'s pick Herr up and toss him in the jug. The rest camp in Caserta is located directly across from the King's Royal Palace. We have a big time here for five days.

It's getting towards evening of the fifth day when we get back to our camp near Benevento. When we get to the company area, we see Big Barnsmell and Old Allah walking around in circles with full field packs on their backs. "What in the hell did you guys do now?" I ask. "Oh, we got drunk and called our new platoon leader Lt. a----- a bunch of names. That's why we have to walk around with these full field packs till midnight every night," they reply.

Next day as we go out to train, I meet the replacements that had come in while I was on pass. We got a lot of them in the machine gun section as we are organizing another squad for the 50 caliber that we recently got to use against a new German weapon, the "Dootlebug Tank," which they are using at Anzio. The Dootlebug is a midget tank filled with high explosives and operated by remote control from the German lines. They send this tank up to our positions, then explode it, doing considerable damage.

The replacements we get in the section are as follows: Weeks, Valley, Mancia, O'Neale, Portman, Fahr, Waugh, Westbrooks and a boy from Alabama by the name of Hicks. The guys in the platoon make it so tough on our new Platoon Leader, Lt. A------ that he gets transferred out. Now for Platoon Leader we have Lt. M-----, a stern, serious sort of fellow, he seems to be.

The 2nd Platoon has a new platoon leader that is liked by everyone. His name is Lt. McGinn. Next day Black Rufe, 4th Platoon sergeant, his brother Pape, 3rd Platoon sergeant, and Lennie Holtegaard, 2nd Platoon sergeant are commissioned 2nd Lieutenants. Black Rufe gets transferred to M Company. Pape and Lennie are transferred to L Company. Lloyd Doe, being the senior staff sergeant in the 4th Platoon, gets promoted to platoon sergeant succeeding Black Rufe. I then succeed Lloyd Doe as machine gun section leader. Old Allah succeeds me as 2ⁿᵈ Squad Leader, Brady still has the 1ˢᵗ Squad and Macky takes charge of the new 50 caliber squad.

The next two days we spend packing up preparing to move. We haven't been told for sure where we're going, but from all indication we can hardly be going any other place but Anzio. I don't get to know the replacements very well before we leave, but I have found out that Hicks is my biggest problem child. We get on trucks and head for Naples to a staging area where we stay for the night.

It's late the following afternoon when we get aboard an L.C.I. It's just getting dusk as they hoist anchor and we leave Naples Harbor. As we sail out into the blue Mediterranean, we can see a scarlet flash beaming above Naples. It was a picture like we have seen in books but never in reality. That glowing flare above Naples was Mt. Vesuvius. Right at this particular time Mt. Vesuvius was erupting violently. Once again, the red-hot lava was pouring down on the ancient ruins of Old Pompeii, and some of it was even hitting the new, modern Pompeii. As we get further out to sea, the red glow from Mt. Vesuvius grows dimmer and soon disappears entirely from our view.

The entire 3ʳᵈ Battalion was aboard the L.C.I., and K Company is the company that gets hooked for guard duty and I get hooked for the sergeant of the guard for the duration of the voyage. I establish my guard C.P. in the cab of a six-by-six, which is on top deck of this L.C.I. I go to sleep. When I awaken, it's early next morning. The L.C.I. standing still. I look out to the beach and see a badly battered and beaten town. The early morning air above Anzio was literally dotted with barrage balloons.

We disembark about an hour later and start marching to an assembly area. At the Anzio Beachhead we know we can't march very far or we'll be in Jerryland. When we reach our destination, we all dig in. Hicks, my problem child, has lost all his equipment, so I have to round up some more for him. The Luftwaffe was out that night bombing Anzio and ammo dumps. Next day I draw a big supply of ammo for the section, and it really loads the boys down. I tell hicks, "You are 4ᵗʰ ammo carrier of the 2ⁿᵈ Squad. Old Allah is your Squad Leader, and you do what he tells you to do." Hicks stutters, "Gosh 'o mighty damn, looks to me like ya'd let a feller rest once in a while and not keep him runnin' with ammo all the time."

That night all our officers go up to the front to reconnoiter our positions. Next day they give us the dope. Lt. Doty tells us, "We are moving up tonight to relieve the 3rd Division," as he points it out on a map. Lts. Foto and McGinn are laughing and joking, but Lt. M----- has a serious look on his face. We then go back, give the dope to the men and prepare to move into the line. I call the section together and tell them they'll have to travel silently, and when we get there, we'll be pinned down in our holes all day. And anybody that is seen during daylight, friend or foe. Hicks raises his hand, signifying he has a question. "Ya gotta get out of your hole to shit, don'tcha?" "Not if it's during daylight. You shit and piss in a can or a box or something. When night comes, take it away and bury it," I reply. "Ah, ah, ah, it seems a feller should be able to shit if he has to, gosh oh mighty damn," Hicks mumbles.

It's plum dark when we start for the front that night. We cross Mussolini Canal, and they start laying artillery on us. It was the first fire the newest replacements had been under, and they start bunching up. Lt. M-----, who had been leading us, hits the dirt and is somewhat reluctant to get up and push forward out of the impact area. I can see this is causing the replacement to become nervous.

I walk up and down the dispersed section column and tell each man individually, "Let's go. We won't get hurt as long as we're movin'." We get out of the barrage with no casualties and reach the left flank, the company's position that we are to relieve. The 3rd Platoon takes this sector. I leave Brady's squad in the 3rd Platoon sector in a very good position. The rest of us move on till we come to a wine cellar that is used for the company C.P.

Old Allah's squad is placed about 50 yards to the left of our company C.P. Between Old Allah's squad and the C.P. I place Macky's 50 caliber squad. The holes here have three inches of water in them, so we have to bail them out. Macky and I clean out a hole, and before daylight we have it fit to live in. We then sleep for a couple of hours. We were awakened by a concentrated artillery barrage, so we just brew some mud and sweat it out.

When darkness finally comes, I go over to the company C.P., get a new password and strike out for Brady's squad. I find all of Brady's squad in good shape, then return to Macky and Old Allah's squads, gather up a carrying party and go back to the dump for rations and ammo. When we get back and have the rations and ammo distributed, I hear the voice of Lt. M----- call, "Sgt. P.T., come with me. I want to go down to the mortar section." So, we start hiking for the mortar section's positions. Every time the Lieutenant would see a bush or a stump, he would hit the dirt, call me over and say, "See that German out there?" He does that several times before we reach the mortar section and about as many times on the way back. We barely make it back before daylight.

Next night I get orders to move my two 30-caliber squads over on the right flank in the 2nd Platoon sector, but leave Macky's 50-caliber squad where it is. I go over alone first to reconnoiter the positions. I then come back and get Brady's and Old Allah's squads. I put Old Allah's squad on the extreme right flank between K Company and L Company. Brady's position is in the corner of the line near a lone pine tree. We then go back to the dump to bring up supplies of rations and ammo. Again, we barely make it back before daylight. I stay with Old Allah's squad as that is most distant from all other C.P.'s. Old Allah and "Jimmie the Fence" stay right in the gun position. The rest of them are dug in on either side of us. I have a sound power phone connected to all C.P.'s so we have good communications.

Every night we can hear a bold bunch of Jerries not far out in front of our positions. It sounds like they might be putting up barb wire entanglements. One particular Kraut was continually whistling the tune "I'm Riding On A Ferry," seemingly for our benefit. We figure all he's up to is to draw fire from us so that he will be able to pick out our positions so we let him continue with his solitary serenade. However, Old Allah counters by whistling the tune "I Can Get Along Without You Very Well." At the first sign of darkness every night Hicks emerges out of his diminutive fox hole, sneaks up to ours and whispers, "Ah ah ah I wanta can a bread."

As soon as it got dark enough, I would go over to the 2nd Platoon C.P., which is situated in a straw shack. There I would shoot the bull with Lt. McGinn,

"Ole, 2nd Platoon sergeant, and "Good Deed," 2nd Platoon right guide. When the password for the next 24 hours comes out, I would go over to see how Brady's squad was making out. There was a great deal of heavy artillery landing around Brady's squad. The replacements were pretty jittery.

By that time, it would be time to gather up a detail and go back to bring up food, water and ammo. The supply dump is quite a ways back, and this 2nd Platoon sector is most distant from it. When we get back with the supplies, Good Deed and I sit down in the open field and break down the rations. We get these ten-in-one rations, and they're quite difficult to break down into small groups as we had to do here. After getting the rations to Brady's and Old Allah's squads, it's usually beginning to break day and we crawl back into the conceal-ment of our holes in much the same manner as groundhogs until darkness once again appears. This is the routine we go through for the next 45 days.

We are here about a week when I get orders to move Old Allah's gun to a different position, which I'm glad for. I never did like this position anyhow. We work as fast as we can all night digging these new positions. Lt.----- even sends us a couple of mortar men to aid us in the digging so that we'll be able to finish it before daylight. Old Allah chuckles over the fact that we have mortar men working for us. "The mortar section has always shit on the machine gun section. Now were shitting on them, oh happy day," Old Allah says with a tone of revenge in his voice.

In this new position Old Allah's gun is used as a breakthrough gun. It's located about a hundred yards to the left rear of the 2nd Platoon C.P. It's a perfect position for the mission to which it is assigned. We have some super deluxe fox holes. Over the top of our holes, we have heavy planks. Above the planks is a double layer of sandbags. Here we lay in our holes and shudder, sweating out one barrage after another. "Anzio Annie" is the name we hung on the big one that seemed to say, "You you" as it comes toward us.

The top of Hicks' head was black and blue from jumping up, hitting the top of his hole every time a shell came in. Shortly after dark each night Hicks is bound to come into our hole for an hour or two and relate his day's experience. "I was playing black jack with the 'tother feller. The I bet him all my ammunition, thinkin' if'n I cheat a little I can get the rest of the stuff back. And whattya think, the 'tother feller done, he done beat me just lke if'n I hadn't cheated at all." "Who is this other feller?" we ask Hicks. As we know he's alone in his hole. "Oh, 'tain't sure'nough nobody at all. I just make like there is so'n I won't get so lonesome," Hicks replies.

Next night as we are down at the ration dump for supplies, I see a big fellow with an overcoat standing in the darkness. He comes over, slaps me on the back. I turn around, see who it is and say, "P.J., you old son of a gun, when did you get back?" "Last night. Where do I go from here?" P.J. replies. I was glad to have P.J. back, for we sure can use a man like him right now. On our way back we stop at the company C.P., Lt. Doty tells P.J., "I've got a good job for you. Take over a section of machine guns in the 1st Platoon sector." So, I lose P.J. again.

I then stop at Macky's 50-caliber squad and find they are all making out okay. Lloyd Doe is up at the C.P. standing at the entrance when the Krauts send in a hail of bullets from their indirect firing machine guns. They're landing all around Lloyd, but he doesn't move an inch. I call over, "What the hell you standing in that impact area for, Lloyd?" "Oh, I'm just trying to get hit so I can go to the hospital," Lloyd replies with a tone of disgust in his voice.

Lt. M----, 4th Platoon Leader, has been wounded and sent to the hospital. The Little King has just returned from the hospital after spending much time recovering from a shot in the ass delivered by the 168th back in the Montequalla area. First Sergeant Bennie goes home on rotation so the Little King once again takes over his old position as top kick.

One night the company gets some new replacements. The 2nd Platoon gets most of them. "Ole," 2nd Platoon Sergeant, tells them before they go to their holes, "If you have to shit during daylight, you can shit in your helmet or something, but don't get out of your holes." One replacement obeyed Ole's command, but instead of doing it in the outer shell of his helmet he does it in the liner. That night when he was picked to help carry rations, he just nonchalantly dumps out the contents of his helmet and places it back on his head. That night we could always tell where he was from the foul odor of his helmet. Lt. Knox, the former 3rd Platoon Leader who left us with a case of trench foot way back when we were in the Volturno River area, has just returned from the hospital and takes over as 4th Platoon Leader succeeding Lt. M----.

In front of our position about 500 yards stands the remains of an old beaten down house. We have been pasting it with artillery and mortar fire ever since we've been here, but there are still Jerries there. This house is technically known to us as "Y House." Tonight the 2nd Platoon is to raid Y House. They have a rough fire fight, but all return safely before daylight.

We've been here about five weeks now. Old Allah, Jimmie the Fence and I are very tired of looking at each other's filthy dirty bearded, homely faces—five weeks without eve washing our faces and hands, let alone shaving. Water was too scares for the likes of that. Water here was only to be drank or to brew mud. We brew mud almost constantly all day, mud that was so strong it turned a new mess spoon green as soon as it was dunked it in the inky liquid.

What keeps our morale up most is what we read in the *Stars and Stripes* every morning. About the first thing we turn to is the popular cartoon "Up Front," by a very talented guy who knows his stuff by the name of Bill Mauldin. His cartoons were so true to form to the life of the dough foot that any old combat Doggie might think he is looking at a picture album of his own outfit. If Bill Mauldin had some trouble with the high brass, his popularity among the ranks of a combat outfit would more than compensate for it. Also, a friend of the Doggie was the great columnist, Ernie Pyle. We always turned to his column for a plug a dough foot sometimes likes to hear.

Lt. M----- and Phees, who is now our platoon runner, come over one night. Phees is bitching because he has to follow the Lieutenant around. "He sees more stump patrols than anybody I ever seen," Phees grumbles. They tell us 1st Platoon Sergeant L.S. got it today, which made our morale drop considerable. L.S. (Lee Sobse) was one of the original K Company National Guard boys. He was young in years, but behind him were many considerable months of carrying out a burden of high responsibility as a very efficient N.C.O. His leadership and caring for his men were exemplary. Ahead of him were the commissioned ranks, and a commission could be hung on no finer man or soldier. The loss of L.S. by his loved ones and his outfit was a loss to mankind as well.

Next night Brady is sent back to the kitchen area to attend a special mine school. I move over and take charge of his squad personally during his absence. There I stay in a hole with one of the new replacements, Johnnie Mancia. He's a young kid from Pennsylvania of Italian descent. When I see him in daylight, I could see the horrors of war getting him down. I boiled a cup of mud, took a sip and say, "It's damned good stuff. Ya' better have some," pushing the dirty, caked-up canteen cup towards him. He backs away, makes a face saying, "No thanks." I could read the expression on his homesick, beardless face like he was thinking, what a dirty bunch of guys you are.

After some silence he starts talking. "Sometimes I almost go crazy. I think I can't stand it another minute, and I want to get up and run before another burst of shells come down on me. But I sweat it out till evening, when I look out of my hole and see you come walking towards us, carrying your carbine in one hand and your helmet in the other." (At Anzio I never wore my helmet when making the rounds, but carried it under my arm, as I could hear so much better that way.) "Then you come into our holes, talk to us and explain things. When they throw a shell, you just grin. When you leave, you walk like you're not scared of anything. Then I'm not scared either. That's the only thing I have to look forward to day after day, is the time when you come every night. I always feel better then."

Them were simple words that Mancia spoke that night, but I'll not forget them as long as I live, in spite of the fact that he was so very wrong about me not being scared. But somehow it gave me a good feeling and made me feel sort of warm inside to know that I might be doing that much good anyhow. Besides, there are times when the ego of an old dough foot sergeant can stand a lift. I guess it's things like this that keep them going.

Every night after that I made my stays with the boys a little longer. By the time Brady come back, Mancia was drinking mud out of the same cup with me, and smiled a little when a shell came close. Speed was the gunner of this squad, and he done a wonderful job of keeping the morale of these replacements up. He made it as good for them as he possibly could, helping them make their holes more inhabitable, sharing with them the ample supplies he invariably has stowed away in his pack. And his ability to create a friendly, hospitable atmosphere wherever he is, regardless of the situation, I think was Speed's greatest gift to his buddies. That man has a heart as big as a house. When Brady comes back, I return to my old C.P. in Old Allah's position.

Another thing the *Stars and Stripes* keeps us posted on is the big Russian offensive. They've just taken Karkov and Kiev. We have a map of the Russian front pinned to the side of our hole, and every day we draw a new line with a pencil, representing the latest advance of the Russian offensive.

Rumors are now going around that we will be relieved in a few days, so our morale picks up somewhat. The 168th Infantry Regiment is the reserve regiment of the division, and they are the ones who are supposed to relieve us. Shortly after dark one night a runner comes up to our position and tells me to get ready to go back to the kitchen tonight, as Lt. Doty has picked me to go on a five-day pass way back to Caserta. I can't quite figure this out, as I had a pass just before we left Benevento. Nevertheless, I don't argue with anyone about it, so I go over to Brady's squad and tell Brady to take charge of the section while I am gone. I then go to the company C.P. and ask Lt. Doty, "How come I get a pass?" Lt. Doty grins a little and says, "Last week I sent Ole and Good Deed from the 2nd Platoon, because they have the toughest job on this beachhead. This week I'm sending Sgt. Ingraham of the 3rd Platoon because he has been leading a patrol between here and the 2nd Battalion every night since we've been here through damned tough country. He deserves a break. And I'm sending you just to get rid of you for a while. Now get the hell out of here." Ingraham and I walk back to the battalion C.P. and hook a ride on a weapons carrier that takes us back to the kitchen area.

"Ducky" is the only one up when we step into the Kitchen tent. He brews us some mud and shoves us some bread and jam and we eat and talk for quite a while before going to bed. Next morning, we wash and shave for the first time in six weeks, get on trucks that take us to Anzio where we board an L.S.T. which takes us to Naples. The L.S.T. leaves Anzio as soon as it begins to darken. When we wake up next morning, we are in Naples Harbor.

Here we disembark, get on trucks that wheel us right through Naples and on to Caserta, where we go to the rest center directly across from the King's Royal Palace that is now used as 5th Army headquarters. Ingraham and I find

Caserta pretty dead, so we spend most of our time out at Santa Maria just a few miles north of Caserta where we keep ourselves very comfortable by drinking cognac and going from joint to joint. Ingraham is a swell egg and enjoys this routine very much. At the end of our five days, we go back to Naples, where we once again get aboard an L.S.T., and we head back to Anzio. We get off the L.S.T. and go to our kitchen, where we learn that the 168th relieved the 135th a day or two after we left them. Ploopie tells us K Company is dug in around Mussolini Canal, which is the reserve position of the division, and are now enjoying a well-earned rest.

That night Ingraham and I go up to the company's positions with Ploopie as he takes water rations up. Mussolini Canal is nothing but a big concrete ditch filled with flowing water. Along this canal the company has some deluxe foxholes. It's a moonlight night, and as I near the 4th Platoon area I can see the boys are out training in the moonlight. They're doing calisthenics by squad. Lloyd Doe and Lt. Knox are standing by the hold watching them as I walk up. "What the hell you got the boys out this time of the night for, Lloyd?" I ask. "It sure as hell ain't my idea," Lloyd replies. I then shake hands with Lt. Knox, who refrains from twisting his handle bar mustache just long enough to shake hands. He then proceeds to twist it more vigorously than ever, saying, "Them machine gunners of yours can stand a lot of training."

Next morning is nice and sunny as we cook up our ten-in-one rations for breakfast. I've had these new replacements in the section for about two months. I talked to them every night while we were at the front and learned to know them by voice, but this was one of the first time I had seen them all good during daylight. I knew all their names, but didn't know which name belonged to which guy. However, it didn't take me long to get to know them well after being with them a few hours in daylight.

Macky points them out for me saying, "That short, stout one is O'Neal. The tall, thin feller is Portman. The pigeon-toed one is Waug. The guy with the southern accent is Fahr. The big overgrown kid that's always singing those negro spirituals is Westbrooks. The quiet guy over there that's always willing to do a little more than his share is Weeks. The guy over here brewing mud is Valley."

"And that one," Macky says, pointing at the feller with the egg-shaped head— "You needn't tell me who that one is," I reply, and then call out to the feller, "Hicks, come over here." "Gosh O mighty damn, whattya say, Sergeant," Hicks replies with a beaming smile. "Who gave you that haircut?" I ask, viewing his flat top scalp that has a perfect V cut in the middle of it. "Oh, that was that Old Allah and P.J. thinkin' they were doin' something smart, gosh o' mighty damn, looks if'n they don't care what I look like, do it," was Hicks' mournful reply.

While we are in this position, we train every night. When we fall out into platoon formation each night, my section is always late, so every night I receive a royal ass-shewing from Lt. Knox. We're here a few days when we march back to our kitchen area where we can enjoy some hot meals. When we get back to the kitchen, Ploopie has some good hot chow for us. We then proceed to dig holes to sleep in.

Macky, Lloyd Doe and I dig a big one together. Lt. Knox tells us to send a man over to dig a hole with him. We respond to his request by sending the one and only Hicks over to him. They dig their hole right next to ours. Soon we are all comfortably bedded down in our holes. We then hear roar of Stukka's and Messerschmidt's approaching to deliver their nightly raid. As the ack-ack guns open up on them, we pay very little attention.

We pull the covers over our heads and start dozing away, thinking the Luftwaffe was only after the ships in Anzio Harbor. But the planes were soaring around in circles directly above us now. Ack-ack was bursting right over our heads and flak was falling all around us. We put our helmets on and proceed to go to sleep again, when we are aroused by several terrific explosions. BANG! BANG! BANG! Lloyd Doe just rolls over and murmurs sort of drowsily, "They don't care where they drop them damn things, do they." Now we can hear Hicks and Lt. Knox talking in their hole next to us. Hicks says, "What ya shakin' fer, Lieutenant, are ya scared?" "I'm not scared, I'm just cold," we hear the Lieutenant reply. Thinking there was no damage done, we go back to sleep. When we get up next morning, we learn that several men from the company were killed by the bombing, and L Company's kitchen had a direct hit and there was a lot of damage in the battalion that we had anticipated at the time it happened.

PREPARING FOR THE BIG PUSH

Seeing this isn't a very peaceful place to be, we move to a wooded area where we are in perfect concealment. Here we are told we're going to make a small-scale attack. In fact, the attack was to be so small that only K Company would partake in it. Nonetheless, a small attack can sometimes turn out to be the roughest ones, and this attack had every indication of being just that. We get our orders in the finest detail and train intensively for the coming attack. The mission of the machine gun section was to be the toughest assignment of any unit in the company. Lt. Doty and Lt. Knox explain it to me as we study maps closely.

Lt. Doty says, "There are three houses about 1600 yards in front of our lines. There is a knoll to the left rear of the left house. You have to get your section up there first and start firing on that house, your mission is to draw attention and fire while the 3rd Platoon comes closing in on the house from the left. If our primary plans come off successfully, the 3rd Platoon will take and occupy the house. As soon as that is done, you quickly take your guns out of action and withdraw about 300 yards to the rear.

"You then cut to the left, follow this ditch for about 500 yards, cut to the left again and go forward about 200 yards, set up your guns to fire on the extreme right house, doing the same mission for the 1st Platoon that you just got done doing for the 3rd Platoon. If all this comes off successfully you withdraw again about 100 yards, then cut to the right and start picking your way to the middle house, which is the furthest out. If the Krauts in that house haven't already withdrawn, you'll assault the house with your machine gun section while receiving support flanking fire from both flanks by the 1st and 3rd Platoons.

"Besides your machine guns you will have a B.A.R. team and a bazooka team from the 2nd Platoon attached to you. I want you and at least four other men from the section to be armed with tommy guns, have your two squad leaders armed with .03's equipped with grenade launchers, and make sure all the men have beaucoup grenade enforcements sent up." Lt. Doty then folds up the map and kinda grins a little. I was a little bit mad about this time and said, "I've got a light machine gun section, not a battery of mobile howitzers and a battalion of commandoes. How in the hell do you think we can do all that in such a short time?" "I know it's a rough assignment, P.T., but that's an order," Lt. Doty replies, looking me in the eye.

We spend the next two days simulating this attack over and over. These two days are causing me to become old very fast. This is to be a dawn attack, and the preceding evening we are preparing to move out when Lt. Doty sends word for all non-coms to report up to the company C.P. We all expect Doty to give us some last-minute details or something. When we get there, we find Doty sitting on the hood of a Peep with that cocky grin on his face. He looks us over and says, "I bet you guys would be glad if you didn't have to make this attack." There was a harmonious reply of men's voices saying, "Yeah."

"Well, you don't. It's been called off indefinitely," Doty says, and everybody heaves a sigh of relief as it must be admitted, I believe, every one of us were going into this attack with a great deal of reluctance and were not one bit sorry about the fact that it had been called off. Lt. Doty then pulls out two quarts of Scotch and says, "Drink this and forget about the attack, boys." When I get back to the section, I get as big a kick out of telling the boys the attack was called off as Lt. Doty did telling us. Lt. Knox comes up vigorously twisting his mustache and says, "I'm glad that's over with. That attack had me worried."

Next night we move to another reserve position, which is along a wooded creek where we stay for about four or five days, then move back to the wooded area again to the same place where we trained for the attack that never came off. Here I get rid of the 50-caliber machine gun and dissolve the 3rd squad, making two big 30-caliber squads. Macky is now section runner and radio man. Lange returns from the hospital after being gone for quite some time with a case of trench foot. The young replacement, Johnnie Mancia, has now taken on all the character of a battle-torn veteran. As he is so dark, I hung the nickname "Midnight" on him.

We all know the big push is about to begin, but we don't know exactly when. The 88th and the 85th Divisions have now arrived in Italy and are fighting on the southern front. The 36th Division has now arrived at Anzio and will be in reserve for the big push. We learn that the 3rd Battalion will be the reserve battalion of the 135th on the first day of the big push. On the second day we will attack through the 2nd Battalion. The initial push on the southern front takes place one day preceding the initial push at Anzio. The 135th Infantry is to work in conjunction with the 1st Armored Division to form a unit to be known as Combat Command A. This attack we didn't fear so much, but were almost eager to drive the Krauts back and away from our diminutive beachhead and push our way northward. We are confident that this will be an all-out, well-coordinated offensive.

It was on a nice moonlight night that we moved out to an assembly area to the rear of the 2nd Battalion. Just before dawn everything is silent. We could hear dogs barking across the limited expanse of Anzio Beachhead. At the first hint of gray above the mountains that made out the rugged eastern horizon, the early morning burst into flame and deafening noise. The push was on. Allied artillery was pasting the steel like ring around the Anzio beachhead with tons of shells as fighter bombers were flying overhead, dropping eggs and spitting lead at German defenses.

We follow the 2nd Battalion, and they break through the enemy's first main line of resistance and cross the Cisterna-Cappoleone Railroad. The men of the 2nd Battalion were bringing back many prisoners. It was a perfectly coordinated attack. Immediately east of the railroad is where we push through the 2nd Battalion and go on the assault. Here the Germans start retaliating somewhat. Three of the 1st Armored tanks were knocked out, and they were throwing aerial bursts at us that were bursting about 15 feet above the ground.

Brady gets wounded in the leg before we can get out of this hot spot. I tell Macky to take over Brady's squad as we get up to advance again. Lt.

Doty was calling me over the 536 radio. "Sunray to Dog 1, Sunray to Dog 1, over." "Dog 1 to Sunray, Dog 1 to Sunray, over," I reply. "Bring unit to front, bring unit to front, Roger," Doty comes back. "Wilco," I reply, and we proceed forward. When we reach Lt. Doty, he has us set up to cover the left flank of the 1st Platoon. After that is done, Lt. Doty shows me on a map where to advance to. "You shift to the left and you should be able to get to Highway 7 as soon as the 1st Platoon does, if you don't run into anything too tough. We'll all join forces on the other side of #7."

We advance slowly. The grass was high and snipers were pecking away at us from several angles as we bypassed them. At one spot we were pinned down temporarily by machine gun fire. We set up and give them some counter fire as I called back to the 60mm mortars to fire on them. The mortar men delivered some very accurate fire and soon silenced the enemy. We then continue our advance. We pass an abandoned Anzio Annie, the gigantic artillery gun that almost drove us all pyscho on the beachhead. It made us feel somewhat better to know that they had to leave it behind. We hit Highway 7 near a big bridge where the grade was high. The section lined up along the bank of the road. To our left front there was a great deal of machine gun fire. The 1st Platoon had crossed #7, so I say to the men in the section, "Let's go one at a time over the hump."

It took quite some time for the entire section to get across the grade, but we had cut #7 and now joined the 1st Platoon where we push to capture a Jerry aid station full of wounded Jerries. The company then reorganized and we continue on to capture an old castle that was our final objective. By now the enemy was completely routed in this sector, and we proceed to set up a line of defense for the night.

Lt. Knox and myself, both in very high spirits and enthused over our success on the first day of the new offensive, are now full of aggression. We grab onto a General Grant tank of the 1st Armored Division, climb aboard and go way to hell and gone out in Jerryland with the tank men on a sort of combat reconnaissance mission. We seen not a sign of a Jerry. We return to our positions and find many tanks of the 1st Armored emplaced in defilade positions covering the terrain out in front of us, which completely constituted a perfect defensive setup for the night.

In this position we find several huge caves. Lt. Knox, Lloyd Doe, Leo Schular and I decide to put the whole platoon in one cave and spend the night in peace. Next day finds us in reserve, as other units have pushed through us. But we still had a few casualties in the battalion as some fighter planes from our own Air Force bombed and strafed M Company. However, incidents such as this have become so common that the dough foot has accepted it as just another hazard he has to put up with in warfare.

That night we again start on the attack. We are still working with the 1st Armored Division as Combat Command A. We stop at an assembly area where we get a couple of hours rest. At dawn we're on the attack again, following tanks of the 1st Armored Division. The company was scattered thinly over a wide area, and as we progress forward, we become still more thickly scattered as our frontage was increasing rapidly due to the fact that we were pushing forward in a cone-like manner to cover the terrain in such a way broad gaps developed between units.

We advanced what seemed to be a great deal of distance when I completely lost contact with other units of the company. We then sit down in a defilade area and take a break as we didn't want to get too far out in front with just a machine gun section. Soon the mortar section pulled up behind us. Behind them was Lt. Foto with Company Headquarters Group. AS Foto comes up to the head of the column I ask, "Where the hell are we?" Lt. Foto drags out some maps, and after looking at them for some time says, "You know as much as I do, but we'll try going along this ravine." So, we start out again with Lt. Foto leading. We go a good distance, winding our way through gullies and ravines till we get to a place where there are a bunch of cherry trees loaded with delicious red, ripe cherries. It was unanimously chosen by all that we should stop and feast on these cherries so we all disperse, having nothing but a good feast.

Speed exclaims joyfully, "Say, these are better than my Ma's angel food cake." The Little King has a whole helmet full already. About this time, Jerry machine guns open up on us from all angles. P.J. nonchalantly says, "Them crazy bastards would wanta fight just when we find these cherries." As the bullets spray around us, Speed hollers back to where the fire is coming from, "Blow it out your ass, will ya', Herman." The Jerries are firing at us from a rock house about a hundred yards to our left front. We continue eating cherries as a tank from the 1st Armored pulls up and proceeds to level the house from which the fire is coming.

The trajectory of the 75 screeched as it passed over our heads and hit the old house with a bang. The 75 on the General Sherman was barking fast, and the old house was soon nothing but a pile of rubble. Shortly after that a skirmish line from L Company came up from the rear with rifles at high port. They were attacking the ground that we had been on for several hours and had captured and done away with a lot of Krauts that we had bypassed. Then Black Rufe comes up with his machinegun platoon from M Company. "What the hell are you guys doing in L Company's sector?" "K Company is about a thousand yards to the left," Black Rufe states.

We then continue forward and to the left when we reach the sector where the rest of K Company is. We find them set up in a temporary defensive position. I set the guns up along a ditch, then go over to where Lts. Doty and Knox are. They were studying maps. Lt. Knox was twisting his mustache like an old Irish washwoman wringing out clothes. He says, "We're going so good now, I think we ought to cross this creek and take that hill on the other side." "That's what we're supposed to do, but I think we'll run into a little trouble over there. This will be a straight infantry attack, for armor will be unable to cross the creek," Lt. Doty replies.

Then he goes on to say, "Alert your men we're going to try it. 2nd Platoon will be the assault platoon supported by the machine gun section." It's just getting dusk as we start the attack. We cross the creek and the assaulting 2nd Platoon's M-1's are barking violently. Hand grenades are popping like popcorn. The Jerries are retaliating fiercely with their rapid firing machine guns.

As we advance up the hill, we pass many helplessly dead Krauts lying on the ground that the riflemen of the 2nd Platoon had knocked off. I take the machine gun section to the right along a bank to get away from in-coming artillery.

Here we set up our guns and commence firing at a column of enemy reinforcement troops coming up a trail. It's getting very dark now, and I can hear the panting voice of our platoon runner call, "P.T., P.T., Lt. Doty wants you to set your guns up on the point of the hill."

I know the Germans are bringing up armor. The men in my section are firing an important mission here, so I decide not to take them up. I ask P.J. to go along with me. P.J. and I follow the runner to the crest of the hill. On the way up the runner gets knocked off by artillery. When we reach the point of the hill, I can hear Lt. Doty barking orders. He's just a few yards in front of a Jerry tank when the tank fires its 88. Lt. Doty didn't get hit by the shell, but he was so close that the muzzle blast from the Jerry 88 burned his face quite badly. I then see a bright flash to my right as the 2nd Platoon bazooka man scores a hit on the Tiger Tank, knocking it out. But a moment later, I seen his head fly back, and the gallant bazooka man crumpled over dead.

I could hear the motor and track noise of German tanks and SP guns all around now. The 2nd Platoon was pulling back. P.J. and I were about two yards from an advancing Jerry tank, and we lit out and ran back to where the section was. I was glad I hadn't taken the section to the point of the hill with me. When we got back, Doty had given the order to withdraw to our old position across the creek. We went back small units at a time. My section was third to leave. We had a couple of Jerry prisoners to take back with us.

Soon the whole company was back. And as the late moon ascended over the eastern horizon, we had a fairly stable defense built up back on our side of the creek. I heaved a sigh of relief and was thankful that we got back in as good a shape as we had. The 2nd Platoon suffered quite a few casualties. Good Deed Arneson, right guide of the 2nd Platoon, and I contacted L Company C.O. to make sure we had contact on our left flank. Good Deed felt pretty bad about losing so many men in his platoon, but even at that we had killed more Jerries in that battle than the Jerries had killed of our men.

Even though we had to withdraw, we done plenty of damage. Those of us who weren't on guard then laid and went to sleep. I had slept about an hour when the platoon runner woke me saying, "Wake up your men and get ready to move." "What the hell? Another attack?" I asked. "Nope, we're getting relieved by the 36th division and pulling back to the rear," was the runner's reply. So that made us all feel much better as we packed up.

The 36th came up about an hour later and relieved us in place. The company assembled in a draw to the rear, and we started marching to the rear. It's noon the next day when we reach our destination. We sprawl out and immediately go to sleep. Here, Lt. Doty, who now sports a nice new set of railroad tracks on his collar as he has been promoted to Captain, goes to the hospital for treatment on his burnt face, leaving Lt. Foto in charge of the company. Lt. Knox takes Foto's place as company executive, so we are now without a platoon leader.

Next day we move out. We shift to the left of our previous sector, which in this case would be north. We get to an assembly area, have a few hours rest. When darkness came, it again found us on the march. We have not been told where we are going or what we're going to do when we get there. After marching all night, dawn found us still marching single file over perfectly flat, open terrain. As we have not yet been told what our mission is, we are beginning to wonder what the deal is as we hear the sickening noise of an artillery duel to our left.

We take heggir interval between men and are a bit skeptical about being in the open like this in broad daylight. I stepped to the side and looked up to the head of the column and seen it was disappearing one man at a time into the huge gully. I was at the head of the 4th Platoon and had just gotten into the gully and out of sight when I heard the Jerries open up on the remainder of the column that had not yet reached the concealment of the gully. The men then poured in fast. The packs on some of the men were riddled with gun bullets. Some of the men were wounded.

We all get to the bottom of the gully and seek the best protection we can find. Speed comes up and says, "Boy, the old man just about got his combine that time around." He shows me where a Jerry 30 Cab had pierced right through the middle of his canteen. "What I can't figure out is why they didn't open up on us before," I asked. "They must not have seen the head of the column," replies Lloyd Doe. "Naw, they just felt sorry for us for being so dumb as to walk in the open like that. The Jerries figure anybody that's that dumb, won't hurt 'em any," comments Old Allah.

Just then, Hiss, Bang! Hiss, Bang! There was a mortar barrage on us all up and down the winding gully. Some artillery shells manage to find their way into the gully too. The whole 3rd Platoon was caught in this gully. Everything was congested, and it was impossible for the men to spread out. Every shell that came into the gully was bound to do a lot of damage, and it did. The Germans had seen us walk into this gully. They hadn't fired on us for they wanted us to all get in this gully which they had their mortars and artillery zeroed in on. It was a trap. They had us right where they wanted us. We couldn't advance nor we couldn't withdraw.

We are pinned down, down helplessly here sweating it out, many men getting killed and wounded. L Company tried to go over the top two times to secure a place from which to fight back. Twice they were driven back. They went up the third time and stayed. K Company was in reserve and remained in the gully. The 45th Division was on our left flank and were also taking a beating. Nevertheless, our boys were bringing back many prisoners. We were up against these fanatical die-hards of Hinrich Himmlies' SS troops. And as these SS prisoners came stringing back through the gully in their fancy SS uniforms, Speed would ask each one of them, "Are you Herman from #609?" Speed would never forget the Jerry by the name of Herman on Hill 609 back in Africa.

Then Speed would look at me and say, "Shall I mop him one?" and double up his fist and hit each Jerry in the head as hard as he could, sending the SS men sprawling in the mud by the force of his powerful blow. It is about 3:00 in the afternoon when K Company is told it's up to them to break this deadlock, as they have been in reserve up to now. Either make or break.

Although we had been in reserve, we had taken a terrific beating in this gully that is now known as Bloody Gulch, and the waters that trickle through the rocks from the creek that flows through the gully shows a faint tine of red from the blood that was spilt here.

We are to go over the top into hell as we know the enemy has so much the advantage on us in this particular deal. It made us all half sick to think of it, and cold sweat was standing out on us. I believe I hated to make this assault worse than any other in the whole war. It got the best of Lt. Foto, who was acting as Company Commander in Lt. Doty's absence. He went psychoneurosis and was evacuated. Lt. Knox keeps his bearings and assumes responsibility of Company Commander. Lt. Knox designated the 3rd Platoon to be one of the assault platoons. Lt. McDaniels was about to break. Finally, he bursts out, "It can't be done. I'm not going. I'm going to the rear. Any man in this platoon that wants to go along, follow me."

Like Lt. Foto, Lt. McDaniels became psycho and went to the rear. His acting platoon sergeant followed along with others. The 3rd Platoon was small now. Only one man out of my sector had cracked. Lt. Knox calls Sgt. Ingram and I under the bridge. Lt. Johnson, the 1st Platoon leader is there. Knox says, as he lifts a shaky hand up to give his mustache a final good twist, "1st Platoon attack on the left. Machine gun section in the middle. 3rd Platoon on the right. 2nd Platoon in reserve." And he then looks up at tall, unwavering Sgt. Ingram and says, "Will you lead the 3rd Platoon?" "I suppose," Ingram replies coolly. As we got ready to go, Lt. Knox says, "This attack will separate the men from the boys in K Company."

I holler at Ingram, "This isn't going to be as much fun as we had on pass." Ingram grinned back and said, "I think this is the last attack I'll have to go on." With that, we were out of Bloody Gulch and over the top, going in a skirmish running and flapping through a veritable hail of bullets as the mortar shells were bursting among us.

Mackey calls up to me, "I'm hit." "How bad?" I called back. "This hit me," Mackey says, holding up a piece of jagged shrapnel about six inches long. I then rushed back, tore his pant leg open, and find a wound about the size of a pen. "You had me scared when you showed me that big hunk of shrapnel, but you got a million-dollar wound," I said. Mackey went back to the medics, and I told Speed to take over the squad as we get up to advance again. The gallant men of the two rifle platoons then made the close-up assault on the enemy with hand grenades and bayonets, routing the Jerries out of their fortified position. My section shifted to the right to set up on the 3rd Platoon's left flank. The Jerries had withdrawn, and we had conquered the hill.

I took my section in an evacuated German trench. It's dark now, and I tell Speed to bring his machine gun. "Put it here," I say, patting the ground where I want the gun. But instead of patting the ground, I patted the leg of a man. I got up to examine the man lying prone, face down across the trench. He's an American, a tall fellow. I remove the helmet from his head. As I tip the helmet, about a quart of crimson blood flows from it. I turn his face and see who it is. "No, you'll never have to make another attack, Ingram," I say as Speed and I lay a shelter half over his dead body. Everyone is tense that night. The company captured about a dozen arrogant SS men on the attack. Next morning, we didn't attack on account of the heavy casualties we had the night before.

We are forced to stay in the trench so we couldn't be observed by the enemy. As the day grew older, it became very hot. From our position we could see the dead bodies of six Americans along with Ingram scattered in our area. As the sun beat down on them, the bodies swelled and began to stink.

At early dawn the next morning, we get attack orders. I get my orders from Lt. Johnson, 1st Platoon leader, as my section is to support the 1st Platoon, which is the assaulting platoon. When we move out, we follow a ditch going single file with big intervals. As we march along, the little guy with the cocky grin comes up sporting his new railroad tracks. "When did you get back, Capt. Doty?" I ask. "Just in time to kill a few Jerries," the young captain replies.

We get to the end of the ditch. The 1st Platoon spreads out in a skirmish line. I call back to my squad leaders, Speed and P.J., "1st Squad left, 2nd Squad right." Then machine guns opened up on us from all over. Grazing fire was coming back in the ditch along with most of Speed's squad. Speed, Dick Jewit and I hit the dirt in the open and are pinned down. After about 15 minutes I get up and crawl back to Capt. Doty, who is about 25 yards behind us, to get some information.

When I get back to Speed and Jewit again, I see Speed rolling in the dirt, moaning in pain. His left shirt sleeve was soaking with blood. Jewit and I get him quieted down after quite a struggle. When we tear his shirt sleeve open, we see a nasty wound from a ricochet bullet right through the middle of his forearm. We dress the wound, and I tell Speed, "Your old man almost got that combine this time. But he'll never get it now, for you'll never have to fight again." I tell Jewit to help Speed back to the medics.

The enemy is laying mortar and artillery on us now, so I beat it back to the ditch where the rest of the machine gunners are. Men from the 1st Platoon are pulling back now. One at a time they run past us. They had to withdraw, for not only was the Jerry artillery dropping on them but also our own, for the artillery from the 45th Division was posting our area all to hell. After the 1st Platoon had withdrawn, I realized my section was out in front all alone. So, we set up our guns in the best places we could find, which weren't very good, and every man put on the alert. They kept harassing us with artillery and machine gun fire all day.

I now put Jewit in charge of the 1st squad replacing Speed. Later that day I sneaked over to Capt. Doty, and again Col. Mearns had just been up to see Capt. Doty and had just left when I got there. Doty grinned a little and says, "The Colonel just told me K Company was the furthest out in front and is the spearhead of all Allied Armies in Europe, and your section is the spearhead of K Company." For a minute I was kind of proud of my little machine gun section, that right at the present time represented the furthest advance of Allied Armies in Europe.

The next moment there was a hiss of an incoming artillery shell that burst very close to us, and I lost all my proudness immediately and call to Capt. Doty, "I think I'll go back to my section now." I just got back to my section in time, for they were now laying a terrific mortar and artillery barrage on us. Midnight got wounded, and I told him to head for the aid station as fast as he could, for I had just received a message from Capt. Doty over our 536 radio that there was a big counter attack coming on our right flank. Most of our power was on the left, and our right flank was very weak with just the mortar section and remnants of the beaten 2nd Platoon.

We had to get back to our old position and make a stand from there or be wiped out. The 1st Platoon had already left, and I followed with my section. Shells were bursting all around us. The Jerries were closing in fast. They lifted their artillery and were now spraying us with assault machine gun fire. Fortunately, we had a ditch to follow back to our old position. We were going on the double as fast as we could go. Two of our tank destroyers (M-10) were here, but both were knocked out.

We all made it back to our position okay. All but one. That was Valley.

During the course of the counter attack in its ferocity, I was unable to keep personal contact with the men in my section. When we got back to make our stand at our previous position, the only man in my section I could not account for was a likeable young fellow who was a recent replacement named Valley. However, afterward Lloyd Doe told me and our superior officer, that while he was pulling the mortar section back, he seen Valley in the gun turret of a knocked-out M-10 tank destroyer manning a 50-caliber machine gun against the oncoming Germans in an act of gallantry that may have been instrumental in repelling the counter attack. Whatever happened after that is unknown. The only assumption we arrived at was that after that heroic action, Valley "blew his cork" and went psycho, for he was later found in the rear echelon AWOL.

He didn't show up at our old position. We immediately set up and commence firing. The Jerries are very close now. We had run through about a hundred rounds when we first heard the sweet sound of our own artillery whistle over head and land out in front of us.

During the next half-hour we watched and witnessed one of the most terrorizing scenes of destruction that could possibly take place. But this scene of destruction looked beautiful to us. For it was our own artillery slaughtering the attacking Germans. Now we could not see ten feet in front of us. It was a picture indescribable. For every 240mm, 155, 105, 75, 90mm, 8-inch howitzer, 4.2-inch mortar, 60 and 80mm mortar in this sector was concentrated on the area immediately in front of us, throwing tons upon tons of high explosives and phosphorous on the enemy. The powder smell was sickening. White phosphorous smoke was so thick you could almost cut it with a knife, along with deafening noise that put a ring in our ears.

Through the smoke, about 10 feet in front of our position was Col. Mearns, our Battalion C.O. He came up to our gun and said calmly, but with a tone of Nazi hatred in his voice, "Give 'em hell, boys. If it's fightin' they want, we'll really show 'em how to fight. We're giving them the worst damn beating they ever had in their life." When the Colonel turns around, we all see he is bleeding like a stuck hog from the neck. He is wounded badly, but he is still going; personally directing his battalion to beat off one of the most vigorous full-scale counter-attacks the enemy had ever attempted.

We told the Colonel to have his wound taken care of, but he would listen to no one, and kept his battalion calm but deadly throughout the battle. When the barrage finally ended and the smoke and dust cleared somewhat, we could hear many Jerries, some crying in pain. Others were calling out, "Komrade, Komrade," and come running with their hands up to surrender. One particular Jerry was so scared, he jumped into an old well that was about 15 feet deep. One of the rifle men from the 2nd Platoon was shooting at the helpless Jerry down the well. He emptied his clip on him, but missed him every shot. In disgust, he throws his rifle to the ground, finds a rope, lets it down to the frightened Jerry and helps him out of the well. When he gets him out, he looked at his prisoner and says, "Now I suppose you're happy, you elusive son-of-a-bitch."

I can still hear Capt. Doty say, "go back to your old positions. We'll make our stand there." And we did just that, not yielding a foot of ground, but instead slaughtering and capturing many crack Nazi warriors of Hinrick Himmler's SS troops who grit their teeth at the sight of the Red Bull patch on our sleeves. But I would like to point out the men who through their wisdom and bravery made this stand a success. There was Sgt. Jack Plumber, a squad leader from the mortar section, whose alert eyes first seen and recognized the counter attack and warned the rest of the company as he desperately fought them off. And Capt. Sashay, our artillery observer, who laid down and directed the most destructive, perfectly coordinated artillery barrage ever delivered in Italy at such a timely moment. Without this artillery we would have lost all. And Col. Mearns, who in spite of being severely wounded, calmly walked around during the course of the battle giving fighting courage to the men of his battalion and directing them to repel this vicious threat in which we might well have lost so much, along with countless other G.I. jobs. 🐂

AFTERMATH

Next day it's warm and sunny, not a live Jerry in sight, but many dead ones. There is beginning to be a very disagreeable odor from the dead bodies, German and American. As we look at the terrain in front of us, we can see it is literally dotted for as far as we can see with shell holes. I don't believe any of them were over ten feet apart. That morning the 100th Battalion and individual battalions out of our division that are completely composed of Hawaiians and men of Japanese descent passed through us, and we watched them advance in front of us and far as we could see, the little yellow men advanced unopposed 'til they disappeared into the distant horizon.

Yes, the Jerries had put everything they could muster together into this counter attack. At the failure of their counter attack, the Jerries apparently from all indications had withdrawn a good distance. I believe up to now I have failed to mention that the southern forces and the forces at Anzio have joined. This happened several days ago. And anyone now can drive on Highway 7 all the way from Anzio to Sorento peacefully. During the day after the counter attack we're walking around searching all the dead Jerries for souvenirs. O'Neale would take off in search for booty, wobbling his chubby ass to and fro' as he walks. He would return with an armful of equipment consisting of everything from soup to nuts.

The whole battalion has had a tremendous amount of casualties in the past few days. Our manpower is down to its lowest ebb. In order to still carry on as an organized fighting unit, K Company and L Company go together, making two strong rifle platoons. The 1st Platoon is all K Company. The 2nd Platoon is all L Company, and there is no 3rd Platoon. L Company's weapons platoon throws in with us. So out of the two beaten companies, 1st Company, minus one platoon is born. To the right of us, just below the Alban Hills lies the town of Lanvio, which has now fell to the 2nd Battalion of the 135th.

The counter attack we had last night is known as the Lanvio Counter Attack, and takes its place along with previous bloody symbols of World War II that we have went through: Bloody Gulch, Cassino, Mt. Pantano, 609 and 409, Fondouk and Kasserine. In the afternoon, we withdrew from this position and gather in an assembly about two miles to the rear of Bloody Gulch. Here we draw rations and ammo. When darkness came, we were again on the march. We walk several hours till we get to an area where we lie down and get some rest before daylight. Next morning, we get on trucks. These trucks take us through Lanuvio, through the Alban Hills to the town of Albano, near Lake Albano. The trucks take us to a big, swell park right in the center of Albano. There we dismount trucks, flap in the shade of towering evergreens near a big pool with a huge overflowing fountain in the middle of it. When evening came, we were again on the march. We marched right down the blacktop highway, one column on each side of the road.

We march fast and cover many miles. None of us enlisted personnel know for sure where we are, but we know we are heading for Rome and are getting quite near to the Eternal City, for we see signs along the highway with the word Roma printed on them. We're dog tired from the long hike as we pull off the road where we encounter some Jerry machine gun fire that soon explodes. It was about 4:00 A.M. when we laid down and got some rest. At dawn we were up again back on the highway and on the march. Some of the boys were still half asleep as we marched. We were sweating as the hot sun was beating down on us as step by step, we were nearing the city that we had fought for as our ultimate objective all the way from the beaches of Selarno.

We now can see the colorful buildings of ancient Rome. As we march into the heart of the Ancient City, we get an ovation from the Romans that was superb. Italian people of Rome freed from years of Nazi domain as they were shouting wildly, they packed the streets so it was difficult for us to pass through. Throwing flowers at us, pretty Roman signorinas running up and kissing us, made our morale pick up somewhat in spite of our utter fatigue. There was a continuous roar of applause and hand clapping, "Bravo Americano, multi bauna Americano, teliski Mussolini yenti bouno. Vivi Americano, Englise, Italiano," were the words you could hear from the happily excited Romans. Older Romans we could see were making religious gestures and making crosses over their hearts as if they were thanking God for being liberated from Nazi domain.

We marched past the historic ancient Colosseum, one of the oldest landmarks in the world. We reach the Tiber River, which flows through Rome, and there we stop and take a much-needed break. Here, tired doughboys flop down and drop off to sleep immediately, with no more enthusiasm over the Eternal City than over a mountain village. After about an hour's rest, we begin moving around. Realizing we had taken the Eternal City, we now wonder what it looks like, so some of us go around to different places in Rome.

Mackey and I got back just in time. Mackey is already recovered from his wound and came back to the company last night. The company got ready to move out of our platoon. Lloyd Doe, Platoon Sergeant, P.J. and Old Allah didn't make it back in time, so we left them behind. Big Barnsmell Slink was also left behind. We march across the Tiber and out of Rome, heading north on the blacktop highway as we did before we got to Rome. In the city of Rome, we didn't have a shot fired at us.

After going some miles north of Rome, we pull off the road and stop for the night. After we are settled and laying down resting, we see a skirmish line of American infantrymen advancing on us with fixed bayonets from the rear. They were attacking the ground we had already taken. They passed through us. The attacking infantry were units from the 36th Texas Division. Next morning, we are told the 135th is to hook up with the 1st Armored Division again to form the units of Combat Command A. Our mission is to make a mechanized spearhead advance as far north as we can, as fast as we can. Other units of our division are to spearhead along the coastal sectors to make a swift plunge for the port city of Civitavecchia on to Tarquinia and points north.

The 168th and 133rd Infantry Reg. are to take care of that. We get on trucks of the 1st Armored Division and head north in a column of six-by-six, scout cars, half-tracks, General Grant tanks, German tanks and tank destroyers. We head north at a rapid pace. Every so often, forward reconnaissance elements of the rapidly advancing column would run into some disorganized Jerries. After a brief fire-fight they would bring back some prisoners and the column would continue on its mission. Passing through towns, Italian civilians would go wild with joy of being liberated and would throw wine at us. Some of the boys were pretty well buzzed up on wine.

We stop for the night. We are happy, having a good time chasing the fleeing Nazis back at such a rapid pace without running into any real opposition. We figure if all the war could be fought like this, it would be nothing but a good deal. The best part was, we got news tonight. Very good news it was, too. For the long-awaited second front had now come to being. The Allies had invaded Normandy and were progressing satisfactorily. This put our morale on a new high.

For after nearly two years of bitter fighting, it gave the boys a feeling that somebody else had a share in America too and were willing to fight for it. It didn't matter to us that all the bloodshed spilled by a mere handful of American divisions during the last two years of bitter bloody fighting that led to the eventual conquest of Rome, only made the bottom of the third column on the second page of the newspapers back home. To most people, the war had just begun, but to the battle-torn veterans of Africa and Italy, it merely had taken a new phase. Although some were bitter, everyone was happy to be able to read the big headlines in the *Stars and Stripes* about the new bighead in Hitler's Festung Europa.

Early the next morning we are on trucks again, and the mechanized column is on the move again traveling northward at a rapid pace. Along the highway we pass many abandoned German vehicles that have been destroyed by our Air Force. As we go through small towns along the highway, we ask the Dagos where the Jerries are. "Tediscki tuta via diedi minvet," the Dagos would reply, meaning the Germans left ten minutes ago. We go on like this for four days when we come to the town of Oriola, where we stop for the night. Here, my machine gun section sets up on a crossroad forward of Oriola to form a roadblock.

That night, Old Allah, P.J., and I go up to the village ahead of us that as yet has not been captured. We figure there are no Jerries there anyhow so we walk into the village just for the hell of it. We were invited into many Italian homes for wine in this village. There were no Jerries around that we could see. The last house we go into we find a Jerry soldier sitting at the table drinking wine. "Are there any more of you birds around here?" we ask the Jerry. The Jerry answers us in good English, "I'm the only one." We didn't know whether to believe him or not, but we didn't much give a damn 'cause we weren't out looking for them anyhow.

But we tell the Jerry that he better come back with us, and he gives us no argument. He was about the most sensible Jerry I had ever talked to, 'cause he said Hitler was an asshole. Next morning, we delivered our prisoner to the Company C.P. This morning we didn't get on trucks and continue to our spearhead, but we stayed in Oriola. I pulled my section back into town from the roadblock and joined the mortar section, who were leisurely cooking up in the city park. Lt. Knox is dashing madly up and down the street on a captured Jerry motorcycle. He's going so fast his long mustache is sticking out behind him like fins on the tail of a P-38. He's as happy as a kid with a new toy.

After stealing some extra good rations from a colonel from the 1st Armored, a very nice meal is enjoyed by each and every one in the section. After a while P.J. and I decide to explore a mansion up the street. Most of my section goes along, carrying their carbines and pistols. "This is some pup tent," Old Allah comments as we go inside. There is no one there, but a lot of swell furniture, broken wine bottles and big vats of wine with the plugs pulled out. The contents of the casks covered the floor of one room. Jim Fenstemaker was fairly drooling at the mouth and says, "That's a dirty rotten shame, 'ya know that?"

We then find three large hand-painted pictures about 3 x 4 of none other than the three little darlings, Adolf, Herman, and Hinrich. We then place the portraits against a bank, and walk back about fifty yards. Here is where the men in my section really got some of its best range work, for one and all opened up on the terrible trio with carbines and pistols. When we finished, each one of the men in the picture looked like they had chased a fart through a keg of nails.

We got an ass-chewing from a major from the 1st Armored when he came up, but that didn't bother us much.

When we got back to the company area, we see a lot of French soldiers. Many of them were Arabs. We then learn that the French are here to relieve us. Generally, we are very happy about being relieved, but this time we didn't want to go, for we were actually enjoying the type of warfare we were doing the past few days. We figure if we get relieved now, they must have another tough assignment for us. But there is nothing we can do about it, so we load trucks and by 4·00 P.M. we are moving back south. Just before we get to Rome we cut to the right and head west to the coastal section where we turn north again at Civitavecchia and go all the way up to Tarquinia where we find a bivouac area in a wheat field and proceed to erect pup tents. Mackey and I pitch one together, which is the best in the company, located right in the shade of an olive tree.

In this area we train. Two men out of the platoon can go to Rome on a one-day pass each day. Many men are coming back from the hospital. Lt. McGinn, the good-natured 2nd Platoon leader, came back. Ted "Pete" Peterson came back after being gone a long time. Pete is talking a blue streak about the good time he had while he was gone. Oscar Kotz, who got the nasty big wound way back on Mt. Pantana also returned. "I just about had 'em talked into giving me a job in the rear with P.B.S. Then they shipped me back," Oscar said with his same old good-natured chuckle. We always kidded Oscar about losing his P.B.S. job after that. P.B.S., incidentally, stands for Peninsular Base Section. The troops in P.B.S. have it extra good, as they sit back in all the nice rear echelon cities like Naples, Caserta and Rome, driving truck or something.

We get a big bunch of replacements in this area, and we surely needed them. In the 4th Platoon we get several. They all go to the mortar section, as I still have plenty of men in the machine gun section. One particular fellow that catches everybody's eye is "Tiny" Bower, who weighs close to 300 pounds and can play a guitar and sing like nobody's business. Leo Schular, the mortar section leader, points at him with pride and says, "Don't ya wish you had a man like that in your section to tote a machine gun around?" "I'll swap you Hicks for him," I reply.

In this area not only the company but the whole battalion undergoes quite a change. We get a new platoon leader by the name of Lt. Darling. L Company and K Company now dissolve the partnership they had formed after the terrific beating of Bloody Gulch and Lanuvio counter attack. As the replacements brought the companies up to strength, K Company organizes a completely new 3rd Platoon. Lt. Hayden, a new officer, is named Platoon Leader. Pete takes over the newly organized platoon as Platoon Sergeant. Right away Pete makes one of the new replacements a squad leader. This replacement's name is Jim Huffman. Pete says, "Jim is the next thing to Superman." Capt. Doty leaves the company and takes over new duties as Battalion S-3. Lt. Knox takes over as company commander. Lt. Johnson is Company Exec. Lt. McGinn is 2nd Platoon Leader. Lt. Royster has the 1st Platoon.

Here we are issued a new type of machine gun made to operate something like a B.A.R. Capt. Doty asked me how I like them. "Not worth a damn, and none of the boys in the section like it either," I reply. "Take 'em back then and use your old ones," Doty tells me. Lt. Knox thinks they are good and wants us to keep them. I argue with him for about an hour one day. Finally, Knox gets mad and says, "You take them guns, 'cause I'm the one that's running this company," and walks off twisting his mustache vigorously. Then Col. Mearns, who just came back from the hospital, comes up and asks, "How do you like the new guns?" "No good," we all reply.

"I don't know what they would be good for unless it's to probe for mines," the Colonel says with a chuckle as he walks off. P.J., Mackey and I then gather up Buck Rogers guns and take them to the supply tent and tell "Pugly," the Supply Sergeant, we want our old guns back. Pugly says, "That's the kind you're supposed to use now." "Colonel's orders to get our old ones back," I reply. So Pugly and Jeep, the Company Articifer, get out our old guns for us. Pugly then tells me, "If you don't keep your man Hicks from losing all his equipment he'll have to go without. He's lost six helmets in the last two days."

When we get back to our pup tents, I send Hicks down to Pugly for a hundred different items just to make Pugly mad. Pugly and I have a lot of fun keeping Hicks on the run between the supply tent and my C.P. I would send

Hicks down to Pugly for a bullet spacer for the machine gun. Pugly would send him back with a message for me to return the key for the bazooka.

We are in this position ten days when we get orders to move up and relieve the 36th Division. We get on trucks and go a good distance north to an assembly area. At dawn the next morning we are on the attack going through a solid mass of brush single file. We advance all day without meeting any opposition. Next day we shift to the right towards Cecina. We are to the left of Cecina, the 133rd Infantry is fighting bitterly to capture the town of Cecina itself. We now run into fairly stiff opposition consisting of artillery and machine gun fire. There we set up a defense for the night. My section sets up the 3rd Platoon sector. When we went back for rations and ammo that night, Midnight was at the ration dump waiting to go back with us as he just returned from the hospital. Next day the sun comes out hot. "Big Jim" has his squad placed between my two machine guns, and he really has them on the ball. I talk to Pete and Lt. Hayden. Lt. Hayden is a swell egg. I haven't seen Lt. Darling, our platoon leader, since we came to the front.

That afternoon we get attack orders. I get my orders from Lt. Hayden, as the 3rd Platoon is the assaulting platoon, and my section is to be attached to the 3rd Platoon. We have a stream to cross. Immediately across this stream is a wooded area. The stream is wide, but shallow. We run across it as fast as we can one at a time. The water is only knee high. We receive some machine gun fire, but the entire company, with the exception of the mortar section who sets up behind the stream, gets across okay.

As soon as we get across, Lt. Knox calls for me to set up the left flank. When I get there, he changes his mind and orders me to set up on the right flank as someone had reported a counter attack coming from the right. The rumor is that there is a lot of armor in this attack. We have a section of M-10 tank destroyers with us (2 T.D.'s). This T.D. outfit is fresh from the States. They already have the T.D.s across the stream in good position. The word "counter attack" apparently had scared the new men in the T.D.s for without another word they lit the explosives in the T.D.s and blew them all to hell and ran to the rear. That was the last of our anti-tank support. Lt. Darling was across the stream and already had a fox hole dug so deep I could hardly see him curled up in the bottom of it. The predicted counter attack caused plenty of excitement, and I don't know why, for it never did materialize. On our tiny beachhead across this stream, we set up a stable defense for the night and are not threatened in the least by the enemy.

Next morning at dawn we are on the attack again. We advance to the left towards Cecina, which the 133rd, our sister regiment, are still fighting for from the south. Scattered Jerry machine guns make our progress slow, and at many different times hold us up temporarily until we can route out the stubborn kraut-eaters, then we continue our advance. We are still at midnight when we enter another small village. Here we set up a defense for the remainder of the night.

Next morning finds us on the attack again. Once more the machine gun section is attached to the 3rd Platoon. We pick our way through grape vineyards until we see a town situated high on a lofty mountain. Right in the center of this mountain town is a conspicuous building that stands out from the rest because of its enormous size, and it is built like a castle. We get to a group of farm buildings near the base of this hilltop town when the Jerries open up on us with machine gun fire. The 2nd and 3rd Platoons are temporarily pinned down, but soon maneuvered so that the whole company was immediately at the base of the hill.

They throw some artillery at us here. We set our machine guns up and fire back at the Jerry machine gun nests. Here we duel it out with them all day, but they were unable to hurt us and vice-versa, although P.J. had to change barrels on his gun several times. When darkness came, we started the assault on the town. We sneaked cautiously up the slope of the mountain, taking the long way around and entering the town from the right. I heard a few bursts from tommy guns and popping of hand grenades from the attacking 1st Platoon. The next thing, the whole company was mustered by the castle. This castle covers an entire city block and is several stories high. All three rifle platoons move in and occupy this castle along with part of I Company and M Company.

I try to get my machine gun in there too, but nothing doing. Lt. Knox orders me to set up a roadblock covering an approaching trail. We set up behind a paved road where it was very hard to dig in. We build rock barricades and camouflage them with brush. We then find a building which has two-foot-thick rock walls facing the side of incoming artillery. There are several beds in this house, and all that weren't on guard soon put them to their proper use. Next morning as we cook up, things seem peaceful, but we can still hear from that diehard machine gun nest that we were with yesterday stubbornly firing out of his pillbox, which is now below us. About noon we get a word by runner of a counter attack coming right flank.

We quickly change our guns to fire down a ravine. P.J. leaves his gun on the road and cuts loose from there. I take the 1st Squad's gun up on a bank, back of the road behind P.J. and I had the ammo bearers running to keep us supplied with ammo. The little 30's were jumping up and down as we run through about 1600 rounds through each gun. M Company's heavy water-cooled machine guns to the left of us were barking equally as loudly, and the counter attack was soon broken up. I ceased firing and looked at the smoking sizzling hot machine gun. It suddenly reminded me of the Homely One when he was section leader back in Ireland.

When the guns were all cleaned up and polished for Saturday's inspection, the Homely One would proudly say, "Ain't they purty tho," but right now I patted it and thought to myself, "pretty, hell. Just effective." That was the last threat we got from that flank. Next day was the 4th of July. It was a fairly peaceful day. The Jerry machine gunner behind us is still in his pillbox, firing away as hard as ever. From now on we just ignore him. There is one old Italian woman around this house we are in. She seen Oscar pissing on a bush and shortly came running after Oscar with a white enameled pisspot in hand.

That evening we get orders to attack down the street. I Company is to take all the buildings on the left side of the street. K Company is to take the ones on the right. Again, my section is attached to the 3rd Platoon, which is the assaulting platoon. We're up against the fanatical SS troops again. Big Jim's squad is the spearhead of the 3rd Platoon. With a sledge hammer in his left hand and a tommy gun in his right, he knocks down doors, then bounces in throwing hand grenades and firing his tommy gun. If any Jerries were in there, they were readily taken care of by Big Jim.

By the time we have taken over the third house, we figure we have gone far enough. The machine gun section and the 3rd Platoon occupy the same house. We set our machine guns up inside, firing out the windows. We can hear Jerries in the next room. Sgt. Parent, right guide of the 3rd Platoon, spies a grand piano in the corner of one of the luxuriously furnished rooms. An expert piano player, Parent sits down and starts beating out Roll Out the Barrel. Soon everybody is singing. The Jerries in the next room evidently enjoyed it. At least they didn't make any complaints.

These buildings we are in are richly furnished apartments, four stories and many rooms. Each squad has a room. Nice, well-equipped kitchens, luxurious dining rooms and modern, furnished bedrooms. So, in spite of the Jerries in the next room, we make ourselves comfortable in these fancy apartments that formerly were occupied by Fascist big wigs.

Next day we explore the kitchen. We find good supplies of spaghetti, tomato sauce, cheese, fine wines and other foods. From the back yard Old Allah captured three young chickens and one rabbit. Soon we are frying chicken and rabbit and spaghetti on the tile charcoal burner. We then prepare the dining room for a banquet. Out of the walnut buffet we drag out some fine, gaily colored linen which we spread on the walnut table with a napkin at each place. We then set the table with fine china, glass, and silverware. Mackey then brings in two long, red candles mounted on beautiful candle holders that he places at each end of the table. As soon as we lit the candles, a shell from a Jerry 170mm hit the bathroom to the right of us completely demolishing it.

Old Allah says, "Them dirty son of bitches, I was going to take a bath after dinner." "The concussion blew the damned candle out," Mackey complains. Dinner is now ready, so the entire section takes off their helmets and sits down at the table. It looked awful good, but the dirty, unshaven bloodstained G.I.s around it sort of spoiled the scenery. Everyone is exceedingly polite and everyone is addressed by rank.

Mackey holds his little finger out smartly as he passes the spaghetti to Old Allah, saying, "Would you care for some more spaghetti, Pvt. Whitworth?" "Thank you, Pvt. Mackey," Old Allah replies. When we are all done eating, the tablecloth is picked up at the corners, folded over the dishes and thrown in the corner with a swish.

The dishes are now all gone, and the house is getting smaller every day as heavy Jerry artillery is taking the rooms out one at a time. One day O'Neale was on guard at the machine gun, which is on the second floor. I was wondering why O'Neale didn't come down to get a new relief as he had been up there for quite some time. I decide to go up and see that the trouble is. When I get to the place where the stairway used to be, I find it's gone, knocked out by an artillery shell.

I look up and see O'Neale sitting behind the machine gun, the room below him is gone. "How in the hell am I gonna get down from here?" O'Neale asks. I then stack up some furniture to make the machine gun accessible. The 3rd Platoon and the machine gun section are now crowded in to three small rooms, when we decide it's about time to acquire another apartment. Big Jim, with a sledgehammer, tommy gun and grenades, says, "Come on, 2nd Squad, let's get another house." About a half hour later Big Jim returns saying, "Okay, you guys can come in to the next house now." So, we take up new quarters and proceed to make use of new equipment again.

Lt. Knox, who enjoys his comfort as well as the rest of us, also likes this town and hates to leave it as he has a super deluxe apartment for his C.P. The battalion commander isn't satisfied with the progress we are making and calls Lt. Knox on the radio, ordering him to attack and take the rest of the town. "Okay," Lt. Knox replies and commences to twist his mustache vigorously. Then he calls back to the battalion commander, "Big counter attack coming from the left front, cannot advance." The battalion commander called for us to attack several times. Lt. Knox could generally find a counter attack brewing somewhere. The Knox Counter Attack soon became a byword throughout the company. The name of this town we are in is Rosignano. From this hilltop we look to the west to where not far away lies the blue expanse of the Tyrrhenian Sea. On the beach is a modern resort town, which is known as Rosignano By The Sea. The town we now are in is known as Rosignano On The Hill.

We are here about a week when we really set out to clear the rest of Rosignano. After several short but rough skirmishes, we have the street cleared and all the Jerries run into a huge cave at the end of the street where they can block our advance. We cannot figure out how to get them out of this cave. Finally, Lt. Knox decides we should use a pole charge. A pole charge is nothing but a long pole with about 20 pounds of TNT on the end of it that is ignited by prima cord.

Big Jim volunteers to be the one to use it. The 3rd Platoon gets right up to the entrance of the cave. Big Jim hollers in at them, "Come on out. We will send you back to the States. They'll treat you good there." "Cha, dey treat us goot in Berlin too," the Jerries reply. "Okay, you sons of bitches," Big Jim replies as he pushes the pole charge in the hole, pulls the igniter and BANG! The entrance to the cave is closed. The Jerries are either dead or wish they were. Now the whole town is ours. Next day we are drinking wine, anisette and other fine drinks as we enjoy our last day in Rosignano. Dead Jerries and knocked out German tanks are strewn up and down the street. It wasn't with regret when we observed SS insignia on their uniforms.

Next morning, we advance north of Rosignano. For the first time in a long while the 4th Platoon stays together as a unit with the machine gun section leading, mortar section following. Platoon Sgt. Lloyd Doe is up at the head of the platoon with me. "Where is Lt. Darling?" I ask Lloyd as we march along. "He's back with company headquarters," Lloyd replies and goes on to say, "We got another new officer in the platoon. Now you can have an officer with your section. You'll be the new one. Lt. Darling will stay with the mortars." "I sure would like to have an officer so he could take some of the responsibilities, but if he's like some of these 90-day wonders we've been getting lately, I'd just as soon go without," I reply to Lloyd. Lloyd then says, "I don't know how he'll be. Oh, here he comes now."

I look at the man and see he's pretty fair sized, nicely built and has a pleasant smile on his face. As he approaches, Lloyd Doe says, "Lt. Wigle, meet Sgt. Walund, machine gun section leader." The Lieutenant and I shook hands, as saluting in this outfit at the stage of the war was kind of forgotten. Lloyd Doe dropped back to the rear of the platoon. As we walk along, Lt. Wigle and I carry on a conversation. "I'm pretty green at fighting. I've got a lot to learn from you guys," the Lieutenant says. "You'll catch on real quick," I reply.

We are winding our way through a gully now. The column stops for about a half hour. No on knows why. While we are sitting along the banks of the gully, I see Col. Mearns walking back from the head of the column, for Col. Mearns was always up front. As he gets closer, I can see every once in a while, he stops and says a few words to the boys along the way. When he gets to us, he stops and says in his dead voice, "So long men. I'm going to have to leave you. I'd rather stay with the 3rd Battalion, but it seems 5th Army wants me somewhere else, and I know Major McSween will make you a good battalion commander." He then continues on his way. I turn to Lt. Wigle and say, "There goes one of the best battalion commanders we ever had." Along with Col. Swenson, Col. Mearns got a chicken put on his shoulder back at 5th Army Headquarters and is now a full-fledged colonel.

When we get up to advance again, we don't go far before they start laying some artillery in on us. I can see Lt. Wigle acts differently than most new officers under fire. He keeps cool, takes the necessary precautions but doesn't dive for a ditch and remain there as some do. Instead, he walks up and down the section column to see if anyone is hurt. Jimmy Fenstemaker and Waugh out of the machine gun section are wounded. Lt. Knox is wounded. Major McSween, who just took over the battalion is also wounded. Capt. Doty now take over the battalion.

Lt. McGinn assumes command of the company, replacing Lt. Knox. Fortunately, we are near a ditch, and we get the entire section concealed in this ditch where we are forced to stay for the remainder of the day. Mackey again is back at his old job as section radio man, as Wiegle came from the hospital and took over his old squad which Mackey had been leading during Wiegle's absence. I'm glad to have Mackey back as radio man, for he's a lot of company, especially when we are pinned down as we are today. During the day Mackey, Lt. Wigle and I sit together in the ditch and talk as shells burst around us.

NICKNAMES

Lt. Wigle tells us he was a concert violinist in civilian life and played with the Detroit Symphony. He had studied the violin in Salzburg, Austria. Wiegle came over to where we were. "We're going to have to call you by your nickname from now on, Wiegle, because your name is too much like Lt. Wigle's. So, from now on, you're to be known to one and all as Brady," I tell him. Wiegle likes to be called Brady, as it brings out the Irish in him, of which he is so proud. Brady always claimed he's Irish, but Old Allah says he's a cross between a red fox and a snapping turtle.

When darkness came, outposts were set out on top of the hill that is now cleared of Jerries. The machine gun section is ordered to set way out in a forward outpost. I complain to Big Jake, 1st Platoon Sergeant, about this and he gives me a B.A.R. Team for support. Lt. Wigle offers to take his turn on guard. I tell him, "The only officer that ever did guard duty in K Company was Lt. Sad Sack, and you don't want to be like that." Lt. Wigle then goes back and stays in the company C.P. with Lts. McGinn and Darling. The night was peaceful and uneventful.

Next morning finds us again on the attack. Our final objective is supposed to be the port city of Leghorn (Livorno), which is still many miles from where we are now. We make very good progress this day. The terrain we are on now is not really mountainous, but a mass of rolling high hills, an excellent place for armor to operate on, and we have a tank battalion attached to us. We advance all day with tanks. We don't encounter any opposition until about sundown when we run into some jerry machine gun fire.

We get to a crossroad when we are greeted by a large band of ragged Italians who had rifles of all kinds of makes and caliber. Some had long knives. Some of them were just kids, some were girls. One girl in particular was noticed by all as she was pretty good looking. She was carrying one of those British Bren guns, which is the equivalent of our B.A.R. The fellow who apparently was the leader of the group, spoke up first. *"Bouna sierra,* Americanos, we are partisans. We just chased Tediski off this hill." "You look like a bunch of asshole bandits to me," Old Allah comments. We then set up a defense for the night.

Next morning at the first peep of dawn, the 2nd Battalion passed through us, and we stayed in our position as we were in reserve for the day. As we lay around in the sun this day, I think to myself, I've really got a good section now. Lt. Wigle helped to make it a lot better. Mackey as radio man, P.J. and Brady make excellent squad leaders and such old faithful gunners as Old Allah and Oscar, Lange and Jewit. Although I miss Speed very much. The ammo bearers are all good and have a big time with each other. They call one another in this manner: "The Week," "The Brown," "The McNeil," "The Waugh," "The Portman," "The Hick," always adding the work "the" before their last name. Jim Fenstemaker is known to one and all as Jimmy the Fence, as if he were one of the characters out of a Damon Runyan novel.

That night platoon and section sergeants are called up to the company C.P. to be briefed for an attack, after which we are on the road headed for an attack. We march on the road all night. As the morning sun broke over the eastern horizon, we were entering a village by the name of Gabbro. We stop in this village long enough to brew a cup of mud and then we're up and at 'em again. We wind our way down from the hill where the village of Gabbro is situated. Before us is a huge mountain that is nothing but a mass of rocks. The 1st and 3rd Platoons are the assault platoons followed closely, of course, by the ever-present machine gun section.

Making their way through deadly machine gun fire, the grim-faced riflemen of the 1st and 3rd Platoons maneuver up the steep, rocky mountain and route out the ornery kraut-eaters. The hill is now ours. The machine gun section gets orders from the Company C.O. who at this particular time is Lt. McGinn, to set up on the forward slope of this hill to beat off any potential counter attack. Lt Wigle then says, "Company K machine gun, let's go." The men in the section by now had dispersed into various places that afforded them protection from the incoming artillery that was increasing by the moment. "Wait a minute, Lt. Wigle, let's look over this position before we take the entire section out there," I say. But Lt. Wigle wants to take the section along right now.

After arguing a few minutes, he finally concedes to my wish. Lt. Wigle and I then sneak over the top of the hill. One look at the other side was enough for me, for there was no forward slope to this hill. It was a sheer drop off that was almost a cliff, and bare as a billiard ball. If we took the section out there, we would be seen immediately. It would be impossible to dig in. Direct fire from the deadly Jerry 88mm would knock us out with the first round. "We can't set up here, Lieutenant," I say.

"We're going to have to. It's the C.O.'s orders, and I'm going to see that it's carried out," Lt. Wigle replies. I argue back to him, "I'm sure when we tell the C.O. the circumstances, he wouldn't want us out here. We can find a position from which we can defend this hill just as well without getting unnecessarily knocked out and that's exactly what will happen if we set up out there." "You've got to expect to have casualties in war," the Lieutenant replies. I come back, "Yes, but this position is useless." "Go back and get the section. We're going to set up here," Lt. Wigle replies firmly.

Artillery is landing all around us now. Both of us were subject to being hit at any moment as we lay in the open arguing. "PLEASE, Lieutenant, will you listen to me? You're a nice guy and all that, but you're a bigger fool than I take you to be if you put the section out there. You're brave, but stupid. Your bravery makes me feel like a coward, but I won't allow the section to go out there," I pleaded. "Okay, I guess I can't do a thing with you," the Lieutenant replies as we run back off the slope of this hill to the company C.P. where Lt. McGinn is in a ditch. I relate the situation to Lt. McGinn. Lt. Wigle is now agreeing with me. "Don't set up out there by any means, set up wherever you see fit," Lt. McGinn tells us. So, we set up our guns on the right flank. All the men that are not on the guns are protected well by a big ditch.

There is a tremendous amount of mortar and artillery fire landing on this hill, and the Company has had many casualties. I was glad that I had talked Lt.

Wigle out of setting up where he wanted to and the boys in the section thanked me for it. "Croatenpecker" Daloes, a squad leader from the mortar section, came running down off the hill as fast as he could. When he got to where Mackey was, he was completely out of breath. "What's the matter, Croatenpecker?" we ask. "Oh, I just seen a mortar shell come at me. Believe it or not, I seen it while it was still in the air. I couldn't get away from it. It landed right by my feet. It was a dud, but it still scared the daylights out of me. If it would have been live, I'd be nothing but a grease spot now," Croatenpecker tells us breathlessly.

The name of this hill we are on now is known as the Hill of Ill Fate—not a very pleasant, but appropriate, name—for it has been somewhat ill fate for K Company. On top of the gruesome name of the hill, we get a new password for the next 24 hours, which has a cheerful ring to it—Coffin Nail. "I wonder who them rear echelon geniuses are that think up all these gay titles," Old Allah comments. Lt. Wigle has been moving around viewing the situation most of the while. He comes back and says, "I've got to thank you, Sgt. Walund, for talking me out of setting where I wanted to. L Company sent a patrol out there and suffered a lot of casualties."

It's getting towards evening when Lt. Darling calls me from his subterranean foxhole to set up in another position so I go to where he sent me to reconnoiter the situation leaving the section in place. When I get there, I see Lt. Black Rufe Stratmoen, who has his platoon of heavy machine guns place here. "You need some help, Rufe?" I ask. "No, we can take care of everything here for the next two hours. Then the 2nd Battalion is coming up to relieve us," Black Rufe replies in his familiar calm way. I talk to Black Rufe for a while, then go back to the section. There was a bright beam on the men's faces when I tell them they don't have to move and that the 2nd Battalion will relieve us as soon as it gets dark. It had been dark about an hour when the 2nd Battalion came up to relieve us. We then marched a short way to an assembly area to the left rear of the Hill of Ill Fate where we flop down immediately and get some much-needed rest.

Next afternoon we are marching for another attack. We're stopped by Jerry machine gun fire and artillery at dusk. We stop and set up a defense for the night. It's about noon the next day when the battalion C.O. gives us attack orders which state "don't stop until you take Leghorn." K Company marches down a mountain trail single file with a flank patrol on either side of the column. At dusk we are again pinned down temporarily by machine gun fire. After a brief skirmish the Jerries left, and we continued on our mission. We march along for several hours without being molested. We figure we have probably by-passed a good many Jerries. We stop and disperse in a grape vineyard.

The 1st Platoon send a reconnaissance patrol forward into Leghorn. The vital port city lies less than a mile ahead of us. The port of Leghorn is a prize objective for the 5th Army. The loss of Leghorn for the Jerries will greatly impair the German war machine in Italy, as it has been a major supply base for them and it will be valuable to us for the same purpose. The reconnaissance patrol returns about an hour later, reporting they didn't see any signs of Jerries in Leghorn. The Italian people that were left in Leghorn told the patrol, "Tadeski tuta vied" late that afternoon after sabotaging the docks.

There is a tint of grey on the eastern horizon as we enter Leghorn. We don't go very far into the city when we run into a group of nice buildings. The buildings looked inviting, so we decided we have gone far enough. The Italian people invite us in and give us their spare rooms. Tired and sleepy, most of the men soon drop off comfortably in deep slumber. The 100th "Go for Broke" Battalion from our division is supposed to be closing in on Leghorn from the right so we figure to let the reliable men of Japanese descent clear that sector of the city.

Next day we wake up about noon. Ploopie already has his kitchen tent set up in Leghorn so we have a good hot dinner. Lt. Knox returned from the hospital. We hear there has been an Allied landing in southern France near Marseille, Toulon and Nice. We've been expecting this, for they took the 3rd, 36th, and 45th Divisions out of the 5th Army and held them in a staging area near Naples for quite some time. We all knew they weren't going to make a USO outfit out of crack fighting veterans such as they.

In Leghorn, Tiny Bower, the big replacement in the mortar section, found a guitar and keeps us and the Italian people well entertained with his melodious singing. There's a new division in Italy to take up the slack of the loss of the divisions that went to southern France. It's the 91st Division.

Next day Big Barnsmell Slink, Old Allah and I decide to set out and see what Leghorn is really like. As we walk up the streets, we can see many demolished buildings that the Jerries had blown up before evacuating. They apparently left in a hurry for we see many of their signs reading "ACHTUN MINEN" still standing in various places. "Real polite of them to let us know where the mines are," Old Allah comments. We see a jeep load of rear echelon MPs drive in, but we beat them to it. Out of some boards we made signs reading "Leghorn off limits to P.B.S. and MPs" and "Leghorn off limits to all rear echelon personnel."

We run into a couple of fellows from the 100th Battalion who tell us they have found a Jerry brewery in tact with three vats of genuine German beer. "Time's a wasting," states Big Barnsmell, and in a swish we are in the brewery. There already was a bunch from the 100th Battalion there. Big Barnsmell turns a spigot on a vat, Old Allah and I remove our outer shell of our helmets and hold them under the foaming spigot. When we have three helmets full of the sudsy brew drawn, we sit down in a cool place and proceed to drink.

When that is consumed, we fill them up again. With chin straps buckled, we carry the foaming liquid up the street as if they were buckets. We now are in a very good mood indeed. We wander around town for a while. Every building is blacked out, but we came to one big fancy home where we seen a light. There is a big, high iron fence about ten feet high around this home. The gate is locked, so we proceed to climb over the fence and knock on the door of the house. An Italian man came to the door and invited us in. He immediately served some spaghetti and vino. We eat and visit with him for a couple of hours and then leave, crawling over the high steel fence again.

It's about midnight. Old Allah spies an Italian car parked in an alley and says, "I'm going to bed," and crawls into the old Fiat and goes to sleep. Big Barnsmell and I don't desire to sleep in the old Fiat so we start walking to the house that the platoon was staying in. When we get there, no one is around. Our outfit had moved out. "I kinda thought they would, but we couldn't pass up all that free beer," I comment to Big Barnsmell. The Italian mamma of the house shows us to a nice bedroom where we go to sleep.

Next morning when we get up, we are hungry. Ploopie had moved his kitchen so we couldn't get any chow. Big Barnsmell and I walk uptown again. When we get to the square, we see a lot of commotion. There's a vehicle standing there that looks like a circus wagon. As we get closer, we can read the printing on the side of the vehicle, which states "Stan, the doughnut man," and there is a big red cross on it. Big Barnsmell and I lose no time to get in line and get some coffee and doughnuts from "Stan." This is a Red Cross club mobile that follows fairly close to the front passing out coffee and doughnuts to tired, hungry G.I.s. It's run by a lively little guy who talks a blue streak as he cheerfully hands out coffee and doughnuts, and Stan, the doughnut man won fame among G.I.s in Italy.

After eating many doughnuts and several cups of coffee, we set out in search of Old Allah. We go back to where two "Cabbarinis" were that we had met the day before. They made signs that Old Allah had left that morning in a jeep. We then catch a weapons carrier from M Company, which takes us back to the battalion kitchen area which is located several miles south of Leghorn. Old Allah is already at the kitchen tent drinking mud.

After the usual razzing from Ploopie, Pugly, "Jeep" and the cooks, we go over to rear battalion C.P. to see if we can get transportation up to the company, which is now many miles north of Leghorn. There is no transportation available, and we don't feel too badly about it. When we get back to K Company kitchen, we are greeted by Ole Evans, 2nd Platoon Sergeant, Good Deed Arneson and Lt. Black Rufe Stratmoen from M Company, who have just come back from the companies as they have been selected to go home on this month's quota of T.D. T.D. stands for temporary duty in the States. It's a 30-day furlough plus traveling time, then they come back to their old outfits. They're pretty happy about going home. Old Allah tries to dishearten them by saying, "That's the last thing I would do right now is to go home. The submarine menace in the Atlantic is terrific. As soon as you get on that boat, you're a dead duck."

With Ole, Good Deed, and Black Rufe gone, it doesn't leave so many old boys left in the outfit. Although Big Barnsmell, Old Allah and I are pretty sure we'll be the last ones to go, there is a faint glimmer of hope that even we may someday return to the States.

Next night the battalion furnishes us transportation and takes us up to the company. As we go through Leghorn, several long-range artillery shells land in the city. These shells pack a terrific wallop, just like Anzio Annie, only these are known as Leghorn Lizzy. We go many miles north of Leghorn before we get to where the company is holding a defensive position just on this side of the Arno River. From all indications the Krauts now hold everything north of the Arno River barrier, and we hold everything to the south. We stop first at the company C.P. I see Lt. Knox twisting his mustache, so I decide not to report to him I don't want to report to the Little King, for I figure he's in a bad mood anyway seeing his brother, Black Rufe, getting to go home before him. His other brother, Paper Ass Stratmoen, is also on his way home with a wound that he received at Bloody Gulch. However, we now have an extra 1st sergeant, a new replacement who joined the company just north of Rome. His name is Groble, who looks more like Abe Lincoln than Abe looked like himself.

So, I ignore the Little King and report to 1st Sergeant Groble instead. "It's oaky. Your machine gun section is over there," the extra 1st sergeant replies. So Old Allah and I go to the machine gun section, Big Barnsmell goes to the mortars. The boys in the section, including Lt. Wigle, rub it in a little. They say if our section leader can take a couple days off, we should be able to do likewise. Lt. Wigle tells me the deal, shows me where the guns are set up covering a road with crossfire. After making out a guard list, I crawl under a bridge with Macky and go to sleep.

Next day I see the terrain in daylight. We are on perfectly flat ground. About a mile ahead of us flows the Arno River. To our left flank and just north of the Arno there is a pretty fair-sized city which has a tower in it that leans crazily to one side. Yes, that was the tower that Galilei Galileo, the Italian genius, dropped apples to prove his theory of gravity. It was one of the seven wonders of the world. The city is called Pisa, and that tower we could so plainly see was the famed Leaning Tower of Pisa.

Lt. Wigle goes out and picks grapes and other fruits for the section. That seems to be his hobby. Later on that day O'Neal, Portman and Fahr ask if they can go up ahead and investigate some farmhouses. At the word yes, O'Neal straps his 45 on his hip and wobbles his chubby ass up the road followed by his inseparable comrades Portman and Fahr. They're gone several hours when Macky and I decide to go up and see what they are doing. We go into a nice farmhouse and find a table full of fresh-cooked grub. "What are we waiting for," Macky says as we dive in.

There is fried chicken, fresh vegetables, fruit and eggs and wine. When O'Neal, Portman and Fahr return saying, "Look who's eating our grub. And to think I fried that chicken southern style," Fahr drawls out in his southern accent. But there was enough for everybody. After we ate, we went back to our position. We find the company alerted to move. We didn't like the sound of it at first, for we thought it meant crossing the Arno and attacking beyond. But we found out later we were getting division relief, which makes us all exceedingly happy. For the entire division to get relieved could mean a pretty good rest. We've not had division relief since we left Benevento.

ROSIGNANO BY THE SEA

We move out during daylight, one squad at a time. Each platoon is to take a different route. After the three mortar squads had left from the 4th Platoon, Lt. Wigle take Brady's 1st squad and pulls out. Fifteen minutes later I pull out with P.J.'s 2nd squad. The company all assembled in a wooded area about four miles to the rear, where we get on trucks which take us to our final destination. We roll right through Leghorn and follow coastal Highway 1 until we come to a beautiful resort town by the sea. This town is none other than Rosignano by The Sea, the town we could see from Rosignano on The Hill. Here we turn sharply to the right and up a hill to a wooded area and stop. We get off trucks and can see a light in the kitchen tent with Ploopie standing in the doorway, which looked mighty good to us. We were assigned to our platoon areas where we pitch pup tents and then go up to the kitchen and enjoy a hot supper.

A bunch of the old original men lingered long at the kitchen after supper talking about old times and departed buddies as they sipped mud that was so black it made tar look like milk. Phees, who has a new job as stove mechanic in the kitchen, asks me, "Wanna make a bet that you won't go home next month?" "Sure, here's five says I don't," I reply. We each give Pugly a 500 lire note, telling him he's to hold stakes. It's late when I get back to my pup tent. Mack is sawing wood a cord a minute as I flop down beside him.

Next day everyone is at ease and happy. The boys in the section are having fun with each other. P.J. and Old Allah are giving "the Hick" a fancy haircut again as Oscar shaves his eyebrows off. Westbrooks is singing a holy-roller song. Portman and Fahr are playing catch as O'Neal wobbles up and down the area. Jimmy the Fence just returned from the hospital and is greeted by The Brown,

The Lane, The Week and The Waugh. Jimmy the Fence looks at The Brown and asks, "What color is shit?" "Brown," the others reply harmoniously. "You mugs are just bucking for a fat eye," The Brown replies. "Humpty dumpty" is trying his best to disassemble a machine gun in the shade of an olive tree, and in disgust blows his top. Midnight is talking Dago to an Italian senora when Adams emerges with one of his fantastic inventions.

Brady is bragging to Jewit and Bartlett how good his '34 Plymouth that is sitting in a garage back in Grand Forks, North Dakota is. Lt. Wigle makes his rounds to each group, laughing and joking with them. As Macky sees the battalion doctor walk by, he immediately proceeds to peel a banana he doesn't have.

After that, he picks imaginary grapes out of the air and pretends to eat them. He does that to try to induce the Doc that he is psycho or a Section 8 case so he can be reclassified and sent home. When the Doc gets out of sight, Macky says in disgust, "I'll be a sad sack. I failed again, but I'll make it one of these days. Next time he sees me I'll be embroidering my shelterhalf." That's the general picture of what the machine gun section of the 4th Platoon was doing on this first day of division relieve near Rosignano by The Sea.

Leo Schular, who is right guide of the 4th Platoon as well as mortar section leader, brings supplies over to us and sits down and talks for a while. "I'll swap officers you," Leo says. "Oh no you won't. Everybody in the machine gun section likes Lt. Wigle too well," I reply. I guess Leo just had another run-in with Lt. Darling.

There has been an expeditionary force from Brazil arrived in Italy. Lt. Knox has been sent to them on detached service to give them some battle schooling. Lt. McGinn is now acting as Company Commander. Ploopie and the cooks have got a Dago working in the kitchen. They picked him up in Leghorn. We call him "Renardo the Pison." He also has the job of company barber.

This is the best rest area we've ever been in. We have very little training, good eats and shows every night. We have now organized a Sergeant's Club for the first three grades in the battalion. Each man donates 15$. We rent a nice big house in Rosignano by the Sea that is located right on the beach. We have a bar and manage to keep it well supplied with gin, white lighting, cognac and various wines. We also employ a bartender. We have a big party at the club almost every night. Pete thinks this is wonderful and he practically lives at the club. Lloyd Doe, Leo Schular and I make it almost every night.

Lloyd Doe is told he has been selected as the man from K Company to go home on next month's quota of T.D. (30-day furlough.) Lloyd is very happy about this. He will remain with the company until he is about ready to sail, as we are in a rest area anyhow. Leo takes over as 4th Platoon Sergeant when Lloyd leaves. Croatenpecker will succeed Leo as mortar section leader and I will be right guide on top of still having the machine gun section.

The British 8th Army has now taken the great cultural city of Florence and are now fighting north of the Arno River.

Once we get word to act as an honor guard for Winston Churchill again, as he was going to be in Rosignano by The Sea. He was making a tour of Italy upon returning from the Tehran Conference. We line up along the streets and present arms as the Prime Minister rides by in a command car followed by Generals Marshall and Clark. We then return to our bivouac area.

Not long after the Churchill incident we leave Rosignano by The Sea, much to our disliking. We move close to the town of Castle Florentino, which is not far from Florence. We bivouac in an open field and have a regular training schedule each day, and night problems most nights.

We are here about a week when my turn comes up for a five-day pass. Big Jake, 1st Platoon Sergeant, and I go to Rome the next day. It was quite a long trip from near Florence to Rome in the back end of a six-by-six. We left early in the morning. It was about 4:00 when we pulled into Rome. We stop by a group of colorful ultra-modern buildings surrounded by countless numbers of statues. This was the 5th Army rest center in Rome. The name of the place was Foro Mussolini (Mussolini Forum). It was the pride of "Ill Duce's" expanded construction program to set an example to the rest of the world that Italian architecture took second place to no one.

It was built for the purpose of holding the next world Olympic games and all kinds of sports fields decorated the grounds. The flags of three nations waved proudly over the grounds. Old Glory was on the right, Britain's Union Jack in the middle, and France's Tricolor was on the left. They had retreated at 5:00. Big Jake and I were coming from the shower room. We stopped and saluted as the band played the Marseille, and the Tricolor was lowered. *God Save The King* was played as the union Jack came down. And finally, the *Star-Spangled Banner*, as the Stars and Stripes descended. It was a colorful ceremony.

The next day Big Jake and I set out to see what makes the Eternal City eternal. We find the Italian taxis are doing a big business. These taxis are mostly horse-drawn carriages. We engage one of these and let the driver act as a guide, who takes us to points of interest. He took us to Vatican City, where we went through St. Peter's Cathedral and various other places throughout Rome. An Italian kid guided us to a house. When we get in, we see a big tall soldier dressed in a uniform that we had never seen before. He wore a big red star on his cap. I looked over to Big Jake and say, "I bet that guy is a Yugoslavian, one of Tito's partisans." At that, Big Jake turned to the soldier and let out a spiel. I don't know what it was except that it seemed almost every word ended in "ski." The Yugoslav understood Big Jake perfectly. Big Jake could speak the Slavic language fluently, as his parents came from there. Being unable to understand the conversation, I turned my attention to an Italian signorina.

After five glorious days it was time to go back to the outfit. We left Rome about 6:00 in the evening and arrived at our bivouac area about six in the morning. Next day we are out in the field training again. Big Barnsmell has left the mortar section for what he calls a more honorable profession, that of being mule skinner for the company. From now on, each company is going to have their own mules to make sure our ammo and rations will be brought up when we're fighting up in the rugged Appenines.

A couple of days later we move again. We go through Florence, cross the Arno and bivouac north of Florence. In this area Lloyd Doe leaves us to start his journey homeward and Leo Schular takes over the platoon. We're here only a couple of days when our relief is over and we load trucks and again head for the front. We get to an assembly area about four in the morning. Some of us get a couple hours' sleep before dawn when we start on the attack. Just as we start the approach march, the Jerries crippled our battalion incredibly. It was a prize blow for the enemy when they knocked out practically our entire battalion staff. Yes, Col. McSween, Capt. Doty's Battalion S-3 and Lt. Baily's Battalion S-1 got tangled up in a mine field.

Col. McSween lost a leg. Capt. Doty got a large share of his lower body blown to shreds and Lt. Baily was also wounded seriously. None of these men died, but we never seen them again as they were later sent back to the States to recover. They were all good men, and we hated to lose them. Capt. Doty, we all knew so well. He had joined us way back in Ireland as our platoon leader in time for the invasion of Algiers, North Africa and was now acting as assistant battalion commander. Litter squads carried the wounded officers to the rear. We gulped a little and felt small and helpless in their presence. Some men cursed a little and looked up at the high ground that concealed the hated Jerries. "Who is going to run the battalion now?" we all ask. Regiment sent down a new Lt. Col. To command the 3rd Battalion whose name is Col. Joyce. He looked old to us for being in a combat outfit. He had no previous experience in this war and was a fairly recent arrival from the States.

After reorganizing somewhat, we continue on our mission. We come to a stream immediately in front of a town. Our sister regiment, the 168th Infantry, had already taken the town. We are to push through them and take the rolling hills beyond. We stop by a stream and brew mud before moving on. Lt. Wigle is no onger just with the machine gun section but now has the mortar section as well, for Lt. Darling was sent to R Company. Lt. Wigle now has the entire 4th Platoon.

We get up and are on the go again. We enter the town and see the name of it is Barbarino. As we enter the town, little did we realize how important Barbarino would be to us in future months. We found the natives suffered severe casualties. We move right through the town and follow a stream for a short distance northward. We stopped by a destroyed bridge. We were marching a long single file and the weapons platoon was at the rear of the company column. They pass messages back from the head of the column by each soldier repeating the message to the man behind him and passing it back in that manner.

Now I could hear the message being passed back. When it got to the middle of the 3rd Platoon, I could already make it out. It was a message I always hated, but always come on every attack. I could hear the men in front of me repeat faintly, "Sgt. Walund forward." It sounds more clearly as each man passes it back. I could have went right away, but I waited until the man immediately ahead of me looks back and says, "You're wanted forward."

I then reluctantly proceed forward to confer with Lts. McGinn and Wigle to get the dope. I went to the bottom of the blown-out bridge where Lts. McGinn, Hayden and Morgan, along with Sgts. Big Jake, Pete and Leo Schular were studying maps. Lt. Wigle tells me as he points it out on a map, "Lt. Morgan will attack on the left side of the creek with his 2nd Platoon. Lt. Hayden will attack on the right side of the creek with the 3rd Platoon. I will take Brady's 1st machine gun squad and support the 2nd Platoon. You'll take P.J.'s 2nd machine gun squad and support the 3rd Platoon." With that, we're off in a skirmish line advancing cautiously over the rolling terrain. We encounter a small amount of machine gun fire, but we take the hill comparatively easy with no casualties. We then set up a defense for the night.

Lt. Wigle is busy directing mortar on Jerry positions on the next hill. He has Croatenpecker with his rapid-fire orders. About midnight we get orders to move. We take our guns out of action and follow the creek back to Barbarino. When we get to Barbarino we just stop long enough to draw a fresh supply of ammo, rations and fill our canteens in the pitch-black darkness. We head north again out of Barbarino, only this time we head way to the left of the place where we had fought the previous afternoon. It seemed as if we had walked over the rough terrain in the blinding darkness. Just as we silhouette ourselves over a knoll, we hear Brrrrr Brrrrr from the rapid firing Jerry machine guns that seemed incredibly close. Everyone hit the dirt. They had us stopped cold, so we hurriedly disperse, dig in, conceal ourselves and set up a hasty defense before daylight. In fact, we were unable to get all this done adequately before the illumination of a new day was upon us.

In the early dawn we could see the precarious position we are in. We're right below a steep terrace hill in a big gully. The Krauts were up on the hill looking down on us. They knew we were in this gully and they rained artillery and mortar fire on us all day long. It was just another one of those days that were just plain hell. Men getting killed and wounded all around you, and you wonder if the next one is going to be you. The Jerries have a stronghold on this hill, which is known as Hill 458 on the map. On top of this hill are several buildings. We have been pasting them with artillery and mortar fire, but Kraut fire still pours from them. We have our two machine guns set up on a bank firing up the hill into the buildings, but we would have done just as much damage as throwing rocks at the moon. Lt. Wigle is very anxious to take this hill and get out of the hot spot we're in.

Lt. Hayden went back to Florence on a five-day pass and Pete got wounded, so that left right guide Sgt. Haugen in full charge of the 3rd Platoon. Lt. Wigle has one method of attack figured out, then he finds something wrong with it and thinks up another one. Just at dusk the 1st Platoon attempted a frontal assault on the hill and were driven back with heavy casualties. At midnight a carrying party was organized to go back for more ammo and rations. It was a rough old grind carrying the supplies back over the rough terrain in the jet-black darkness. By the time we got the ammo and rations distribute, the early morning sun was peeping over the Kraut-held hill.

About noon we started another attack again. We are driven back by the stubborn Jerry paratroopers. About 4 o'clock found us organizing for another attack. This time the 3rd Platoon was chosen as the assault platoon, and it looked like Sgt. Haugan was hooked to lead the 3rd Platoon assault. The 1st Platoon was to be echelon to the right rear of the 3rd Platoon. Lt. Wigle called me over to where him and Sgt. Haugan were making out last minute details. "We'll follow the 3rd Platoon and cover their right flank," Lt. Wigle says to me. Sgt. Haugan is a very good, capable soldier with much combat experience. He wasn't wavering a bit on the new burden wished onto him, but I can see he is very skeptical about the attack. Lt. Wigle then turns to Sgt. Haugan and says, "Say, I wish you would let me lead this attack. I'd really like to." "I'd sure like to have your help, but this is my job and I'll do it," was Haugan's reply. Lt. Wigle pleads with Sgt. Haugan to let him lead the attack, and finally Haugan yields to the Lieutenant's wish.

Our preparatory artillery barrage had just begun. We organize our respective units and follow the barrage closely up the hill, Lt. Wigle leading the attack.

We go through the mined area and follow the terracing of the hill. The ground was being raked with vicious machine gun fire. I seen it. Wigle hoist himself over the bank into full view of the enemy and dash madly for their positions, his carbine barking violently. Sgt. Shaw was the next man over the top, but unfortunately, he crumpled to the ground almost immediately. He was already dead as I passed him.

I ran and flopped behind a haycock. A Jerry evidently seen me, for he fired tracers into the haycock and set it on fire so I was forced to make a mad dash to the next bank. I motioned for the rest of the section to pull up along this bank. We are right at the Jerries' positions now. They are just above the bank. Lt. Wigle and the 3rd Platoon are even further ahead than we are. As I peered carefully over the bank, I seen a Jerry come out of his hole and start running to the rear. I aimed hastily. I think the bullet only hit his gas mask, but he hit the dirt. I call for him to come down and give himself up, but he only lies there.

I then call The Lange over, who can speak German fluently. "Tell him to come down, we'll treat him good," I order Lange to say. The Lange then lets out a lingo of German, and the Jerry comes down with his hands up to surrender. To the left of us another was coming with his hands up to surrender to a man from 3rd Platoon. P.J.'s sharp eyes sees a potato masher in the upraised hand of the oncoming Kraut and hollers to the man from the 3rd Platoon who was covering him, "Shoot the son of a bitch." The rifleman obeyed by putting two rounds from his M-1 through the head of the Kraut. The Kraut flopped face down, throwing the potato masher ahead of him. But everyone escaped injury from the exploding grenade. We already had accumulated a good number of prisoners, and dead Krauts were visible in the area.

I can hear a lot of fire coming from the house on the extreme right. I call to the section to get ready to move. We turn our prisoners over to the mortar section to take care of and pick our way up the hill. The firing has died down as we near the house on the right. Here I meet Sgt. Haugan, and he says to me breathlessly, "All the Jerries are in the cellar of that house. Lt. Wigle chased most of them in there himself and went down after them with his carbine.

They drilled him through the stomach." "Is he dead?" I ask. "No, let's go get him out. I think we can save him," Haugan replies. Haugan, many more men and myself rush to the cellar steps where we find Lt. Wigle lying mortally wounded half-way down the cellar steps, paralyzed from the hips down. He still had that smile on his face. He must have been in great pain, but he didn't let on. He only pleaded, "Throw down a grenade that will get 'em."

We realize, however, that if we throw down a grenade, it would impair the Lieutenant as well as the Jerries if it were to explode in the confined space. We denied him his request. "It doesn't matter about me," he replies. The Jerries in the cellar realize they are beaten and surrender. We manage to get Lt. Wigle out and put him on an old bed spring to be carried back to the medics. Lt. Wigle still had a smile on his face as we put him in a room of a battered down house. He looked up to me, and I had to swallow as he said, "Well, Walund, we got the hill. You know, I really feel like I accomplished something today. It makes me feel good to know that I was able to do something. The only thing I hate about it is that I'm going to have to leave K Company."

He was silent for a while. Then he said, "Will you have my musette bag sent to the medics? I'd like to have it while I'm in the hospital." "I sure will, Lieutenant. And please hurry back," I manage to say. I gave the musette bag to O'Neal and had him carry it back to the aid station along with Lt. Wigle. We made the Jerries carry him back on the bed spring, and when they handled him a little too rough, we threatened to shoot them. I follow them back to where the mortar section was where I see Leo. As they carry the gallant Lieutenant by, Leo just mutter's, "God damn 'em!" and swallows kind of hard.

Now we had to hurry up and organize a stable defense for the night. Already the Jerries were starting to counter attack on the right flank. We hold our ground, but our ammo supply is getting low. It's plumb dark as I go over to the center house where the company C.P. is located. Here I see Lt. McGin, who is sick enough to be in the hospital but is still up here running the company. He's telling Ike, the company radio man, to call back to battalion headquarters. Ike is a very good radio man and doesn't beat around the bush to anyone, be he general or private.

When battalion headquarters tells him that are presently unable to get ammo up to us for some reason or other, Ike blows his top and replies back over the 300 radio, "You bring ammo up and bring it up damn fast or we'll pull back and shoot hell out of the battalion headquarters." We got our ammo and held the hill. Later some of the men from battalion HQ told us Col. Joyce had said, "K Company will have to get a new radio man. That man that talked tonight is a maniac and not fit to talk over the radio." But everyone in K Company tips their helmets to Ike as a radio man.

The Jerries kept counter attacking strongly on our right flank all night long, but every attempt "Tediski" made to regain the hill were repulsed. They apparently withdraw in the wee hours of the morning, for the next day we neither seen or heard from a Jerry. Later on, that day we moved around somewhat. We walk to the rear of the hill and view yesterday's bloody battlefield.

One particular scene was one that I hope I never see again, even though the subject of the scene was the enemy. Here we found a wounded Jerry that apparently had laid out there all-night suffering. At noon the next day he was still alive and conscious. He was lying on the ground. On the left side of his face, we could see nothing but a clot of blood. On the right side of his face, his eyeball was hanging out of its socket. With his one good hand he was feeling for his other mangled hand, which still had two fingers. He would count his two fingers, "Ein, Swie," as he searched for the others that weren't there. On top of all this, he had a nasty wound in the thigh. How he survived this long and still was conscious was almost a miracle.

John, a fellow from the 1st Platoon, was with us. John was a German who had left Germany in 1938, for he hated Nazism and everything connected with it. John said something to the mortally wounded Jerry in German as he reached into his first aid packet and brought out a tube of morphine. Then in English he says, "Here iss something goot for you," as he shot morphine into the arm of his suffering ex-countryman and soldier. He had killed many of his ex-countrymen during his combat of this war, but not enough to suit him. John had two brothers in Germany. One of the fellows asked John what he would do if he would run into his brothers in this war. "I would kill them like anyone else," John replies sternly.

From there I went over to the building the company was using for a C.P. When I went into the room, I see the men from company HQ were most all in the room. Some of them were cleaning their rifles. There was a crack from a carbine and a chunk of plaster off the wall immediately behind me fell to the floor. One of the men from Company HQ's carbine was accidentally fired. The trajectory of that bullet didn't miss my head over two inches. Big Jake, 1st Platoon Sergeant, was lying on an old bed in the room sleeping peacefully, when another man from Company HQ accidentally pulled a pin from a grenade, and rolled it under Jake's bed. Bang! It exploded. Big Jake woke up somewhat startled, looked at the man from CO HQ and says calmly, "Cripes. If it's my job you're after, okay, but don't go about it that way." Big Jake and I then decide it may be safer up fighting the Krauts than to be in a house occupied by the CO HQ, so we go back to our units.

About 2 o'clock that afternoon we get word to attack to the left of where we are now. Our objective is only about a mile to the left of us. It's a group of farm buildings at the base of a hill. We can see them plainly from this position. We don't believe there are any enemy in this sector. Nevertheless, we take the usual precaution by advancing on the objective tactfully, with assaulting platoons going in skirmishes. The machine gun section sets up on a knoll to cover the advancing rifle platoons and give supporting overhead fire if necessary. We watch the rifle platoons get to the objective without a shot being fired. We then take our guns out of action and proceed to the objective. When we get there, we find most of the company lying around the farm buildings leisurely brewing mud and cooking up.

That night we learn that other units are now out in front of us putting us in a sort of semi-reserve, so we bed down in an old barn and make ourselves comfortable for the night. Next day we clean our weapons and make our requisitions.

The Little King has now reached his lifelong aim, that of being a commissioned officer, as he went back to a rear division where they pinned brass bars on him and pronounce him a 2nd Lieutenant. He is transferred to M Company following in the footsteps of his brother Black Rufe. 1st Sgt. Groble is now in full command as the first soldier of K Company. Lt. McGinn, who is acting as company commander in Lt. Knox's absence says, "I'm sure sweating it out. Knox can't come back soon enough to suit me." We get a new 2nd Lieutenant by the name of D'mitri transferred in from M Company to succeed Lt. Wigle as 4th Platoon leader.

An epidemic has hit the machine gun section. Brady, Jewit and Midnight all went back to the medic's dead sick. I tell Old Allah to take charge of Brady's squad. We get attack orders that night. We're now up to the Germans' strongly fortified winter line that is located in some of the ruggedest part of the Apennine Mountains. This line is known as the Gothic Line, a fortified line that "Smiling Albert" Kesserling has been preparing ever since the initial landings at Salerno. We are told we're not going to make a whole scale on this line, but individual companies will infiltrate through the line. Disorganize and route our Jerries in that manner, as our G-2 maps show the Gothic Line to be very deep but irregular.

As we are lined up ready to go, Old Allah asks everyone he sees, "Are you going to give the supreme sacrifice this time?" That reminded me of what John L. Sullivan, the West Virginia hillbilly, used to say in his southern accent, "The Bible say the lion and the lamb went up the hill. It say the lion came back, but don't say nuttin' about the lamb. And that's the same thing gonna happen to you if you keep going up these hills. Some day you ain't comin' back either." We put out our last cigarettes and start marching single file over a high rugged mountain that is dense with brushy forest. Just to walk over this terrain in daylight with no load would be difficult, let alone total darkness. We had to maintain contact with the man ahead of us or we would be lost. Sometimes the head of the column would go to fast for the heavily loaded weapons platoon which was in the rear.

We would have to pass the word up the column, "Not so fast. 4th Platoon losing contact." The head of the column would then stop and soon pass the word back, "Are they all caught up yet?" and soon we are on the go again. We were coming down off the steep, rugged mountain and it was hard to hold back to keep from plunging to the bottom. It was full dawn when we finally reached the bottom and start up another hill. We get about half way up the next hill when they lay artillery on us. We then disperse and dig in the best we can in the almost solid rock. Here we sweat out another day when you want to blow your top, but somehow you manage to hang on.

Here we find the Jerries are using "screaming meemies" again—the German name for the six-barreled mortar that heaves a projectile about the equivalent of our 105 mm, is Neblewerfer. This is the first time we have run into any since Anzio. At Cassion the Jerries almost drove us all psycho with them. We call them Screaming Meemies on account of the weird, demoralizing sound they put out. They fire six rounds, one after another. They are electrically discharged, and when they are set off it sounds like someone is cranking them out on a machine that has badly worn gears. The six shells have a wide dispersion and pack a terrific wallop. The one consolation we have is that they aren't very accurate.

Shortly after dark that night they lay another concentrated barrage on us, inflicting more casualties. The 2nd Platoon was hit the hardest. Among their casualties was John, the fugitive from Nazism. Lt. McGinn was wounded and Ike, the company radio man was critically wounded. Lt. Hayden just returned from a five-day pass in time to take over as company commander, succeeding wounded Lt. McGinn. We remain in this position this night. Next day we sweat it out again, having more casualties, until about 5 o'clock when we organize to infiltrate. We withdraw off this hill and follow a gully to the right, go over another hill where we reach a big ravine where we receive some mortar fire.

It's pitch dark when we get out of the ravine and into the open. We travel slowly and very silently. Each man takes as much interval as he can without losing contact. Yes, we were infiltrating all right, for we had already went a good distance into the Gothic Line. Many yards possibly, even miles, to our rear we could hear the report of rapid firing Jerry machine guns that we had by-passed. One consolation we had was that no enemy artillery would fall on us. We had went quite a ways when a bright flare went off right above us. We all hit the dirt and remained motionless. When the first flare went out, they sent up another one.

We lie perfectly still on the ground for about a half hour. They evidently didn't see us, for we received no fire. It was going to get daylight pretty soon, so we had to do something. We couldn't be caught in the open in daylight right in the heart of Jerryland. We shifted to the right to a wooded area that had sort of a shallow ditch in it that afforded us fair concealment. Here one lonely American infantry company set up an all-round security defense right in the heart of a Corp area of the Wermacht.

It was beginning to get cold and misty. Fortunately for us, visibility was poor and that was one of our prize assets at this particular time. We are here about an hour lying low and silent, but very much on the alert when in walks five Jerries very unconcerned. We get the drop on them as they are right inside our perimeter. We capture them without making too much noise. They were very much astonished to be greeted by a company of Yanks in what they thought was their rear area. They think that there may have been an airborne landing behind their lines. We never had to fire a shot all day.

As evening drew near, we had captured close to a dozen prisoners who just politely dropped. We found out where F Company from the 2nd Battalion was and sent our prisoners to them. At 5:00 we began to infiltrate still deeper. We are moving along in a thick mass of brush when I hear a snap as a branch of the tree above me was shot off, and machine gun bullets were landing all around us. We hit the dirt. The fire was coming from our direct rear. One man from the 3rd Platoon was killed instantly by the sudden spray of bullets. We get up to advance again. We don't go far when forward elements of the company run into some Jerries. There was a brief but furious exchange fire and we continue on our mission.

When I get to the place where the skirmish had taken place, I see three dead Jerries sprawled out on the sloppy wet ground. We shift to the left and go up a small wooded hill where we silently dig in our self-secure defense for the night. Early next morning we walked up to our position. We called for them to surrender, but they objected and started firing on us with "Schmitzer machine pistols." As we dug in and they were in the open, we had the edge on them. Shortly after that, they are lying harmlessly dead in front of our position. If any in my pack. Jerries seen us here, we done our best to kill them. Otherwise, they would report our position, which may mean that the whole company could probably be wiped out or captured.

We are getting hungry now as we are getting low on rations and little hopes of getting any for a while. My section was now very small, and so many had went to the medics with wounds and sickness. P.J. had also went back to rear division to act as a witness to a court martial. I told Adams to take charge of P.J.'s squad during his absence. Oscar, Jimmy the Fence and Westbrooks were the only other men left in the squad. In the 1st squad only Old Allah, Bartlett, Fahr and The Hick remained. Later on, that day I found a can of C ration biscuits in my pack. One can contains five biscuits. By breaking each piece of the hard tack in two, each man in the section could have half a biscuit, and that's what we done. Each man licked his chops after devouring his morsel of hard tack that would never be eaten if there was anything else. Late that afternoon we can see some of our infantry attacking to the left of us and cutting diagonally in front of us.

We feel much better. We know now that we are no longer alone out in Jerryland as the whole line moved up and passed by where we were. We all hope that we will never have to infiltrate again. That night Big Barnsmell Slink comes up with his mules loaded with rations and water. "Big Barnsmell, you are a hero." Old Allah cries out joyfully at the sight of food and water. "I thought you crazy bastards had infiltrated all the way to Berlin. The Colonel didn't even know where you were," Big Barnsmell retorts.

After the rations and water is distributed, we are on the march again going forward and to the right to where we were. Big Barnsmell follows along to make sure he doesn't lose us again. We are not exactly on the attack as we are to move up behind the 2nd Battalion's newly conquered position. We get to the base of a big mountain, dig in and set up our guns as we don't know for sure what the deal is. I only have two men from the section on guard at a time.

Next day we learn that there are friendly troops on top of the ridge above us, so we relax and spend the day in reserve. Lt. D'mitri takes a patrol out to try and contact the 91st Division. I take the 2nd machine gun squad up the hill and set up to cover the patrol. We remain in this position again this night. Next day Lt. Knox returned after being on detached service to the Brazilian forces for quite some time. We all wonder when the "coffee merchants" will come up to the line. Lt. Hayden is happy over Knox's return as he no longer has the responsibility of being company commander. Here the machine gun section gets bigger again as several men returned from the hospital.

Darkness finds us again on the move. We wind our way over mountains and down gullies till we come to a group of abandoned buildings. Lt. Knox likes his comfort, so we decide to remain in these buildings until dawn when we make an attack on Hill 813. It's cold and rainy and we are glad to get some shelter. I got three men transferred to the machine gun section from the rifle platoons. They are namely: Lusk, Kaughman and a tall slim fellow from the Lone Star State that we call Tex. At dawn we're on the attack. The 2nd Platoon is the assaulting platoon so the machine gun section is naturally attached to them. It's a nice sunny day. We do a good distance single file when the Jerries open up on us with machine gun fire. There is a gully ahead of us, so we make a mad dash for it. The entire company is soon in the gully.

Lts. Knox, Hayden and Morgan try to figure out a method to attack the hill. It is finally decided that Lt. Morgan will lead the 2nd Platoon in the assault on the hill. At the base of the hill are two houses that are apparently full of Jerries, as machine gun fire has been pouring from them all day. We set our machine guns on the bank and start firing at the houses to support the 2nd Platoon. Lt. Morgan comes up to where the guns are just before he starts the attack. "Keep firing into the windows of the houses. If you can silence the guns, it'll help a lot," Lt. Morgan tells me.

Lt. Morgan is a very good officer. He has the friendship and admiration of all the men in his fighting 2nd Platoon. "We'll keep 'em hot, Lieutenant," I tell him as he starts the assault. We kept 'em hot, all right. We ran through most of our basic load, which is 2400 rounds. We silenced the guns firing from the windows. I like our Browning machine guns. Not just because I'm a machine gunner, but because it's the most accurate long range small arms weapon on either side. Every burst is put right where it is aimed. We done some very accurate firing that day. We now can see the 2nd Platoon closing in on the houses from the right, so we have to cease firing for the protection of our own men. The 2nd Platoon Sergeant Earl Smith called back by radio, "Objective taken."

We take our guns out of action and move up to the two newly taken houses. It's dark now, and we don't attempt to take the rest of the hill, but build up a defense at the base of it around the buildings. Several men from the fighting 2nd Platoon were killed on this attack. Lt. Morgan is missing. No one from the 2nd Platoon seems to know what happened to him. Next morning, his dead body was found to the left of the house. Another gallant man had given his life so that a hill could be taken.

That morning most of the company is grouped in and around these two small buildings. The Jerries are still on top of Hill 813, which we now call Cemetery Hill, as there is a cemetery and a shrine on this hill. The mortar section are firing their mortars on the Jerry positions on top of this hill. Sgt. Jack Plumber, an expert mortar man, scored a direct hit on a Jerry machine gun nest. It was about noon when we organize to make an assault on the hill. The 3rd Platoon is to be the assault platoon. We are getting a lot of machine gun fire from the left, so I take the 2nd squad which is led by Adams at the present time. We pick our way half way up the hill, then set up to silence the fire coming from the left as the 3rd Platoon assaults the hill.

Pete leads the attack. The 1st machine gun squad, which is now led by Old Allah, is left in mobile reserve to be used wherever necessary. As we fire to the left, we can see the brave riflemen advance slowly up the hill. I seen Big Jim sneak up to a Jerry position and pull the gun right out from under a Jerry's nose and demand, "Come on out." The 3rd and 1st Platoons took the hill and were now reorganizing on their newly taken objective, but I knew they had several casualties in the battle.

I look up the trail and see O'Neal come running down the hill. "What's the trouble, O'Neal?" I ask. "Our squad started on the attack. They caught us in the open and poured it on us. Portman is wounded bad. Bartlett is too, but he ain't as bad as Portman's," O'Neal replies. "Where's Old Allah?" I ask. "He's fixin' Portman and Bartlett's wounds. They're only up ahead a little ways." I then follow O'Neal up to where they was. Bartlett had a leg wound, but was able to walk. But Portman would have to be carried, as he was wounded in the chest and right arm badly. "There's no need to take the rest of the squad up the hill.

If Pete needs machine gun support, I'll ask the CO if he will ----- M Company's water-cooled guns up," I tell Old Allah, as his squad is now very small. Old Allah, O'Neal, Fahr and I then put Portman on a shelter half and carry him back to the C.P.

We find Lt. Knox is also wounded, so Lt. Hayden is again in charge of the company. Pete comes down off the hill and tells us it won't be necessary for the machine gunners to come up the hill until they can travel under the cover of darkness. When darkness came, I go up the hill with Old Allah's squad. We set the gun up right on the edge of the cemetery. In the moonlight I can see two knocked out Jerry tanks below us. I then go back to Adams' squad and help them out on guard.

I am on guard at the gun when Sgt. Sam and Doc, a medic from the 3rd Platoon, come by carrying rations. When they get about a hundred yards away from me, I hear the explosion of a hand grenade. Then a cry "Help! Help!" At first, I wondered if they have been ambushed by a Jerry patrol, but the grenade sounded like ours. I make a dash to where they were. When I get there, Leo and Macky are already there. Doc is already dead. Sgt. Sam is crying in pain. After examining him, we find the cheeks of his buttocks blown to shreds. We put him on a shelter half and carry him down to the C.P.

The wound was caused by grenades he was carrying in his canteen pouch. The pin from one of these grenades evidently accidentally got pulled and exploded the grenades. One of the fragments from the grenade hit Doc in the temple, killing him instantly. Sgt. Sam had a nasty wound, however he eventually came out of it okay for some time later I seen him in Naples, as he was transferred to P.B.S.

The next day we start on the attack again. We wind our way to the right and forward of Cemetery Hill and enter a small, pretty well-beaten-up village by the name of Briscoli. There we encounter some opposition consisting mainly of sniper fire coming from various buildings throughout the village. By the time we get the village cleared, it is dusk. The machine gun section moves in and sets up in a large church on the forward edge of town for the night. We receive a good deal of heavy artillery during the night, but no casualties were inflicted.

Next morning, we have another one of those cold, misty rains as we continue to move northward. We travel a good distance through slush, mud and water when we come to an old Italian farm. The entire company then jams into the larger barn to get out of the miserable weather, take a break and cook up. While we are in this barn, Old Allah finds a chicken. He takes the hen to a pile of hay, makes a nest for it and the hen settles herself in peacefully. Old Allah lies down beside her, patting her and saying, "Now be a nice little red hen and produce for Old Allah." About a half hour later, Old Allah emerges with a nice, shiny egg saying, "And it ain't dehydrated either," as he proceeds to cook the rare hen fruit.

Shortly after that we are on the move again, advancing on the hill which is our objective. After routing out a few Jerries, the hill is ours. This hill is not very high, but is covered with a thick mass of brush that is difficult to walk through and easy to get lost in. At the base of this hill is a barn and a house. All those who are not on guard are sheltered from the miserable weather in these two buildings. When darkness drew near, Lt. D'mitri, Pete, Big Jake and myself go up the hill to view the situation and plan a defense for the night.

One valuable asset an old soldier has is that he can instinctively tell if a situation is dangerous, requires close guard or relax, they have left. They don't want this hill anyhow, for it is of no tactical value to them. Pete, Big Jake and I, after viewing the situation, unanimously choose the latter. Lt. D'mitri, however, being a comparatively new officer, as yet has not acquired this battle instinct and wants to set up a secure defense.

He asks if I can set up a machine gun by compass to fire a certain azimuth as visibility was zero. Pete, being the spokesman of our group says, "It's useless to set up here. We would just disorganize our own outfit by doing so. The hell with the hill. Let's go back down and organize a security at the base of the hill," and that is what we done. 🐂

MOVE BACK TO BRISCOLI

We bed down comfortably in the old barn and spend a peaceful night. Next day we spend cooking up and batting the breeze in the shelter of the old barn. About noon Lt. Hayden receives a message in code over the 300 radio from battalion HQ.

We gather around, and when the code was deciphered, it read: "Move back to Briscoli for rest. 3rd Battalion now in regimental reserve." We are happy, and lose no time packing up. Soon we are on the march through the still cold, misty rain, only this time to the rear of the regimental reserve position in the village of Briscoli.

When we get to Briscoli, we immediately set out in search of buildings that would give us shelter from the cold rain. The houses were pretty well battered from the ravages of war, and most of them leaked from the roof to the bottom floor. We found two fairly dry rooms for the two machine gun squads and one large room for the mortar section. Leo then told me to secure a place for the platoon C.P. With the aid of my all-purpose man Macky, we found a basement full of brush wood and immediately proceed to clear it out.

After working for about a half hour, we have a comfortable "boudoir" rigged up. Leo was mighty pleased with the C.P., so Croatenpecker, Leo, Macky and myself soon make ourselves very comfortable. We also have a neighbor in the room next to us, as Einer, the company mail clerk, has established his post office there. Macky goes to work for Einer as assistant postmaster general. Although Einer has not been previously, it certainly is not because he's no prominent man in K Company, but on the contrary, he's one of the most popular men in the Company.

He's one of the original old men, and is the first with whom I became close friends with in K Company. I first met Einer when we were both newly inducted rookies on the train ride from Fort Snelling to Cam Claiborne. In Claiborne we were tent partners. About the closest way I can describe Einer is that he's the essence of good nature. He's a bespectacled little fellow about 30 that could easily pass for 20. You seldom see him when he hasn't a big smile on his face, singing "Hotcha Chonia" in his happy-go-lucky way. He's one of the big morale boosters in the company, and is highly efficient as a mail clerk. All the men in the company turn to him for letters from home, and Einer is the man who sends the boys' money home safely via P.T.A. Yes, Einer is indeed everyone's friend.

The first night in Briscoli Old Allah brings over a half dozen chickens with their heads neatly chopped off and asks me, "Can you fry 'em?" "I sure can," I reply. We get lard, flour, salt and pepper from Ploopie and proceed to fry the tender chicken in mess kits over Coleman stoves. By midnight it was all fried and a delicious feast was enjoyed by all present. Old Allah was so full he didn't even go back to his own quarters, but crawled in bed with Macky and I.

One day as we are loafing around the C.P., someone walks in and Leo bellers, "Attention." I look up and see none other than Pete, who is sporting brand new gold bars. "They sure as hell aren't very particular who they pin 2nd Lieutenant on these days," we razz Pete. "I only took em' for the whiskey ration every month," Pete replies. In spite of the razzing we give Pete, we are all glad to see him get the commission for he certainly has earned it and will make a good officer.

Later that day all non-coms are called up to the company C.P. to meet our new company commander. When we all get assembled in the C.P. room, Lt. Hayden introduces us to the new officer as Lt. Arie. After Lt. Arie says a few words, Lt. Hayden informs us of the death of Lt. Wigle. There fell a moment of silence throughout the room. There seemed so little any of us could do for such a great man that gave the supreme sacrifice in action above and beyond the call of duty. After the meeting was dismissed, we immediately proceed to write up a recommendation for the posthumous award of the CONGRESSIONAL MEDAL OF HONOR for the valorous Lieutenant.

Brady once again returned from the hospital, which he has made frequent trips to for the last several months. It's plain to see that Brady is no longer the steady, reliable, ever-present warhorse of days gone by. When he returns from the hospitals, he says the medics cannot find anything wrong with him physically, but his buddies didn't have to be doctors with high degrees to know there was something wrong with him. We would watch him walk all doubled up. He would only nibble on food, and lines on his face are getting deep. He's no longer the fiery, ambitious Brady we had known for years. The medics told him he just had a nervous stomach and ordered him back to the outfit, but we knew Brady had just been through too many battles. Offhand, I would say that Brady had seen more combat than 90 percent of American soldiers and was like a machine that was old and worn out from hard, abusive use. However, to some rear echelon people in authority, he had not yet done enough for his country and was sent back for more use.

During the days in Briscoli, I spend much of my time visiting with the two old faithful privates in the machine gun section. Outside of P.J. Ortman and Brady, the two squad leaders, they are the only living symbols present today of the colorful old machine gun section of days gone by. These old privates are Old Allah, who has been acting as squad leader off and on for over a year, and Oscar Kotz, who received the nasty leg wound back at Mt. Pantano, who still goes about his duties as gunner in his good natured, nonchalant way. Being with these two old faithful privates brings back memories of the other colorful men that had dropped out one by one—like Old Tom, the Homely One, Miss Polda and Lloyd Doe. I think to myself now, If I lose Old Allah and Oscar, my morale will hit a new low.

While we are in Briscoli we receive our winter issue of clothing. Mud packs, combat suits, wool sweaters and fur caps. It's good warm clothing all right, but how we will be able to maneuver around with all of it has us guessing. I have come to the conclusion that it's almost an utter impossibility to clothe an infantry man properly. If he has enough clothes to keep him warm standing those long, cold, wet hours on guard on a wind-swept mountain, the next day on the attack, them same clothes will bind him up like he's tied to a pole. And being unable to maneuver and move quickly on the attack is like sending an invitation to an undertaker.

We are in Briscoli five days when we get orders to move up to the front again. It's a cold, rainy, miserable day when we get on trucks that take us through a muddy trail to an assembly area by a group of farm buildings. The entire company manages to crowd into these buildings to seek shelter from the miserable weather. The Italian people in these houses offered us the best hospitality they could. At dusk we get orders to move. It was still cold and rainy as we organized, drew rations and ammo. Leo went to the medics, so I was left in charge of the platoon.

We March all night in the sloppy mud. Dawn found us entering a small village where we stopped. The company C.O. told us to find some buildings to shelter our respective platoons. After finding a suitable place for the mortar section and ²/₃ of the machine gun section, I take one half of the machine gun squad into the room to be used as the platoon C.P. I figure there would be room for half this squad in the room, as Lt. D'mitri platoon leader and Macky platoon radio man and myself were the only other occupants.

Fahr, Jewit and Bartlett were the men I took into the C.P. Fahr found a bed and made it up nice and comfortable, when in walks Lt. D'mitri with Lt. Booth, new platoon leader of the 1ˢᵗ Platoon and his radio man. "What are these men doing in the C.P.?" Lt. D'mitri asks. "They are going to be in here with us as it is too crowded where the rest of them are," I reply. "Well, they're going to have to move out 'cause Lt. Booth is going to have his C.P. in here too," Lt. D'mitri retorts.

I can only recall a few times during my combat career that rage overwhelmed me, but this was one of them times. I bust out, "Stay where you are, men! As long as I'm acting platoon sergeant of this platoon, this platoon comes first. If there's any room after we get settled, okay. But none of our men will get out to make room for men from another platoon." "You seem to forget you're not in complete command of this platoon, Walund. You're just a non-com. Lt. Booth and I are commissioned officers, and we are the ones that will give the orders," D'mitri replies smartly.

It was then I blew my lid. "Officers, hell! Neither one of you would make a pimple on a buck private's ass. I have certainly associated with good officers, but you mugs don't come in that category at all. Now, you can go up and tell the Old Man what I said and have me busted." "Now let's talk sensible, Walund. You can't blow up like this. Maybe there is room for all of us in here," the Lieutenant replies in a calmer way. "There's not room for me in all this chicken shit," Fahr drawls out in his southern accent as he leaves the room, followed by Jewit and Bartlett. I figure I have said to much so I shut my mouth and go down to talk to the men in the machine gun section. If I lost the respect of the two Lieutenants, I certainly won it back from Fahr, Jewit and Bartlett. They never did forget that episode.

Four o'clock that afternoon finds us packed up and, on the move, again. It's dusk when we come to some farm buildings. The company disperses into the various buildings and bed down for the night. Next morning, we are able to get a good view of the terrain that lies ahead of us. About 1800 yards in the valley ahead of us lies a small village. Beyond this village was one prominent landmark that stood out from everything else. The landmark was an enormous mountain. The sides of the mountain were nothing but sheer cliff.

Because of its enormous size, it appeared relatively close but we all knew it was several miles away. We look on a map and see that the name of this huge mountain is Monte Armichi, and from G-2 reports it is a Jerry stronghold and is the dominating ground for miles around. Through a clearing to the left of Monte Armichi we can see the wide expanse of the fertile Po Valley. From what we could see of the valley from this faint distant view, it looked beautiful. Level as a table and literally dotted with brightly-colored buildings. Right at the gateway to the po Valley and at the base of the rugged Apennines, we can see part of a large city. This was the city of Bologna which we were told was our ultimate objective when we went into the line just north of Florence last September.

Now we are close, yet desperately far from the prime objective. Once we get Balogna and a foothold in the Po Valley we could be able to make a mad dash on northward, clearing practically all the remainder of Italy infested with Nazis until we come to the next barrier, the Alps and Brenner Pass. This potential advance across the Po Valley could be much like our rapid advance north of Rome last June. It would be ideal terrain for armor to work in, and ideal armor terrain in Italy is about as rare as a nice guy in an S.S. regiment.

We stay in this position this night. Next day is still raining. As we are lying around in the old barn batting the breeze, a runner comes in and says Old Allah and Big Barnsmell Slink are wanted back at the company C.P. I believe I got to my feet before either Old Allah or Big Barnsmell did. I looked at the two old faithful privates who had for so long had been such big morale builders in the platoon and said, "So long, fellas, it's been nice knowing you." Old Allah just says, "What in the hell did we do now?" and they went out the door. The minute the runner delivered the message I somehow knew they were the ones selected to go home on this month's quota of rotation or T.D., and when they returned, I found my hunch was right.

All Old Allah and Big Barnsmell had to do now was wait for evening to come when Ploopie would bring rations. Then they would ride back to the kitchen and prepare to go home. "It would kinda be too bad if the kitchen truck got a direct hit from an artillery shell on the way back, being you guys are so close to going home," Oscar chides them. The Little King Stratmoen, who has been leading a machine gun platoon in M Company for the past few months, is one of the officers from the battalion selected to go home. Pete, who has just been made a 2nd Lieutenant, takes over the Little King's old job in M Company.

You would think Old Allah and Big Barnsmell would be so happy they would jump for joy over the fact they are going home, but on the contrary. They mope around like they've lost their last friend. I guess they were just now feeling the sentiment of leaving their old buddies. As they left that night, we bid them goodbye and good luck. "Don't wish us good luck. You guys are the ones who need it," was Old Allah's parting words.

Next day finds us still in the same position. I already miss the presence of Old Allay and Big Barnsmell. To relieve the emptiness of the atmosphere, I brew a C ration stew with Oscar. I'm glad Oscar is still around to BS with. After that, I go over to the mortar section to chew the rag with Sgt. Jack Plumber, one of the old-time original men who is almost certain to be the next one to go home from the company. Jack was the one that was cited for gallantry at the Lanuvio counter attack by being the first one to sight and realize the vicious threat. He was awarded the Silver Star for that deed. "Well! Just about 30 more days and I suppose you'll be going home, Jack," I say. Jack just puffs on his ever-present pipe and says, "It will be a cold day in July when I go home," in his calm way.

About 4 o'clock that afternoon we are alerted to move as soon as darkness offers us enough concealment to do so. We are to relieve the 2nd Battalion in place, who are somewhere between the village and Monte Armichi. When Ploopie comes up with rations, he has Leo with him. Leo had just returned from the medics, and I drew a sigh of relief and was glad that Leo was back to take over the platoon. I now return to my own little machine gun section.

It's plumb dark as we marched through the village and continue our trek northward on a winding road. The night was turning cold and misty as we turned off the road into a huge bushy gully or ravine. We are now unable to see our hand in front of our face as pitch black darkness prevailed in this jungle-like ravine this cold misty night. Every man had to have his hand on some part of the man in front of him in order to maintain contact, and even then, it was difficult. We were moving at a snail's pace. In places the brush was so dense, openings had to be cut with bayonets. The ground was irregular—big drop-offs, huge boulders and steep banks to climb.

The only way we could get over these steep banks was for the man on top to lower the stock of his rifle to the man below and help pull him up over the obstacle with his rifle. Every once in a while, you would hear a thump and a splash, after which you could hear the angry disgusted voice of a doughboy murmur lowly, "God damn son of a bitch anyhow." Several times we are forced to backtrack a couple of hundred yards and hit it from another angle. It was still misting, but we could now see the man in front of us more plainly, as there was beginning to be a tint of grey in the little bit of sky, we were able to see through the openings in the brush. A few minutes later, it was full dawn and we stop.

When we look back over the terrain we had just covered in the black darkness, we wonder how the hell we done it with our heavy loads of machine guns and ammo. We find some empty holes that the 2nd Battalion had evacuated, and immediately put them to their proper use as shells were now bursting in the general area. We take turns brewing mud on the four Coleman stoves we have in the section as we await further orders somewhat skeptical of what they might be.

After resting about an hour, we get attack orders. At the end of this weird ravine is a hill. It isn't a very large one. The number of it on the map is #410. This is to be our first objective, a stepping stone to Monte Armichi, which is the prime objective. The 2nd Platoon is to be the v platoon. We set our machine guns up to cover their advance. The 2nd Battalion had apparently taken a beating in this gully, as several bodies of G.I.'s are scattered throughout the gully. Almost automatically everyone started to call this weird gully Death Valley. The name stuck, and as time went on the name became more and more appropriate.

From behind our guns, we watch the riflemen of the 2nd Platoon advance cautiously up the hill. They're about a third of the way up the hill when Jerry machine guns open up on them, and a mortar barrage lands throughout the skirmish line. We open up with our machine guns, firing at what we thought would be the most suitable for their guns, for it was impossible to accurately pick out their perfectly camouflaged positions. The 2nd Platoon took a beating and were forced to withdraw with heavy casualties. Later on, that day, different tactics for taking were doped out. The 3rd Platoon is to maneuver to the right flank following the brushy right bank of the ravine. My machine gun section is attached to the 3rd Platoon on this deal.

It's at 1600 hours when we push off with Sgt. Haugen leading the attack with his 3rd Platoon. We pick our way forward about 800 yards when we get a message over our 536 radios to halt the attack and build up a defense where we are. By the time we get dug in it's dark. Brady is all curled up in a knot with his nervous stomach, and Fahr is sick. I tell them both to go back to the medics, leaving the section somewhat depleted as a couple of the newer replacements had somehow disappeared during the course of events. I tell Jewit to take over Brady's 1st Squad. We're out of rations, and it would be a hopeless effort to try and find the ration dump in this jungle-like terrain on a jet-black night such as this, so we decide to wait until morning.

When morning came, I decide to go on a reconnaissance in search of the ration dump. I take only one man along, Tex Lewis. We go back to where we were the previous day and find the group from company HQ lying around brewing mud. I see broken up cases of rations. I find two boxes with the famil- iar four strips of tape on them, identifying them as property of the 4th Platoon. After the four strips of tape were the initials "M.G.", so I knew they belonged to the machine gun section. Ploopie was always good at making sure each outfit got the right rations. At the ration dump was Midnight Mancia, one of my men that had just returned from the hospital. I was glad to have him back, but hated to see him come at a time like this, for I knew things were bound to get rough soon.

I go over to 1st Sgt. Groble, who looks more like Abe Lincoln than Able looked like himself, and ask him if he has any news. "The company C.O. is back at battalion HQ getting the dope now," Groble replies and then asks, "How many men you got missing?" That's one question Groble never fails to ask. Midnight, Tex and I then start trudging up the side hill with the rations to where the rest of the section is anxiously waiting for grub. As we are eating our C-ration breakfasts, we get orders to continue our attack on Hill 410 with the 3rd Platoon.

As soon as we get organized for the attack, the plan is again changed. The 3rd Platoon gets orders to remain where they are for the time being. The machine gun section is to pull back into the draw and join the 1st Platoon, which is going to attack the hill by frontal assault in much the same manner as the futile of the 2nd Platoon yesterday. After getting the final dope, Big Jake, 1st Platoon Sergeant says, "Let's go," and the 1st Platoon is on its way. Sgt. McCarthy, right guide of the 1st Platoon, brings up the rear, and I follow him with my machine gun section.

I follow echelon to the right rear of the 1st Platoon. We're about half way up the hill when we receive our first machine gun fire. The machine gun section makes a mad dash to a rock bank to the right. We immediately set up our guns and commence firing at a Jerry machine gun nest we have spotted. We keep the Kraut gun somewhat silenced as the 1st Platoon continues to advance. The climax of the battle came when I see Sgt. Earl Smith sneak up to the gun we have silenced, jerk the gun out of the hole with his left hand as he blindly fires his tommy gun into the hole with his right.

Two Jerries came bounding out of the hole with their hands up frantically calling, "Comrade! Comrade!" Altogether five Jerries were captured. The rest withdrew, and Hill 410 was ours. While we were making a frontal assault on the hill, the 3rd Platoon was moving in on the left flank. Unfortunately, however, they got caught in the final protective lines of Jerry machine guns and suffered many casualties. Sgt. Haugen was among them that were critically wounded.

When darkness came it gave us an opportunity to reorganize our defensive setup. We set the machine guns up in evacuated positions of the Jerry's that was between the 1st and 3rd Platoons. After we get a fairly stable defense organized, I see Big Jim, who has taken over the 3rd Platoon after Sgt. Haugen had been wounded, inspecting the position of his platoon. Big Jim is always on the ball, rough and rugged, and is always ready to try anything. Offhand, I would say Big Jim has probably killed more Jerries than any other man in the company. Big Jim is not exactly a young man to be in the infantry. He was nearing the forty mark. The first thing Big Jim says to me is, "Look here what I'm going to send home to my kid," as he shows me a Luger and a P-38 he had captured from some Jerries. "How old is your boy?" I ask. "Sixteen, and damned near as big as I am," Big Jim replies.

Just then we were interrupted by a terrific artillery and mortar barrage, and we all made a mad dash for our holes. The reason I remember that conversation between Big Jim and I is because it was the last one we ever had. The barrage was long and terrifying, but finally came to an end. And as far as I know there were no casualties, as we are well dug in. About an hour after the barrage ended, we get word to pull off Hill 410, as we're getting relieved by a regiment from the 1st Armored Division. Our reliefs, however, were not coming up on Hill 410, but were to take up positions elsewhere. We're glad to get relief from the precarious position we are in, but couldn't quite understand the deal and were somewhat reluctant to walk off and leave the hill we had so bitterly fought for totally unguarded. Whoever's idea it was, we hoped they knew what they were doing.

We lose no time getting off Hill 410 and are soon back down in Death Valley where the entire company is assembled. We start the tedious trek through jungle-like Death Valley, which is now becoming more trail worn and is less difficult to negotiate when you are going to the rear. It was a great relief when we finally pull out of the valley and onto the winding road that takes us back to the village. When we get to the village, we secure buildings to sleep in. The 4th Platoon occupies part of the same buildings as company HQ and C.P. The mortar section is downstairs and the machine gun section is upstairs.

When the machine gun section gets assembled in the small room, I now notice the presence of two men who disappeared from Death Valley. I put on a gruff look and start chewing them out thoroughly for taking off, but while I was giving them hell, I thought to myself, "I can hardly blame them. I would like to have taken off myself." I told them, "Every time a man takes off at a time like that, it makes it just twice as hard for his buddy that stays and fights." After that brief lecture, we all settle into a friendly bull session before dropping off to sleep.

Next morning Ploopie brings hot chow. Einer brings mail and Pugly brings big piles of clothing, including long-handled underwear, socks, etc. On top of that, we get a big bunch of P.X. rations, keeping us busy all day distributing these items.

About four o'clock that afternoon we get orders that take the morale out of everybody. The company C.O. called all non-coms into the C.P... Lt. Arie had a sort of haunted look on his face as he said, "I hate like hell to tell you this, men, but we're going to have to go through Death Valley again and re-occupy Hill 410." "We had it once and were ordered off. What in the hell should we take it again for?" we all want to know. "I know, but orders are orders, and we'll have to carry them out. Our artillery is going to lay down a terrific barrage preparatory to the attack. Now, go back and have your men assembled on the road in ten minutes," the C.O. replies.

I organize the machine gun section minus my two squad leaders, as Brady is in the hospital and P.J. has went to R Company with a bad back. At times like this I miss my old supernumery squad leaders Old Allah, who has went home, and Macky, who is now platoon radio man. So, I have two PFC's, who are very good, capable men, but inexperienced as squad leaders, take over the two squads. These two men are Adams and Jewit. As we are lined up on the road waiting, I get the feeling that I've been getting so much lately. I can't exactly explain it. I never used to get it in the early or middle stages of the war, but now at the mere word "attack," after hearing it thousands of times, now seems to make my stomach do a flip flop, and I want to puke but somehow don't.

The section is small now. It seems it always gets small at times like this. The men seem to take their turns going to the hospital with wounds or sickness or to the rear for some other matters. I selfishly think to myself, "Why can't I get a slight wound or light sickness and go to the rear also." I conceal my feelings by chewing the Hick in the ass for losing his hand grenades. Lt. Arie hollers, "Let's go," and we are off on another attack.

Once again, we go up the winding road, turn to the right and descend into Death Valley. We follow the valley during daylight hours so it is somewhat less difficult. We come to the opening at the other end where we see the familiar contour of Hill 410 ahead of us. We immediately set up our guns on the right bank of Death Valley to deliver overhead fire for the assaulting rifle platoons.

We heard the bark of our heavy artillery guns to our rear open up with a concentrated barrage on Hill 410. I can see the assaulting platoons are half way up the hill now. Heavy Jerry counter artillery was landing all around us now. A couple lit very close to our position. Westbrook, Lusk, Lewis and Kaufman are wounded out of the machine gun section, but were able to walk back to the medics. Leo then comes up to our guns. "How is everything here?" Leo asks. "Westbrook, Lusk, Lewis and Kaufman wounded," I reply. Leo's eyes were big with traces of tears. "What's the matter, Leo?" I ask. "They got Jack," Leo says, hanging his head. "Not Jack Plumber," I reply. Leo nods his head. Another one of the original old men who had come up to fight just too many times. In another ten or fifteen days he may have been on his way home. The hero of the Lanuvio Counter Attack. I remembered now of our last gab fest when he said, "It will be a cold day in July when I go home."

Shortly after that I receive a message that our troops have secured Hill 410 for the second time and get orders to move the machine gun section up right away. We take our guns out of action and start up the hill. Just as we walk out of

Death Valley, I see the dead body of Jack Plumber lying face down half way out of his foxhole. I stopped momentarily and looked at him. I wanted to say something, but didn't. Every other man in the section paused for a moment as they came to Jack. None of them said anything. They didn't have to. The expressions on their faces seemed to say, "So long, Jack," or "Tough luck, Jack old boy."

We follow the right slope until we reach the top of Hill 410. I expected to find that our troops had taken a beating from the artillery, but I didn't realize it was as bad as it was until I seen it with my own eyes. The first dead man I come to is Lt. Barnett, one of the new officers in our company. The others were mostly replacements. I learn that the 2nd Platoon is no longer an organized unit as only a few men remain. I then look for the holes we had dug the first time on this hill. I find mine all crumpled in by a direct hit from an artillery shell. There were only a few usable.

I learn that the 2nd Platoon is no longer an organized fighting unit, as only a few men remain. I then look for the holes we had the first time we were on Hill 410. I find most of them crumpled in from mortar and artillery shells. We set our machine guns in about the same place we had before, then lose no time convincing Hicks to dig a hole in the rocky ground.

We just get our holes dug when the Jerries lay in a terrific artillery barrage. We all hit the dirt and hug the ground for dear life. All but one, that is. That was none other than the Hick. I could hear his voice above the bursting artillery say, "Sgt. Walund, I'ma a leavin'," as he ran down the hill through one of the worst barrages I have ever seen. I think to myself he will get killed for sure, but I'm not going to get out and stop him. About a half hour later when the barrage ended, I could hear the panting voice of the Hick as he came back up the hill. "Ah ah, Sgt. Walund, where's my hole?" I was glad the Hick was alive. I think he could fall in a barrel of shit and come out smelling like a rose. Sometimes I get so mad at the Hick I could break the stock of my carbine over his flat-top head. In spite of the pest and nuisance he is, we have all learned to develop a sort of fondness for the Hick, hopeless as he is.

After the barrage ended, the remainder of the night was spent fairly peacefully. O'Neal and I just laid down in our hole. Next morning as we are heating up our C-ration breakfasts, Lt. Arie comes up with more attack orders. We are to shift to the left to the hill above Death Valley right near the winding road, then go after Monte Armichi as our final objective. So, K Company, set with only two rifle platoons and a badly crippled machine gun section, set out on another attack. There are only seven men left in the section besides myself. The machine gun section follows the 1st Platoon. The 3rd Platoon follows the machine gun section. We pick our way cautiously. When we come to the low spot between Hill 410 and the next hill, we run into a mine field. After a couple of men from the 1st Platoon receive wounds, we maneuver around and get by the mined area with no more casualties.

We pull up and stop behind the small hill near the road, which conceals us from the ----- of Monte Armichi. Lt. Arie calls us together to give us some last-minute dope. The two rifle platoons are to go right down the winding road and capture a group of buildings near the base of Monte Armichi. Lt. Arie turns to me and says, "You set up one machine gun in that old Kraut position on the forward slope of this hill to cover the advance of the rifle platoons." "But, Lieutenant, they'll spot us the minute we get out there," I come back to him. "Get 'em set up right away. We've got no time to lose," the Lieutenant replies.

With great reluctance I say, "Jewit and O'Neal, bring your gun and ammo and follow me. Adams, pull your squad behind the hill and wait." I found out later that Adams, for some reason or the other, didn't get the latter part of that order. Jewit, O'Neal and I creep on our bellies on the broad open forward slope of this hill until we come to the old Kraut positions. Even then we could hardly help from being seen as we are in perfect observation to the nearby Jerries. We get our gun set up and fully loaded as we first see our riflemen stringing up the winding road to our left of us with about a fifteen-yard interval between men. The next thing we heard was a burst from a rapid-firing machine gun coming from the buildings to the right near the base of Monte Armichi. We fire a burst back at them. Now I could see Jerries running from one building to another. I gave them a slight lead and let go with a burst. They hit the dirt. We are getting some machine gun fire back now.

All our troops are on the winding road now in their thinly scattered formation when we hear the ghastly familiar sizzle of an incoming mortar barrage.

The black puffs of smoke and dust arose one by one up and down the road followed by the crack from the explosion and the sickening hum of mortar fins flying crazily through the air. In between shell bursts I could hear a voice on the road call out, "HELP! HELP!" The voice sounded familiar. Then it came again crying, "Lange, come quick and help me." I look at Jewit and O'Neal and say, "If Lange is up there, Adams must have his whole squad there. I meant for them to stay behind this hill. I'm going back and find out."

"It sounded like Oscar's voice," Jewit replies. I then crawl back over the hill. When I get to the rear slope of the hill, I see only two men. One of these was "Blick," radio man and survivor of the beaten 2nd Platoon. "Have you seen any machine gunners back here, Blick?" I ask. "Not since I've been here," Blick replies. Blick still has his 536 radio with him, so I tell him to call the 1st Platoon and see if Adams has his squad up with them. We tried desperately to contact the 1st and 3rd Platoons and company HQ, but were unable to get any of them.

Just then, Leo pulls up to the rear of the hill with the mortar section. As soon as I start talking to Leo, they lay in another barrage on us. Fortunately, there were a few holes in the area to afford us some protection. As I look out of the hole, I see Jewit come running down off the hill. "Here, Jewit, get in this hole quick," I say. As I pull him into the hole, I see he has a wound in his arm, water is running from his eyes and nose, and he is trembling like a leaf. He could hardly talk.

"It's awful. It's awful," was all he could say at first. As I put some Sulfanilamide on his wound he managed to say, "It's awful. We got a direct hit. O'Neal is covered up." I say to Leo, "We've got to get O'Neal out." "I don't know how, but we'll sure try," Leo replies. With our shovels we run over the top of the hill. It's no use crawling anymore. When we get to the position, we can see O'Neal is buried from the waist down. His face is pale, but he's still conscious. He cries in pain, "Please get me out, please." We start digging like crazy in the ground that is packed almost like cement over O'Neal's body from the blast of the shell.

Next thing there was a terrific blast from a shell which burst only a few yards from us. By the time we hit the dirt, there was another one and another.

This kept up until Leo and I were forced to run back over the hill to seek protection temporarily, as we are unable to dig anyhow. The fire we were receiving was from a Jerry self-propelled gun that had moved up fairly close to this position and firing point blank at us with direct fire from its high velocity shells. You don't have time to duck these shells. They are on you before you can hear them. As soon as the firing ceases, we're back over the hill again digging O'Neal out. They start firing on us again, and again we have to run back. This time when we get to the rear of the hill, we see Adams.

"We're in the houses up ahead now, but---" Adams says as I interrupt him. "Who all got hit?" "Oscar is killed," Adams replies. Oscar killed, that almost took everything out of me. I turn to Leo and say, "They got Oscar, but we can't let O'Neal die too," and we are back over the hill again. As we dig, they start firing on us again. I say to Leo, "We've only got one hope, and that's that there may be a gentleman in that S.P. gun. Let's wave a flag or something to try to make them understand we are only trying to get a wounded out of here." We drag out our dirty handkerchiefs and from the ends of the barrels of our carbines, we wave the makeshift banners back and forth madly.

Two more shells land nearby. "Well, that didn't seem to do much good," Leo comments as we continue to dig. After a while, Leo says, "You notice something?" "Yup, there hasn't been a shell land here for a while," I reply. We now have O'Neal mostly uncovered. I look at him and say, "This is going to hurt pretty bad, but you're coming out," as Leo and I grab him by each arm and pull him out. The pain for O'Neal must have been almost unbearable. We carry him to the rear of the hill. Yes, there was a gentleman in that S.P. gun. You wouldn't find a guy like that in an SS regiment. We're up against the Wehrmacht here.

We drag O'Neal to a hole and get a medic to fix up his legs the best he could. At first all we could see of O'Neal's legs was balled up dirt formed into mud by blood. We rip his pants off and clean the blotted blood and ----- of his legs. The more we worked on him, the worse he looked. From the hips down, his legs appeared completely crushed with numerous smaller wounds up and down his body. Leo went back to the aid station to bring up a litter squad to carry O'Neal back.

We had to get him back soon or it would be too late. After the first aid man had dressed his wounds the best he could and administered a shot of morphine, we try to make him as comfortable as possible while awaiting the litter squad. O'Neal kept asking, "Tell me the truth. I'll lose my legs, won't I?" "No, you won't. The medics will fix you up as good as new," I reply very doubtfully telling the truth. Just then I hear Hisssss and hit the dirt just as a mortar shell lands about two yards to the right of me. The burst rolled me over on my back. Everything seemed black momentarily. Water was running from my eyes and nose as I started feeling over my body in search of wounds. To my surprise, I found none. I thought sure I must have at least one piece of shrapnel someplace. As I begin to breathe more freely, my chest begins to hurt. I've had a concussion before, but it never bothered me like this.

Leo comes up with the litter squad and they carry O'Neal away. I think to myself, Oscar is killed. O'Neal has both his legs crushed. Jewit is wounded. Only Adams, Lange, Midnight and the Hick remain in the section. And after that last mortar shell, I'm not much good myself. I turn to Leo and say, "Maybe the American Army ain't beat, but I am." "You better go back to the medics and see what they can do for concussion. Adams has three men. They can take care of one gun. Besides, they can't keep us up here much longer, weak as we are," Leo says.

Jewit and I walk back to the aid station, which is in the village. In the aid station the Doc is very busy with wounded patients. They only take care of surface wounds here, so they send me to R Company and tell me to see the regimental medics there. R Company is a new unit. Although other divisions have R Companies too now, it was originated in the 34th. Each regiment has an R Company for the purpose of taking care of men with everything from concussions to tooth aches or men unable to get the proper shoe size.

A weapons carrier from M Company takes us back to R Company, which is located in some farm buildings about two miles to the rear of the village. The name of the village incidentally is Monsuno. After reporting in at R Company, I meet my old friend Berdeen Sampson, an ex-K Company Staff Sergeant who is not on the permanent cadre in R Company. Berdeen takes me into the kitchen and has the cooks fix me something to eat. In the kitchen I meet Lt. Darling, who has been on the cadre in R Company the past couple of months also. Lt. Darling and I use to have some harsh arguments at times, but we were somehow glad to see each other now.

"Here, I got just what you need," Lt. Darling says as he pulls out a bottle of Scotch. We finish what was left in the bottle. "Now, bring out that bottle of bourbon you got stashed away in your bedroll," I say. "I wish I had one, and we should would," Lt. Darling replies. There were several old-timers from the regiment in R Company, including 1st Sergeant Derby from L Company; Buben Saboe, and old K Company man, and others. After the eats and whiskey, Berdeen takes me over to an old barn where the men are billeted. When we get in the barn a am greeted by P.J., who is here with a lame back, and "Big Gun" Dawson, a squad leader from the mortar section who is here with a toothache. When P.J. seen me, he seemed to sense that things hadn't went too well. "What happened," was the first thing he asks. When I told him, he just went outside and stood there in the moonlight, looking into space for over an hour without saying anything. Oscar and P.J. were very close friends.

The next day I go up the road to a house where the regimental medics are. My chest still bothers me. It's about nine A.M. when I go into the building. One aid man was in the building cooking coffee. "You'll have to wait a few minutes. The doctor is just getting up," he states. As I am waiting, I expect either "Captain "Bill" or Major Mills, our old regimental surgeons to come in. Instead, I see a captain come in that I had never seen before. "What's your trouble?" the captain asks. "Close shell burst concussion in the chest," I reply.

The captain then turns to his aid man and says smartly, "I don't know why I spent thousands of dollars going to medical school when other people can diagnose a case so well." That was a sarcastic remark, but I ignored it. The doctor then puts his stethoscope to my chest. "Don't seem to be anything wrong with you. How long you been in this outfit?" he asks. "Over 3 ½ years," I reply. "Well, if you've been in there that long, this isn't going to bother you. Any pain you have is strictly your imagination." That remark made my bold boil, but I was hurting. And when you hurt, you don't feel like arguing. If I felt like arguing, I need not have come there.

What really burned me up was the insult. His implication was that I might have run off in the face of the enemy or something. I had only went to the medics twice before during the course of 400 days of front line infantry combat—once for yellow jaundice and once for a wound. This incident stays marked in my memory, for this doctor inflicted a wound on me by his remarks that thousands of the enemy were unable to do with all their sophisticated weapons. Maybe he should be cited and awarded a medal from the enemy for inflicting this wound on me. I thought to myself, what a reward to get from a captain lolling in comparative safety and comfort.

I was in R Company three days when I went back to the company. I rejoin the company in the village of Monzuno where they are now located, as they were relieved the day after I left them. The company had only 32 men left when they were relieved. Big Jim Hoffman, the brave sergeant from the 3rd Platoon, was killed just below Monte Armichi. But Big Jim will be remembered by everyone in K Company for his many gallant and heroic deeds. While we are in Monzuno, some of the men return from the hospital, but beat up old K Company is still small. And as we are expecting to go back into the ---at any time, we are forced to draw some men out of the kitchen force to be used for combat duty. I get most of these men in the machine gun section. One of these men is Phees, who was my squad leader way back when. Phees looks at the sky and says, "Well, I'm right back in the machine gun section where I started from."

We are in Monzuno about three days when we get orders to move to a different sector. We are all glad we are going to a different sector instead of going back through Death Valley and Monte Armichi. We go to the right this time. We march a good distance when we enter a village. It's plumb dark, but we manage to find some old buildings to shelter us from the cold drizzle and bed down for the night. Next morning Ploopie is here with hot chow. The name of this village is Anconella. The village of Anconella is situated high on a lofty mountain perched in full view of the enemy.

We have a continuous smoke screen going between us and Jerryland to keep the Krauts from observing all the activity that takes place in crowded

Anconella. We get orders to move out at dusk to relieve the 2nd Battalion, who are in a defense position. Ploopie comes with hot chow again just before we move out. While we are eating, the Jerries lay an artillery barrage on us, resulting in The Lange getting wounded, so I lost another man out of the section.

It is dusk when we start the approach march going single file in a thinly-scattered formation up a winding road. We don't go far when they lay another barrage on us. The company splits up to seek refuge from the incoming artillery and becomes somewhat disorganized. It's about an hour before we get completely reorganized and continue our journey. We cover a good distance before we finally get to our position.

First, we come to a big building that is a house and a barn all in one. Here is where the company C.P. and the mortar section is located. There's another building forward and to the right about 500 yards, which will be occupied by the reserve platoon. About 300 yards straight up the hill from this building are our front-line positions. P.J. has now returned from R Company, so I take his 2nd squad up the hill where we set up a position in the 3rd Platoon sector. P.J.'s and Brady's 1st squad will alternate holding this position.

After P.J.'s squad is in place, I return to the C.P. where Brady has his squad. The machine gun squad that isn't on duty stays in the platoon with Leo, Macky and I. The next night Macky is sent back to the kitchen to act as mail clerk, while Einer is on a five-day pass. Macky is deputy mail clerk, so we are now without a radio man. Next day Lt. Hayden, who is company executive officer, calls me into C.P. and says, "We are going to make ap a reserve platoon with some men from the 1st and 3rd platoons, as we have no 2nd Platoon. The reserve platoon is to be called the 2nd, and you'll move down and act as platoon sergeant of this platoon.

"Although the men in this platoon will rotate, you will always remain in reserve unless you are assigned to some particular mission." This sounds like a good enough deal to me, so when darkness comes, I move down and take over the reserve platoon. The reserve machine gun squad is placed in the basement—the men from the 1st Platoon are in one room, the men from the 3rd, another smaller room is used as platoon C.P.

MANNING'S HILL

As usual, the hill we are holding gets a name. The name of this particular hill is "Manning's Hill." It's named after Sgt. Manning, a man from the 3rd Platoon who has recently been promoted to buck sergeant. And through the right process of elimination is for the present time temporarily acting as right guide of the 3rd Platoon. Being right guide sort of give Manning a big head. He is continually chewing the men of his platoon for some little thing and telling others he will promote them to sergeants. Because there are a few men of his command occupying this hill, he refers to it as "my hill," thus the name of Manning's Hill was christened to our position.

One night I get a big package in the mail. I wonder who it could be from as I anxiously remove mountains of paper in search of the contents. I finally discover two tubes of Barbasol, a roll of toilet paper, a can of C rations and a hand grenade with a note attached saying, "Ha ha, sucker." I knew then it was Macky, who is now acting as mail clerk, playing a joke on me. I spent the next three nights trying to think of some way to get even with him.

We are in this position about ten days. Every day is cold and rainy. I have had it exceptionally good, as I have been in reserve position all the while, but I have always been a little leery of that special mission which Lt. Hayden said may be assigned me. One night about 3:00 A.M. there comes a call over the sound power phone for all platoon sergeants to get on the line. It was Lt. Hayden's voice calling from the company C.P. He sounded happy and sort of excited and happy as he said, "Get this, men, get this." "What in the hell, is the war over?" I can hear big Jake, 1st Platoon Sergeant grumble. "Have your units ready to move by dusk tomorrow night. We're moving back 25 grid squares to the rear," Lt. Hayden states and hangs up.

I was happy over this and thought to myself, 25 grid squares to the rear is a long way back for an infantry outfit. I grab a pencil and paper and figure it out. A grid square is about 1100 yards. 1750 yards to a mile would make it right around 15 miles. "Hot dog," I say to myself, "looks like divisional relief when we get that far back."

We spend the next day preparing to move. At dusk I dissolve the 2nd Platoon and move back to take charge of the 4th Platoon as Leo went to the rear the previous night on a billeting detail. By midnight we are totally relieved, and the company is on the march going single file to the rear. As we march along, the cold, drizzly rain is pouring down on us. We march a good distance when we come to a village. Here, Lt. Arie tells us to find shelter for our platoons while we await trucks. We wait about a half hour when trucks come and we load up and head for our destination.

The rain was beating down on us in the back end of the six-by-sixes, but most of the men were deep in slumber. We are still riding at the first tint of dawn, and by nine o'clock we are rolling into a city. The sun is out now, and we can see this is a fair-sized town. Unlike most other Italian cities, this one is neat as a pin and totally untouched from the ravages of war. We learn the name of this town is Montecatini. We pull up to a street lined with nothing but nice big hotels, stop and de-truck.

Just then I hear Leo holler, "Bring the platoon and follow me." We follow Leo into one of the hotels where he shows us rooms that we will be billeted in—regular beds and everything. I then jab myself in the ass with a bayonet to make sure I'm not dreaming. The clean, tidy hotel rooms were soon a sloppy mess from the soaking wet, dirty combat Doggies who were so tired they flopped wherever they were and dozed off in peaceful slumber.

We spend the next couple days cleaning up and getting thoroughly dry. There isn't much excitement in Montecatini, but it gives us a peaceful rest in class. This isn't a division relief we are enjoying, but only a regimental relief so it's quite obvious that this good deal will not last very long—a week or ten days at the most.

We are here exactly one week when Lt. Arie, our company commander, calls all non-coms into the C.P. to give us the dope on our next move. Lt. Arie tells us we're moving up tomorrow morning to relieve our sister regiment, the 133rd Infantry, who are holding positions on Mt. Belmonte, which was recently captured by the 133rd in a bitter struggle. Mt. Belmonte is to the right of our previous sectors of Mt. Armichi and Anconella and is the closest point to Bologna in our lines. It's the northernmost spearhead in our lines, just eight miles south of Bologna. It's the most vital part of our lines as everything is hinged on Mt. Belmonte. We then go back to our platoons, relate the deal to the men and prepare to move.

By ten o'clock next morning we are on the move. We bid farewell to the immaculately beautiful little city of Montecatini and again head north to the bleak, cold mud, deafening artillery and chatter of machine guns, which is called the Front. It was a long, cold ride in the back end of the open six-by-sixes. By three o'clock we pull to a battered village by the name of Bararola. Here we de-truck and start marching over hills. We march a good distance when we come to a big cliff like mountain. Below this mountain is a group of pyramidal tents which we call tent city.

When we reach tent city, we flop down in the tents for about an hour's rest before we resume our trek to Mt. Belmonte. It is dusk when the company organizes and starts trudging up a huge ravine for Mt. Belmonte. We follow the ravine a good distance when we turn off onto a winding trail. Since we have went over on the defensive, the 5th Army has dug in huge search lights to the rear of our front-line positions, so now when pitch black darkness prevails, these search lights are turned on and the sky becomes illuminated in much the same manner as a full moon on a clear night.

This increases our visibility on these hazardous journeys and enables us to see pretty well what we are doing. We get to the base of Mt. Belmonte where there are some buildings. There the men of the 133rd show us to the dug-in positions and the relief is made. Here the men from all platoons rotate from occupying the positions on top of the hill to the buildings below a more or less non-perilous but tedious routine.

For this brief period, I will abridge the events that transpired and take it up in greater detail later on.

We held the defensive position on Mt. Belmonte for quite some time, then had relief at the tent city near Barbarola and a nice rest period in the village of Barbarino. Then back on the line to the left of Mt. Belmonte for a while. Spent another period in the rain and mud at tent city, then some more time in Barbarino. We then moved over near the Tyreanian coast in the Serchio Valley above Pisa near Via Reggio. This move was to back up the newly arrived 92nd Division. This was the first all colored division in combat. We were there for the purpose of backup in case a veteran division was needed. The move was uneventful, and after that we returned to our old defensive position on Mt. Belmonte.

Although this period was comparatively uneventful, peaceful and reasonably comfortable, ironically for me, this was my most trying time of the war. Outside of the kitchen help, I was about the only original man left in the company. Those who weren't killed or disabled had went home on rotation or temporary duty. I felt somewhat alone. I found myself at the tent city during chow time, taking my mess kit and going off by myself, sitting on a rock and eating alone rather than with the rest of the guys.

When non-coms were called up to the C.P. for potential attack orders, I felt sick to my stomach. When the company commander discussed plans of attack, I found myself sort of turning a deaf ear. I just didn't want to hear it anymore. I guess I was near the point of cracking, as many did before me. I really had to force myself to carry on, but that, I did. Back on the line at Mt. Belmonte, I was able to get myself together and resume combat life with renewed enthusiasm.

During this interim several other old timers have left the company, including Brady. Some of the men that had went home on temporary duty have returned to the outfit, much to their chagrin. Among these are Ole Evans, Good Deed Arneson and Lloyd Doe.

We hold down the defensive positions on Mt. Belmonte in much the same manner as we previously had done. We are here several weeks when we get orders to pull a raid or small-scale attack.

Our orders are to move out at 0400 hours. The 2nd Platoon is to proceed us one half hour. We lie down to try to sleep before taking off. Lloyd Doe wakes me up at three o'clock. We warmed up five cans of creamed beef, a new ration that Ploopie had brought up the night before, and cooked a pot of coffee. I then go over to the next room and wake P.J. and Adams. They get their men organized. P.J. follows me back to the platoon C.P. where Lloyd Doe is dishing up grub.

P.J. looks at me sort of skeptical and says, "What did you find out today, Walund?" I took another sip of mud and found our spot on the map and said, "We follow this trail to the right of the company C.P for about 1000 yards, then turn left and go up this ravine to a small ridge where the 3rd Platoon of L Company is holding a forward outpost. By the time we get there it will be pretty damn light, so the first thing we do is find cover and concealment. The 2nd Platoon has a half hour start on us.

"They should be in place, concealed along a rock wall on the forward slope of the hill. The objective is a cluster of buildings about 600 yards to the direct front of this rock wall. At 6:30 the artillery will start pasting the buildings and laying down smoke while the 2nd Platoon launches its attack. We just sit tight in L Company area. If the attack comes off successfully and the 2nd Platoon gets their objective, Ole will call us in code over the 536 radio to join them as soon as possible to help defend the position against an almost certain counter attack."

"Won't the smoke be a dead give-away?" P.J. asks. "I think it will too. Ole and I were both against it, but that's the tactics they insist on using," I reply. "Have you been anywhere near these buildings on reconnaissance," P.J. asks. "No, I haven't, and neither has Ole. And he's leading the attack," I reply. Just then Good Deed Arneson, right guide of the 2nd Platoon, sticks his head in the door and says, "We're taking off now. Next time you see us we'll either have the buildings or the shit kicked out of us." "Good luck, Good Deed," we all say.

Exactly one-half hour later we load up and take off down the trail single file. The brisk Italian winter air made stepping at a rapid pace a pleasure. There's about a quarter moon, making visibility comparatively good. Everything is peaceful and silent with the exception of sporadic crack and rumble of artillery.

We're just noticing the first tint dawn as we pull up to L Company's outpost, when we deploy along a bank and proceed to improvise rock barricades.

After that, we take turns brewing mud on the three Coleman stoves we have in the section. Macky tests his 536 radio to make sure it is okay. The 2nd Platoon is in position on their line of departure. Radio communication is limited as a matter of caution being so close to the Jerry positions. The enemy could possibly pick up our frequency. P.J., Adams and I talk to the 3rd Platoon Seargent of L Company. He says from the information they have picked up in this position, there are beaucoup Jerries out in them houses.

There was a sudden rumble to the rear, a whistle overhead and a series of cracks out in Jerryland. The barrage was on. From our position we couldn't observe where the shells struck. However, we could see the cloud of smoke above the knoll, so we knew the smoke screen was now laid down. Now it is really on. The Jerries are firing counter battery and laying in a concentrated barrage on the 2nd Platoon's line of departure. The position we are in is not vulnerable to artillery, however mortars can raise hell with us should they decide to fire them in our sector.

Macky's 536 radio is squawking and squeaking, but no words. We can now hear the rapid fire of Jerry machine guns, but still no word from the 2nd Platoon. Apparently, the 2nd Platoon's radio is out of commission, for all day we received no word from them. It was another one of those days that keeps everyone on edge. We have had no communication with the 2nd Platoon for quite some time, making us feel useless and sort of guilty just sitting back and waiting unable to do anything. Sometime later in the day a runner came sneaking back from the 2nd Platoon reporting, "They've got us pinned down so we can't move. We got a couple of direct hits. One man is killed, five wounded. Good Deed is wounded pretty bad." "How bad?" we all ask. "Both legs are in pretty bad shape," the runner replies.

Lt. Hayden and his radio man come up with orders to withdraw as soon as darkness permits us to do so. As soon as daylight began to give way to dusk, we load up and take off back to our old positions. The 2nd Platoon follows closely with litter bearers from the medics. Except for the wounded, both the

2nd Platoon and us head straight for the old rock house. The wounded men were put on an ambulance and taken to a hospital as soon as possible.

I wanted to see and talk to Good Deed before he was evacuated, but still, I didn't. This was one day that I failed to check up on Good Deed as him and I have a verbal contract to check up on each other every day. Good Deed always said, "Walund, you and I are getting pretty old now. We better keep a close check on each other from now on. There ain't many of us old guys left anymore, you know." Ole was the only other old man in his platoon. We jokingly made that agreement when Ole and Good Deed first returned from the states at the end of their tour of temporary duty, and this was the first day we missed contacting each other.

After we get settled in the old rock house, Ole comes in. He had just returned from the C.P. where he had answered numerous questions to Col. Joyce and Lt. Arie. Ole looked haggard and pretty well shook up over the casualties. Ole and Good Deed were probably as close friends as two fellers ever get. They had been 2nd Platoon Sergeant and right guide respectively ever since we first hit Anzio.

"Good Deed wanted everybody to be taken care of first before his self, and he was wounded the worst," Ole said. That's just the way Good Deed had been all through the war. Everyone else's welfare was put before his own. Whenever a dangerous situation prevailed in the 2nd Platoon, you could figure Good Deed would be right in the middle of it, along with the ever-reliable level-headed Ole.

Back at the old rock house, the spirit of the men was not too high due to the casualties of the 2nd Platoon. F Company held down our positions that night and the following day. A good rumor has just come out that we will be relieved soon. After being in this position for seven weeks, most of us older fellows are pretty skeptical and regard it more as wishful thinking.

The following night I go up with Adams' squad where we take over our old positions from F Company, who were mighty glad to get relieved. That night I stayed in one of the positions to help out on guard. Time went fast that night, for 1st Sgt. Groble would give a report on the latest Russian offensive, who are now in Marshall Ivan Konev's sector nearing the Oder River. The official word from Moscow in Stalin's order of the day was exaggerated, and Sgt. Groble would exaggerate even more.

Such as this: "Red Army advances twenty miles on a fifty-mile front, killing 30,000 German troops, knocking out 60 heavy tanks in the last twelve hours. A 600-gun salute fired in Red Square this evening." Well, we figure if one-fourth of this is true, it's still good news. 1st Sgt. Groble would get these bulletins at the company C.P. and relay them to us out in position via sound power phones. The Jerries start laying in a barrage to the unit to our left that seemed to go on for about an hour, but no more than a half-dozen rounds lit in our sector. Just before dawn, P.J. brought his squad up to relieve us, and we made our way back to the old rock house.

When we get back to the old rock house, we find everybody happy and gay, for Leo had just gotten word from the C.P. to be ready to leave for Barbarino that night on a billeting detail as we will be relieved by the 91st Division in a few days. Back to good old Barbarino. That made us all happy again. That night as Leo left, we all told him to get the same family's house for the 4th Platoon that this fine Italian family had so graciously lent us on our previous stays in Barbarino. I shall forever feel indebted to this family for their generosity and hospitality. It must have been and ordeal for them. 🐂

TO THE LAST MAN

That night I went up to our positions with Macky's squad to help out on guard. It was a peaceful night. About 11:00 P.M. while Jimmy the Fence was on the gun and Macky and I were alone in our hole drinking mud, there comes a whistle on the sound power phone. "Calling dog one." Macky picks up the phone and listens to the conversation between company C.P. and 4th Platoon C.P. Macky listens for a while with a dead-pan expression on his face. "Sgt. Groble and Lloyd Doe shootin' the shit," he says. After listening more for quite some time, he looks at me sort of funny as he hangs the phone between two sand bags.

"What's new, Mac?" I ask. He didn't answer at first. After a while he said, "Two men from the company going home on rotation." "Leo and P.J., huh?" I ask. Macky just nods in assent. I could read the expression on his face. It was one that extended sympathy to me. After some pause, Macky says, "How in the hell does it feel to be the last original man in the field left in the outfit?" I reflected on that for some time. Leo, P.J. and I were the last three men outside of the kitchen force that hadn't went home on rotation or temporary duty or disablement or death. Now, Leo and P.J. are going, leaving me to be the last man. I was glad for Leo and P.J., for they certainly deserved it. However, I cannot deny that my emotions weren't somewhat stirred. I think to myself, "Someone has to be last." I don't know how the selections are made for choosing of men to go home. However, I have often wondered.

When Macky asked how it felt to be the last man, it sent my mind reeling back to many days gone by. I can remember as a rookie taking basic training at Camp Claiborne, Lt. Col. Nelson, our Regimental Commander at that time, used to lecture to us on the history of the 135ᵗʰ Infantry regiment and how proud we should be to be a part of it.

Some incident in this history had to do with the quote "TO THE LAST MAN." I found myself now associating myself with that motto. I could remember a conversation I had with Phees on top deck of the *Aquitania* looking out one the blue Atlantic on our voyage to Ireland as the first American division to go overseas on the Atlantic side in World War II. Phees nonchalantly said, "I wonder how many of us will come back, and who will be the first and who will be the last." After all this, I now know. Anybody can thank God to get home at all. Dawn came and Adams brought his squad up to relieve us, and we are back in the same old stone house in a flash.

Next day we prepare to move out as soon as the 91ˢᵗ Division relieves us. The relief began about nine P.M. One platoon would move into place and the other would take off. The 1ˢᵗ Platoon was relieved first, then the 2ⁿᵈ and 3ʳᵈ, then the mortar section and my machine gun section was last. It was midnight before all the machine gunners from the 91ˢᵗ Company were in place, but once they were, we lost no time getting out. Company HQ had moved out sometime while the relief was in progress, so once again we were the last ones off the hill of Mt. Belmonte.

We follow the trail to the rear at a rapid pace and soon we're down at the creek bed, where we splash in and out of the water. We didn't give a damn about how wet we got. We were happy we were going to the rear. As we drew close to the tent city, we could hear the rumble of Peeps and weapons carriers and men's voices. I could tell where KL Company was assembled by recognizing voices. I heard them call for the machine gun section, and Midnight was calling my name. Soon we are right in the middle of K Company's assembly area. "Hawk Shaw" was there with a Peep to take our heavy weapons. Lt. Arie then says, "K Company, prepare to move. Orders of march, 1ˢᵗ, 2ⁿᵈ, 3ʳᵈ and 4ᵗʰ Platoons." With that, we march to our trucking area.

After marching all night, dawn found us in the village of Barbarola. Barbarola is a pretty sad looking little village indeed, being situated comparatively close to the stalemated front for quite some time. It more resembled a pile of rocks dumped into an ocean of mud than a place ever inhabited by man. Of the big church on the corner, only a religious statue remained upright unharmed. The mud in the street was about knee deep, churned up thoroughly by the trudging feet of thousands of G.I.'s and vehicles.

By about 9:00 A.M. we're on trucks heading for a town with a similar name, but a much more pleasant place to be, by the name of Barbarino. We pull into Barbarino shortly after noon. The 3rd Battalion was assigned to an area on the edge of town. K Company had a group of farm buildings. As soon as we get off the trucks, Leo come up and says, "I got a good place for the 4th Platoon." It was a good place to be billeted. There was plenty of room for the entire platoon, with a concrete floor and plenty of straw for bedding.

Next day we spend cleaning up. Renardo the Pison is busy cutting hair. I was waiting in line to have my wool chopped off, when Herr the battalion runner comes up to me and says, "I just got some hot dope from battalion C.P. You're going home too this month. It's official right from battalion. Leo and P.J. are going home on rotation, and another quota just came in to allow one more man to go home on temporary duty and that, of course, has to be you." I didn't really want temporary duty and would have preferred rotation, but I was still glad to get it and could hardly believe it.

The war, from all indications, was rapidly nearing the end. A 30-day furlough plus about 30- or 40-days traveling time would make my absence from the outfit over two months. A lot can happen in that time. The war may end while I'm gone. My hopes were high. I turn to Herr and say, "It's about time you brought me some good news. You've brought me nothing but bad news for the last two years."

Later on, that day, Leo, P.J. and I are called up to the company C.P. where Lt. Arie, Lt. Hayden and 1st Sgt. Groble tell us officially that we are going home. Lt. Arie says, "I still can't see how come you three guys from the 4th Platoon are the last old field men from the company to go home. If I had my choice, I wouldn't send you all at once, but I have no choice. Platoon sergeant, machine gun section leader and squad leader all to leave a platoon at once is not good." "The same thing happened last summer when Ole, Good Deed and From went home from the 2nd Platoon at once," Leo reminded. "Yes, but I didn't command the company then," Lt. Arie replies.

Lt. Hayden chimes in saying, "Lloyd Doe is back now and can take over again as 4th Platoon Sergeant, but who will take over the machine gun section and the two squad leaders?" "It'll have to be Macky or Adams," I reply. It was finally decided that Adams be section leader and Macky and Bartlett, the two squad leaders. When we returned to the platoon, we found it quite obvious that most of the boys didn't like to see us leave. We will remain with the company until we get official word from division to report there.

That night, P.J.'s brother-in-law, who is in a signal company in the 12th Air Force stationed at Florence, drove up in a weapons carrier. We had some Dago Red wine that night, and we all had a merry old time. Next day we go into Barbarino and visit our very good friends, the Italian family with whom we stayed the previous times we spent in Barbarino. When they see us, the men greet us heartily, bringing out the wine jug. The women cried a little, saying they had prayed that we all would come back safely and stay with them again.

We take some pictures with them. They told us to be sure to come back at 8:00 that night for a fiesta. We did come back that night, the entire platoon. They had a big, long table set up with enough spaghetti for the whole platoon. Tiny was there with his guitar, and we had a regular song feast. I swore then that if I were aver able to, I would like to repay these people for all the kindness and hospitality they extended to us. To the 4th Platoon, they were a Godsend.

It wasn't many days after that that Leo, P.J. and I get word to report to battalion C.P., then to division HQ. After turning our equipment in to Pugly, we walk to battalion C.P., which is uptown Barbarino. There, some men from other companies in the battalion who were also going home were assembled. Col. Joyce then comes out and shakes each one of our hands. It was the first time I had ever spoken directly tour battalion commander. "I'm glad to see you men go home in good shape," he said. And from the expression on the old soldier's face, I knew he meant what he said.

Most of us never came to know Col. Joyce as well as some of our other battalion commanders. Col. Joyce appeared older than any of our previous battalion commanders, but there seemed to be a rugged gameness in his slight body, and you somehow knew that most of the grey hair that stuck out below his helmet was brought there by the hazardous job he was fulfilling. I think that was the first time I felt admiration for Col. Joyce, but I did then. We all saluted and thanked him. I think the old colonel felt better when we made it obvious to him that we regarded him as a good battalion commander. We then got on one of M Company's weapons carriers, which take us to rear division HQ, which had a group of pyramidal tents set up a couple miles west of Barbarino.

The next day finds us settled at rear division HQ, so we go into Barbarino to visit the company. There, the boys in the company tell us they are moving out tomorrow. They'll take over positions now being held by South African troops. We tell them, "Tomorrow we'll be back to see you off." Next morning Leo, P.J. and I stand by the mess tent and look towards Barbarino and we decided we didn't want to go back and see the boys head for the front without us. It's a funny feeling, and we all felt the same about it. We didn't want to say goodbye, so we head back to our tent and spend another day loafing and waiting.

That afternoon we get word to have clean field jackets, trousers and shoes shined by two o'clock tomorrow afternoon for a ceremony where we will all be decorated by the Bronze Star Medal. According to the order, we are decorated for some specific action at a certain time, but that was only a necessary procedure for the award of the medal.

I figure, the way they think in headquarters is that these men have been in combat with a front-line infantry outfit ever since the invasion of North Africa and have never did anything outstanding or heroic for which to receive a medal so why not award them the Bronze Star on general principles and for just being there. It was sort of a symbolic gesture of Uncle Sam reaching out shaking your hand, and saying, "Thank you, fellers, you done a good job and we appreciate it."

About noon the next day we start to assemble in a cow pasture, which was to be the parade grounds. When we arrived, there was a detail on the field kicking cow turds off the grounds. The division band was tuning up. We went through one dry run before the actual ceremony.

General Bolte arrived in his two-star Peep. General Bolte, our Division Commander, is a big, good looking military man who at first appearance typifies a rugged, hard boiled American general, one who appears capable of handling any situation efficiently. And he was actually just as he appeared.

We heard the words "Adjutant's Call." The bugles sounded, and we were in position. The band struck up our division march. I don't know the name of that march, but it's one of those things that does things to you. You can't help but feel good and proud and sort of thrilled at its catchy tune. It made us want to get out and march, but we had to remain at attention.

After the band finished the familiar march, they drifted off into a more low, mellow tune. I think all the Italians within a radius of ten miles were watching the ceremony. The Adjutant called, "Technical Sgt. Leo Schular" first, then "Staff Sgt. Lloyd Walund." I walked up to General Bolte, stopped, saluted and took one more pace forward. I felt small, scanning upward into the statuesque general's face. He bent low to pin the medal on me and talked casually to relieve the tension. "What are you going home on, Sergeant, T.D. or rotation?" "T.D., Sir," I reply. "Good. You know we need you old experienced soldiers back in the outfit, and that's why you're coming back," The General states. "Thank you, sir," I reply as we shook hands.

I then saluted, did column right and marched back to where Leo was waiting at parade rest. "Paul J. Ortman," the Adjutant bellers, and P.J. marches up to the General for his medal. Soon the ceremony is over, the cows move back in on the parade grounds, and we return to our tents.

A couple of days later we get word to prepare for our trip to Naples where we will await the ship to transport us home, and this is where I will end the story, for what happened after that is of little significance or interest. I might add that I did have a sort o feeling of discomfort thinking of when my 30-day furlough was up I would return to the outfit and into more combat.

I didn't want more combat. After an incredible nearly 600 days of front-line infantry combat, I had most of the fight taken out of me. I was an old battered soldier, even though at age 24 my boyhood was not far in the past. I don't believe I was as good a soldier for combat as I once was. At this point in time it was becoming more and more apparent that the allies were emerging victorious over the despots that created this whole conflagration and soon all would come to an end.

As for Leo and P.J., there worries were pretty well over, as going home on rotation they were most certain to remain in the States for the duration. But my status was entirely different. All my apprehensions proved unfounded, however, for during my furlough came the colossal news of V.E. day. My worries were over. I would have liked to have returned to the outfit, but not to combat. At the termination of my furlough, I was discharged on points—about 130 of them. ♈

Anyone reporting on such is only able to report on his immediate outfit with any accuracy. A soldier in Europe could not calculate the tasks of his buddies in the Pacific and vice versa. And in many cases 2 Platoons in the same Co. can not account for what the other is doing. Therefore if there are some slight errors in the forgoing, it is unintentional. And in the incidents of the forgoing, I make no claim that other outfits did not have the same or even at a greater extent. I only know what happened there, for I was there.

In conclusion, I would like to have a word with veterans who say it is wrong to talk of war. I have talked to many veterans who do not like to talk of war for it horrifys them. They say they have seen enough and do not wish to discuss it any more. I find almost invariably these men are veterans of rear echelon units. Who were absolutely necessary and were a spoke in the wheel of the war machine — but seen no actual combat. One the other hand I find very few old combat men who do not like to discuss the part they played in the war.

Many of us are lucky. Through the grace of God, we came back unmared from the war. Others were not so fortunate

ABOUT THE AUTHOR

Lloyd K. Walund was born in Leola, South Dakota, in 1920 and grew up in farm country in Forbes, North Dakota, during the Great Depression. He left school after completing the 8th Grade, served in the Civilian Conservation Corps (CCC) and, like many of his generation, he enlisted in the Army to serve the United States during World War II. As a member of the 34th Infantry Division, he spent nearly 600 days in combat in Northern Africa and Europe.

Upon his return to the United States, Lloyd opened and operated the Club Café with his brother in Sheridan, Montana, where he met and married Dorothy Jane Burnett. Lloyd and Dorothy later moved to Anaconda, Montana, where Lloyd was employed with the Anaconda Company until his retirement. Lloyd and Dorothy raised seven children. He passed away at the age of 85 in 2005.